Violence in Context

INTERPERSONAL*VIOLENCE*

Series Editors

Claire Renzetti, Ph.D.
Jeffrey L. Edleson, Ph.D.

*Parenting by Men Who Batter: New Directions for Assessment
and Intervention*
Edited by Jeffrey L. Edleson and Oliver J. Williams

Coercive Control: How Men Entrap Women in Personal Life
Evan Stark

*Childhood Victimization: Violence, Crime, and Abuse in the Lives
of Young People*
David Finkelhor

Restorative Justice and Violence Against Women
Edited by James Ptacek

Familicidal Hearts: The Emotional Styles of 211 Killers
Neil Websdale

*Violence in Context: Current Evidence on Risk, Protection,
and Prevention*
Edited by Todd I. Herrenkohl, Eugene Aisenberg, James Herbert
Williams, and Jeffrey M. Jenson

VIOLENCE IN CONTEXT

Current Evidence on Risk, Protection, and Prevention

Edited by

Todd I. Herrenkohl
Eugene Aisenberg
James Herbert Williams
Jeffrey M. Jenson

OXFORD
UNIVERSITY PRESS

2011

OXFORD
UNIVERSITY PRESS

Oxford University Press, Inc., publishes works that further
Oxford University's objective of excellence
in research, scholarship, and education.

Oxford New York
Auckland   Cape Town   Dar es Salaam   Hong Kong   Karachi
Kuala Lumpur   Madrid   Melbourne   Mexico City   Nairobi
New Delhi   Shanghai   Taipei   Toronto

With offices in
Argentina   Austria   Brazil   Chile   Czech Republic   France   Greece
Guatemala   Hungary   Italy   Japan   Poland   Portugal   Singapore
South Korea   Switzerland   Thailand   Turkey   Ukraine   Vietnam

Published by Oxford University Press, Inc.
198 Madison Avenue, New York, New York 10016
www.oup.com

Oxford is a registered trademark of Oxford University Press

Library of Congress Cataloging-in-Publication Data

Violence in context : current evidence on risk, protection, and
prevention/edited by Todd I. Herrenkohl ... [et al.].
p. cm. — (Interpersonal violence)
Includes bibliographical references and index.
ISBN 978-0-19-536959-5
1. Youth and violence.   2. Violence—Prevention.   3. Violence—Social aspects.
I. Herrenkohl, Todd Ian.
HQ799.2.V56V55 2010
303.60835—dc22
2010016615

1 3 5 7 9 8 6 4 2

Printed in the United States of America
on acid-free paper

ACKNOWLEDGMENTS

The authors would like to thank the following individuals for their help in compiling research for the chapters of this book and for reviewing and commenting on earlier drafts of the manuscript: J. Bart Klika, M.S.W., University of Washington; Ninoosh M. Sadeghi, B.A., University of Maryland; Cynthia Sousa, M.S.W., University of Washington; Lisa Stewart, University of Washington; and Miriam Valdovinos, M.A., University of Washington.

We would also like to thank our colleagues who served as anonymous reviewers of our work for their thoughtful feedback and helpful suggestions. And, our sincere gratitude goes to the editors of the Oxford University Press book series on Interpersonal Violence, Professors Jeffrey Edleson of the University of Minnesota and Claire Renzetti of the University of Dayton, for their guidance throughout the process of preparing our manuscript for publication.

CONTENTS

CONTRIBUTORS

EUGENE AISENBERG, PH.D.
Associate Professor
School of Social Work
University of Washington

JENNIFER BOWMAN, M.S.W.
Community Engagement Officer
NELA Center for Student Success

CHARLOTTE LYN BRIGHT, PH.D., M.S.W.
Assistant Professor
School of Social Work
University of Maryland

SHANDRA FORREST-BANK, M.S.W.
Graduate Research Assistant
Graduate School of Social Work
University of Denver

AMELIA GAVIN, PH.D.
Assistant Professor
School of Social Work
University of Washington

Todd I. Herrenkohl, Ph.D.
Associate Professor
School of Social Work
University of Washington

Jeffrey M. Jenson, Ph.D.
Philip D. & Eleanor G. Winn
Professor for Children and Youth at Risk
Associate Dean for Research
Graduate School of Social Work
University of Denver

Gita Mehrotra, M.S.W.
Ph.D. Candidate
School of Social Work
University of Washington

Granger Petersen, M.S.W.
Ph.D. Candidate
Graduate School of Social Work
University of Denver

Anne Powell, Ph.D.
Assistant Professor
School of Social Welfare
University of Kansas

James Herbert Williams, Ph.D.
Dean and Professor
Graduate School of Social Work
University of Denver

Violence in Context

I

DEFINITIONS AND MEASUREMENT OF INTERPERSONAL VIOLENCE ACROSS SETTINGS

1

THE CONTEXT OF VIOLENCE

TODD I. HERRENKOHL, EUGENE AISENBERG,

JAMES HERBERT WILLIAMS, &

JEFFREY M. JENSON

In a 2001 report from the U.S. Office of the Surgeon General (U.S. Department of Health and Human Services [USDHHS], 2001), then Secretary of Health and Human Services Donna E. Shalala wrote, "The world remains a threatening, often dangerous place for children and youth. And in our country today, the greatest threat to the lives of children and adolescents is not disease or starvation or abandonment, but the terrible reality of violence." Approaching a decade later, her statement remains an accurate assessment of the reality facing many young people in the United States. Sadly, homicides remain a leading cause of death among the nation's youth (Centers for Disease Control and Prevention [CDC], 2007b). Hundreds of thousands of children are reported to the authorities for having been abused, and many more child abuse cases occur but go unreported to the authorities (CDC, 2007a). Countless numbers of children each year witness domestic and community violence, leaving them emotionally traumatized and vulnerable (Gewirtz & Edleson, 2007). Violence is indeed a pervasive and destructive force in American society.

It is difficult to imagine a child, an adolescent, or an adult in the United States who is not impacted by violence in some way. The general public hears almost daily news accounts of local, national, and international incidents of interpersonal violence. Nelson Mandela, in his introduction to the World Health Organization (WHO) *World Report on*

Violence and Health, stated, with respect to the suffering of victims worldwide, "This suffering ... is a legacy that reproduces itself, as new generations learn from the violence of generations past, as victims learn from victimizers, and as social conditions that nurture violence are allowed to continue. No country, no city, no community is immune. But neither are we powerless against it" (WHO, 2002). Mandela's comments capture the sentiments of many in the fields of violence research and prevention. While violence is obviously pervasive here and elsewhere in the world, what we now know about the many causes and consequences of violence for young people places scholars and policy makers in a good position to act on this global crisis. Evidence presented and analyzed throughout this book illustrates some of the many advances in violence research and prevention over the past 20 years or more, as well as some of the more difficult challenges that remain, and that must be overcome, if we are to see continued progress toward a less violent society.

Throughout this book, we examine contemporary topics in violence research and discuss ways to advance an integrated, research-based framework to prevent and reduce violence of various forms across levels and settings. To this end, we place an emphasis on the overlap between different forms of violence and the interaction of individuals with their environment. As part of our review, we examine issues of race/ethnicity, culture, and gender. We also examine and discuss evidence that has comes from rigorously evaluated prevention programs, noting what appears to be working, what does not, and what opportunities exist for further innovation in the design and application of programs. We start and end with an analysis of how violence is defined and how current definitions shape research and practice. Throughout the book, we call for more awareness of the ways in which violence and "context" intersect.

VIOLENCE IN CONTEXT

Violence has become a reality of the human experience. Nearly 1.6 million people in the general population of the United States died from violence in 2000 (Krug, Dahlberg, Mercy, Zwi, & Lozano, 2002). Youth violence is a leading killer of young people aged 10 to 24 years (CDC, 2007b). For African Americans in this age group, homicides remain the leading cause of death. According to national statistics in a recent report by the CDC (2007b), more than 18% of males and just under 9% of females in grades 9 through 12 had been in a physical fight on school grounds at least once in the previous 12 months. Nearly 30% of students had property stolen from them or purposely damaged while on school property. Nearly 8% had been threatened or injured with a weapon. While males engage in more physical fighting, bullying, and street crime (Loeber & Stouthamer-Loeber, 1998) than do females, there is growing evidence that in some forms of violence, the gender gap may be narrowing or at least that perceptions of violence among females is changing (Chesney-Lind & Belknap, 2004).

As noted by Bright and her colleagues in Chapter 4 of this book, there are a variety of explanations for the emerging trends in violence among males and females, although we are far from fully understanding exactly what these trends represent and are only now beginning to incorporate gender into theories of violence etiology and models of prevention.

As noted in several chapters that follow, one of the most robust predictors of aggression and violence in boys and girls is their exposure to violence at an earlier age. More than 3 million referrals for alleged maltreatment are made to child protective service agencies annually in the United States (USDHHS, 2007). And, nearly 2 million women are physically assaulted by an intimate partner (Tjaden & Thoennes, 2000), which translates into as many or more children witnessing and learning about violence in their homes. In short, rates of violence of all forms—those that occur within the family and those that occur outside in the community—remain unacceptably high, and children are paying the price.

Few would argue that the use of violence, from minor acts of bullying and aggression in schools to the most serious forms of assault and rape, is damaging to society as a whole. Victims suffer physically and emotionally, and we all share in the financial costs of treating victims and prosecuting violent offenders. However, the damage caused by violence is not distributed equally among the various segments of the U.S. population. Decades of research have shown that homicides and other violent crimes are concentrated in economically disadvantaged neighborhoods and communities (Gelles & Cornell, 1990; Mocan, 2005; Sabol, Coulton, & Korbin, 2004; Sampson, Raudenbush, & Earls, 1997; Smith & Thornberry, 1995; Wikstrom & Loeber, 2000). Consequently, youth and families of color, particularly African Americans, who continue to reside in greater numbers within these areas, experience more of the day-to-day realities of violence. Statistics show that African American youth are victimized more often than are other youth; they perpetrate violence, on average, at higher rates; and they are arrested and detained for violent crimes in larger numbers (see Chapter 3). Statistics also show that rates of officially recorded child maltreatment are higher for African American families (see Chapter 5).

There are a variety of explanations for why disparities in violence persist. Williams and his colleagues review several relevant theories of, and findings on, disparities in youth violence in Chapter 3 (e.g., subculture of violence perspective, structural perspective on race and violence). Other perspectives have been reviewed and discussed extensively in other sources (Hawkins et al., 1998; Sampson & Laub, 1993). Unfortunately, no single theory or perspective captures all of the reasons why certain groups experience more violence than do others, nor all of the reasons why more has not been done to bring about changes in policies and practices to help address these disparities. Discussions throughout this book add to the conversation about race/ethnicity (and gender) disparities and echo a call heard from other scholars and advocates for vulnerable youth to bring these issues more directly into public view and discussion.

THE BOOK

Research on interpersonal violence has progressed at a steady rate in the past two decades. However, relatively little attention has been paid to understanding the overlap in different forms of violence and to addressing the complex interactions among risk and protective factors for violence that exist within the settings of family, school, and community (Sabol et al., 2004). The tendency has been to focus on explanations at the level of the individual victim or perpetrator, rather than taking a larger systemic view of the problem that considers how micro- *and* macro-level causes, correlates, and outcomes of violence intersect and become mutually reinforcing. Consequently, how we talk about violence remains focused on individual deficits and vulnerabilities and less on the social/contextual and environmental influences that support and motivate violence beyond the individual person. What is needed is a purposeful attempt to shift the conversation toward one that focuses more on the many social and environmental factors that predict and extend from violence a shift that captures more of what we actually know from etiological and evaluation studies. Also needed is a careful examination of the ways that innovative approaches to violence prevention can bring about lasting changes in support of families (and children) who reside in the most disadvantaged communities (Freisthler & Crampton, 2009). This requires not only a look at what "works" in prevention but also an investigation of how to adapt promising programs to different cultures and different communities.

In this book, we compile epidemiological and etiological findings on violence and explore how findings differ according to race/ethnicity and gender. We also examine the overlap of violence across settings and discuss various approaches to prevention that seek to reduce risks and enhance protection at the family, school, and community levels. While chapters of the book do not necessarily adhere to a single perspective, nor are they written from a common theory base, the chapters as a whole represent our best attempt to touch on issues that relate in some way to the notion of "context." What is consistent throughout the book is an emphasis on social influences, environment, and larger systems that predict and help explain disparities in violence, adding complexity to an already complex set of issues, but also promoting ideas that have potential to change how we think about violence as a social problem. We use Bronfenbrenner's (1979) ecological perspective as an organizing framework. However, we also refer to various others theories, including those that focus explicitly on gender and race. Our discussion of prevention models refers specifically to social developmental perspectives on violence and related behaviors in youth. The values of social developmental theory are in delineating the ways in which risk and protective factors relate to violence and in offering modifiable targets for prevention and intervention programs. The theory base also provides useful information on social and environmental buffers, factors that lessen the risk of violence by enhancing protection from risks and individual vulnerabilities or propensities (Pollard, Hawkins, & Arthur, 1999). In Chapters 7 and 8, Jenson and colleagues provide a comprehensive review of research on prevention programs, several of which are derived from a social development perspective and many of which adhere to a public health framework.

The book is divided into four primary sections. We begin with an examination of commonly held definitions of violence in Chapter 2 by Eugene Aisenberg and colleagues. The authors explore how violence is understood and perceived in research and practice settings and examine the underlying assumptions behind common definitions of violence. They also identify the limitations that stem from particularly narrow conceptualizations of what violence is and what it is not. While not adopting a single or uniform definition of violence, Aisenberg and his co-authors make the case for broadening our definitions of violence to include more of what we know about context.

In the next chapters of the book, evidence on the etiology and outcomes of youth, family, and community violence is reviewed. The authors summarize how risk and protective factors work to promote and inhibit violence in families and in the community and explore race and ethnic differences in the risk and protective factors associated with violent behavior. In Chapter 3, James Herbert Williams and his associates synthesize research showing that African American youth are at higher risk of violence and are more likely to be apprehended by police for crimes they commit. Differences extend to the juvenile and criminal justice systems, where African Americans appear to be treated differently than whites, evidence the authors suggest may reflect discrimination and system biases. The authors review and discuss various perspectives to help explain racial disparities in violence and systems involvement and propose several directions for future research and practice, including more rigorous studies to understand violence in relation to the complex risk environments encountered by youth of color.

In Chapter 4, Charlotte Lyn Bright and her colleagues draw attention to the role of gender in the etiology of youth violence by reviewing research findings and various theoretical perspectives on the issue. While the authors report that more boys than girls perpetrate violence, they also find that rates of arrests for boys and girls are changing in possibly different ways. Importantly, the authors devote considerable attention to recent trends that show that an increasing proportion of girls are being arrested for violent crimes. In this chapter, the authors grapple with various perspectives to help explain gender differences in violence, examine the many and varied risk and protective factors linked to violence for boys and girls, and explore the implications that emerge from research on gender differences for policy and systems change.

In the next section of the book (Chapters 5 and 6), Todd I. Herrenkohl focuses on the overlap in child abuse and children's exposure to domestic and community violence, environmental stressors on families, and resilience in child victims. He reports that the effects of violence on children are substantial and often long-lasting, according to results from leading studies. On the question of whether developmental outcomes of violence exposure differ by gender and race/ethnicity, Herrenkohl suggests that the answer remains unclear because so few studies have investigated the issue comprehensively.

In Chapter 6, Herrenkohl continues by investigating the focusing specifically on the topic of resilience for children exposed to violence. The chapter begins with an overview of the construct resilience, focusing on how resilience is defined and measured in relevant studies. The discussion then transitions to what we know about resilience and protective factors for vulnerable children, particularly those who have been exposed to violence of one or more forms. The author asserts that additional research describing the ways in which vulnerable children overcome the odds of negative outcomes is crucial to the development of prevention and intervention efforts. This chapter concludes by summarizing what we currently know, and what we still need to learn, about resilience as a life-course process. Implications for strengths-based prevention programs are also discussed briefly as a lead in to Section 4.

In Section 4 (Chapters 7 and 8) by Jeffrey M. Jenson and his colleagues, the topic of violence prevention is covered comprehensively. The authors examine recent advances and current challenges in prevention science and provide examples of effective school, family, and community approaches to preventing aggressive and violent behavior. From their review, Jenson and colleagues argue that there is sufficient evidence to support the implementation of evidence-based practices in school and family settings but that uncertainty remains regarding which community approaches are most effective in reducing violence on a broader scale. The authors also state the need for additional efforts aimed at adapting programs to fit the needs of children and families from diverse cultural backgrounds.

In Chapter 9 in Section 5, Aisenberg and his colleagues return to examine several fundamental questions about the study of violence. The authors raise important and provocative questions about the meaning and root causes of violent behavior. They examine the role of culture related to the conceptualization and assessment of interpersonal violence within families and communities. They argue that research has frequently overlooked many key aspects of culture, intersectionality, and social power, leading to what he and others believe is a compartmentalized view of violence. The authors propose the need for a multidimensional conceptualization of violence that more fully captures individual identities and aspects of culture.

Chapter 10, the concluding chapter, summarizes several key points from the reviews of literature for the book and hints at next steps in the study and prevention of violence. The chapter details some of the tensions in the field and points to the value of bringing "context" more directly into view as we move toward seeking solutions to this enduring problem.

REFERENCES

Bronfenbrenner, U. (1979). *The ecology of human development: Experiments by nature and design*. Cambridge, MA: Harvard University Press.

CDC. (2007a). *Child maltreatment*. Atlanta, GA: Centers for Disease Control and Prevention, National Center for Injury Prevention and Control.

CDC. (2007b). *Youth violence*. Atlanta, GA: Centers for Disease Control and Prevention, National Center for Injury Control and Prevention.

Chesney-Lind, M., & Belknap, J. (2004). Trends in delinquent girls' aggression and violent behavior: A review of the evidence. In I. Putallaz & K. L. M. Bierman (Eds.), *Aggression, antisocial behavior, and violence among girls: A developmental perspective* (pp. 203–220). New York: Guilford.

Freisthler, B., & Crampton, D. (2009). Environment and child well-being. *Children and Youth Services Review, 31*, 297–299.

Gelles, R. J., & Cornell, C. P. (1990). *Intimate violence in families*. Newbury Park, CA: Sage Publications.

Gewirtz, A. H., & Edleson, J. L. (2007). Young children's exposure to intimate partner violence: Towards a developmental risk and resilience framework for research and intervention. *Journal of Family Violence, 22*, 151–163.

Hawkins, J. D., Herrenkohl, T., Farrington, D. P., Brewer, D., Catalano, R. F., & Harachi, T. W. (1998). A review of predictors of youth violence. In R. Loeber & D. P. Farrington (Eds.), *Serious and violent juvenile offenders: Risk factors and successful interventions* (pp. 106–146). Thousand Oaks, CA: Sage.

Krug, E. G., Dahlberg, L. L., Mercy, J. A., Zwi, A. B., & Lozano, R. (Eds.). (2002). *Statistical annex: World report on violence and health*. Geneva: World Health Organization.

Loeber, R., & Stouthamer-Loeber, M. (1998). Development of juvenile aggression and violence: Some common misconceptions and controversies. *American Psychologist, 53*(2), 242–259.

Mocan, H. N. (2005). Economic discrimination and societal homicide rate: Further evidence on the cost of inequality. *American Law and Economic Review, 7*, 597–611.

Pollard, J. A., Hawkins, J. D., & Arthur, M. W. (1999). Risk and protection: Are both necessary to understand diverse behavioral outcomes in adolescence? *Social Work Research, 23*(3), 145–158.

Sabol, W. J., Coulton, C. J., & Korbin, J. E. (2004). Building community capacity for violence prevention. *Journal of Interpersonal Violence, 19*(3), 322–340.

Sampson, R. J., & Laub, J. H. (1993). *Crime in the making: Pathways and turning points through life*. Cambridge, MA: Harvard University Press.

Sampson, R. J., Raudenbush, S. W., & Earls, F. J. (1997). Neighborhoods and violent crime: A multilevel study of collective efficacy. *Science, 277*, 918–924.

Smith, C., & Thornberry, T. P. (1995). The relationship between childhood maltreatment and adolescent involvement in delinquency. *Criminology, 33*(4), 451–481.

Tjaden, P., & Thoennes, N. (2000). *Full report of the prevalence, incidence, and consequences of violence against women: Findings from the National Violence Against Women Survey*. Washington, DC: U.S. Department of Justice, Office of Justice Programs.

USDHHS. (2001). *Youth violence: A report of the Surgeon General*. Rockville, MD: U.S. Department of Health and Human Services, Centers for Disease Control and Prevention, National Center for Injury Prevention and Control; Substance Abuse and Mental Health Services Administration, Center for Mental Health Services; and National Institutes of Health, National Institute of Mental Health.

USDHHS. (2007). *Child maltreatment 2005.* Washington, DC: Administration for Children and Families.

WHO. (2002). *World report on violence and health.* Geneva: World Health Organization.

Wikstrom, P. H., & Loeber, R. (2000). Do disadvantaged neighborhoods cause well-adjusted children to become adolescent delinquents? A study of male juvenile serious offending, individual risk and protective factors, and neighborhood context. *Criminology, 38,* 1109–1142.

2

DEFINING VIOLENCE

Eugene Aisenberg, Amelia Gavin,
Gita Mehrotra, & Jennifer Bowman

We begin, in Chapter 2, with the fundamental yet complex question, "What is violence?" This chapter provides a broad overview of differing conceptualizations and definitions of violence used by researchers and practitioners in the field. We explore varying criteria used to define violence and consider how the lack of a consensus definition of violence impacts research, policy, and practice. We identify challenges and unresolved tensions with respect to definitions and measurement and investigate the degree to which current definitions integrate context indicators of culture and social power. Finally, the chapter provides several definitions of the various forms of violence discussed in subsequent chapters.

WHAT IS VIOLENCE?

This central question remains differentially defined and understood by researchers, practitioners, criminologists, legal experts, law enforcement officials, and policy makers. The lack of a consensus in definitions across disciplines poses challenges for the study, prevention, and treatment of violence. In this chapter, we will compare several definitions of violence and highlight existing limitations due to the absence of a standard definition of violence.

Notable advances in the study and prevention of violence have been made in recent decades, as discussed throughout this book. Nevertheless, progress in the field has been slowed by the lack of a precise and standard definition that accounts for the myriad expressions of violence. The lack of a uniform definition contributes to fragmentary approaches to inquiry, scholarship, and interventions designed to reduce violent behavior and crime and that often fail to address changing the social, behavioral, and environmental factors that cause violence (Mercy, 1993). Researchers and practitioners tend to study, assess, and treat certain kinds of violent acts, such as youth violence, community violence, child abuse, sexual assault, and domestic violence, in a compartmentalized and disparate manner that mitigates against engaging and examining the broader question of *what is violence.* According to Jackman (2002), "Much as some scholars have bemoaned the lack of cohesion in research on violence ... most scholars have proceeded without hesitation as though the conceptual tangle had been cleared. Researchers commonly refer to a phenomenon called violence that implies a clearly understood, generic class of behaviors, and yet no such concept exists" (p. 388).

In this chapter, we wrestle with the fundamental question, "What is violence?" We focus on comparing existing definitions of violence and highlight how these definitions of violence account in particular for issues of culture and social power. While refraining from advocating for the adoption of a single or uniform definition of violence, we examine the impact that the lack of a consensus definition has on the study of violence and treatment of its harmful effects. As scholars and practitioners in the field, it is critical that we reflect on how we define *violence,* how we use the definition, and how this use supports and/or furthers goals of preventing and intervening in contexts to lessen to violence.

DEFINITIONS OF VIOLENCE

Scholars persistently struggle with definitional issues concerning violence, including (Guterman, Cameron, & Staller, 2000):

1. How should *violence* be defined? By the behavior of the perpetrator and/or intentions, the injurious effects of a perpetrator's acts on others, the circumstances out of which those injurious acts derive, or some combination of these?
2. What constitutes an injurious act? The physical nature or characteristics of the act? Does threatening behavior and perceived dangerousness, not accompanied by observable injury, constitute violence?

Disciplinary approaches also contribute to challenges in defining violence in a consistent way. Sociology, criminology, psychology, social work, public health, and biology are a few of the disciplines engaged in the study of the etiology of violence and associated deleterious mental health and behavioral outcomes. However, to a large extent they do so independent of each other, with each discipline invested in different ways of understanding and addressing violence and violent behavior. Given the differences in history, worldview, mission, and politics across disciplines, often each discipline steadfastly adheres to "protecting their turf," thus diminishing the opportunity to be informed by others' insights and findings and advance the field of inquiry. As Raine and Scerbo (1991) note, the lack of communication between social scientists and biologically oriented researchers, for example, has resulted in relatively few tests of the proposition that the interaction between social and biological factors is more important in understanding violent and aggressive behavior than either factor alone. Thus, lessons learned in different "silos" of research and practice fail to reach their full potential in advancing the field of inquiry and reducing violence. Interdisciplinary approaches to defining and addressing violence hold promise in furthering more effective scholarship and intervention in this area.

A predominant approach to understanding and defining violence has focused on the physical nature of violent acts. Reiss and Roth (1993), in their seminal work, *Understanding and Preventing Violence,* presented the following influential definition of violence:

> The panel limited its consideration of violent behavior to interpersonal violence, which it defined as behavior by persons against persons that intentionally threatens, attempts, or actually inflicts physical harm. The behaviors included in this definition are largely included in definitions of aggression.
>
> The panel's definition deliberately excludes consideration of human behavior that inflicts physical harm unintentionally...even when they occur as a result of corporate policies (e.g., to expose workers to toxic chemicals) that increase the risk of injury or death for some category of persons. Also excluded are certain behaviors that inflict physical harm intentionally: violence against oneself, as in suicides and attempted suicides; and the use of violence by state authorities in the course of enforcing the law, imposing capital punishment, and providing collective defense... (pp. 35–37).

This narrow definition highlights the physical aspects of violence but reduces violent behavior strictly to overt and intentionally harmful aggressive behavior toward others (Volavka, 1999). However, aggression can be more covert and less intentional. In fact, verbal aggression and psychological harassment, while not physically harmful, can cause serious emotional harm to those who are victimized. The above definition also fails to address violence that is self-inflicted as well as structural forms of violence rooted in behaviors motivated by monetary greed, discriminatory beliefs, or calculable personal or corporate gain (Derber, 1996).

The Centers for Disease Control and Prevention (Rosenberg, 1994) and the California Policy Council on Violence Prevention (Final Report, August 1995) defined *violence* as the threatened or actual use of physical force or power against another person, against oneself, or against a group or community that either results in, or has a high likelihood of resulting in, injury, death, or deprivation. This definition is broader and more inclusive than the one given by Reiss and Ross (1993). While both definitions focus on behaviors that involve the use of physical force, the latter emphasizes violence that is self-inflicted and violence that is directed to groups and communities that is either certain or probabilistic.

Olweus (1999) has defined *violence* or *violent behavior* as "aggressive behaviour in which the actor or perpetrator uses his or her own body or an object (including a weapon) to inflict (relatively serious) injury or discomfort upon another individual." Similar to other definitions, violence is thought to involve the use of physical force or power. However, it focuses on violence enacted by an individual and does not emphasize violence committed by or towards engaged by groups or institutions. Additionally, the Olweus definition fails to include verbal aggression or relational/ indirect aggression, such as rumor spreading, cyberbullying, or social exclusion, which are important but understudied aspects of bullying among school-age children (Underwood, 2003).

Underlying the substantial array of definitions of violence are two primary assumptions: (1) violence is motivated by hostility and the intent to cause harm and (2) violence is deviant—legally, socially, morally from the mainstream of human activity (Jackman, 2002). Consequently, the examination and study of violence have been largely relegated to acts that are considered illegal or socially deviant or are associated with social conflict (Jackman, 2002). This individual-centered and criminal perspective remains a dominant paradigm of institutions such as the juvenile and criminal justice systems. These systems typically measure violence by arrest, victimization, and self-report data and address violence through control and incarceration despite the absence of a consensus of what constitutes violence. In doing so, these systems often fail to consider the interaction and intersection of factors beyond the individual, including structural and contextual factors such as poverty, culture, racism, and sexism and other systems of stratification. Consequently, this paradigm of deviance and control reflects theories of violence that similarly focus on the individual person while minimizing or ignoring contextual factors that can contribute to the perpetration of violence and to the harmful consequences that follow at individual, family, and societal levels as well as to how violence is experienced. Unidimensional theories have contributed to a limited understanding of the etiology of violence and violent behavior (DeKeseredy & Perry, 2006) and have reduced our ability to prevent violence and intervene on a more global scale by minimizing or neglecting to address the social effects of violence (Saul et al., 2008).

In its efforts to define violence, the World Health Organization (WHO) (1999) advocated a paradigm shift away from a predominant focus on criminal acts. It broadly defined *violence* as "the intentional use of physical and psychological force or power, threatened or actual, against oneself, another person, or against a group or community, that either results in or has a high likelihood of resulting in injury, death, psychological harm, maldevelopment, or deprivation" (p. 2). This emphasis on the use of power and threats, intimidation, and actual violence is unique in that it promotes the consideration of *feelings* of insecurity and differential perceptions of threat and harm. Also, it includes acts involving deprivation, psychological abuse, and neglect. Such considerations are important due to the fact that acts of violence do not meet uniform interpretation across cultures (Jackman, 2002). For example, in some cultures, acts of physical force against a woman may be acceptable and may not be viewed as domestic violence (Zoucha, 2006).

Other definitions of *violence* include institutional violence and violence due to social inequalities including incidents of "micro-violence," "incivilities," or "micro-aggressions" (Evans-Campbell & Walters, 2006). *Institutional violence*—violence that serves or results from institutional objectives—can take extreme forms, like concentration camps or murders committed by totalitarian governments, or it can be part of a socially accepted economic system or a religious organization's goals. Institutional violence can also be subtle, resulting from acts of discrimination, omission, or deception rather than from force (Iadicola & Shupe, 2003). The term *microaggressions* refers to acts involving discrimination, racism, and daily hassles that are targeted at individuals from diverse racial and ethnic groups. Microaggressions includes acts that are covert (e.g., being arbitrarily pulled over by a police officer) and overt (e.g., being chased and attacked) and daily discriminatory stressors (e.g., name calling) that are based in historical and contemporary dynamics of social inequality (Evans-Campbell & Walters, 2006). Over time, such discriminative acts exact a considerable toll on individuals, families, and communities. For example, Walters (2003) found that among Native Americans, the experience of microaggressions was highly correlated with symptoms of distress in the prior year and over an individual's lifetime.

These varied definitions of violence highlight the complexities of violence and the challenges inherent in understanding it and hence addressing it effectively. The use of varying criteria to define *violence*, the numerous definitions of it, and the multiple expressions of violence become problematic for professionals when screening individuals for treatment, evaluating intervention outcomes, and designing policies to address the serious public health problem of violence. Also, the lack of a common language and definition of violence acts as a major barrier to improving communication between researchers and practitioners. As a result, programs and activities are promulgated but are often uninformed by effective practices and rigorous science.

THE IMPACT OF DEFINITIONS ON RESEARCH AND PRACTICE: COMMUNITY VIOLENCE

We look to the field of community violence to illustrate how the lack of definition of violence is problematic for inquiry, scholarship, and intervention. Researchers have defined and operationalized exposure to community violence in a variety of ways but typically require that the exposure occur outside the person's home and involve being a direct victim or witness of violence perpetrated by an individual who is not a domestic partner or member of a family living in the same home (Linares et al., 2001). Some researchers include hearing about a violent incident from someone who has been harmed by violence or hearing a gunshot, or seeing drug transactions as exposures to community violence. However, as also noted by Herrenkohl in Chapter 5, others object to these definitions as being too broad and thus less meaningful (Cooley-Quille, Boyd, Frantz, & Walsh, 2001; Horn & Trickett, 1998; Trickett, Durán, & Horn, 2003).

The lack of consensus in specifying an agreed-on universe of events that comprise community violence is but one conceptual difficulty in the study of community violence exposure. Another problematic issue arises from research findings that suggest not all forms of community violence exposure are the same, at least when considering their detrimental effects on families and children (Horn & Trickett, 1998; Trickett et al., 2003). In assessing violence exposure among children and adolescents, for example, many survey studies use a rudimentary method of data scaling, namely tallying the number of distinct kinds of events and summing them up to derive a total exposure score. In doing so, these studies assign the same value or weight to different violence exposures. However, being robbed at knifepoint, witnessing a fistfight in the school yard, and hearing from someone of a drive-by shooting are discrete events of violence that likely differ in their severity and impact on children. The failure to distinguish the severity of exposure to different types of acts of community violence makes the use of survey measures problematic for measurement purposes (Aisenberg, Ayón, & Orozco-Figueroa., 2008, pg. 1556). Also, it limits the utility of survey measures for systematic use in clinical settings that wrestle with competing priorities and budgetary or time constraints. As a result, most practitioners, including mental health and health providers, fail to assess for exposure to community violence among youngsters, unless it is specifically the presenting issue or concern.

While research clearly documents that the consequences of exposure to community violence are not the same for all children, differences in effects and symptomatology due to children's perception of an act of community violence are rarely examined (Aisenberg et al., 2008). Exposure to a violent event, such as witnessing an assault with a weapon, may be perceived differently by two youngsters and thus affect them in dissimilar ways. Furthermore, most studies fail to examine the subjective differences between exposure to an objectively more severe act of violence (e.g., witnessing a murder) and exposure to an objectively less severe act (e.g., witnessing someone get beaten up) (Aisenberg et al., 2008).

The lack of consensus in defining and operationalizing community violence by researchers makes it very difficult to generalize results across studies and to some extent has contributed to hindering knowledge development in this area (Aisenberg & Ell, 2005; Guterman et al., 2000).

According to Tolan (2007), the lack of consensus in defining violence contributes to the challenges in differentiating or calibrating violence by seriousness or potential to injure. For example, it may contribute to widely varying estimates of rates of violence perpetration and violence exposure. Including in one's definition of exposure the incidence of hearing gunshots for individuals residing in inner-city communities, for instance, may, because of its frequent occurrence, misrepresent the level of violence that occurs in the community.

The lack of agreement among researchers about what constitutes community violence exposure has fostered divergent understandings among practitioners from an array of disciplines that contributes to fragmentary approaches to the prevention and treatment of youth violence and addressing mental health distress symptomatology among youth and adults. Single focused solutions such as lowering the age that a youth can be tried as an adult for criminal behavior or building more prisons are ineffective in reducing crime and the fear of crime. Also, despite the use of popular one-time, didactic, continuing education courses and training workshops for providing prevention support to practitioners, a body of literature suggests that these approaches are unlikely to change practitioner behavior (Saul et al., 2008).

Ultimately, how exposure to community violence is defined, and by whom, will have an impact on what questions are asked as well as on the findings of associations with other variables, including outcome symptomatology in developmental studies of youth and also adults. A standardized method of defining and assessing exposure to community violence has the potential to facilitate a clearer understanding of the nature and developmental course of community violence exposure in children and families and allow a better integration of findings across studies (Overstreet, 2000). Likewise, a universally agreed-on definition of *community violence* has the potential to enhance systematic assessment across jurisdictions and countries and would facilitate comparison of findings across studies to inform intervention and policy. Also, it has the potential to facilitate effective communication among practitioners and researchers and the development and translation of effective programs that are coherent and comprehensive in their responsiveness to diverse needs and contexts. Realizing this potential would likely have a positive effect in addressing persistent disproportionate representation of youth and adults of color in punitive systems of care such as the criminal justice system and the child welfare system as well as disparities in the access to and utilization of mental health and other social services.

The definitional issues of community violence are interrelated with similar definitional issues concerning neighborhoods. As noted by Williams and colleagues (Chapter 3), Herrenkohl (Chapter 5), and Jenson and colleagues (Chapter 8), research has recognized that structural characteristics of neighborhoods such as neighborhood cohesion and the capacity for informal social control may influence community-level mechanisms that have consequences for adolescent behavior (Browning, Burrington, Levethal, & Brook-Gunn, 2008). In particular, the effects of structural deficits on local institutions, neighborhood attachments, and network ties may impede the ability of community residents to achieve common goals, including the informal social control of neighborhood youth (Sampson, Raudenbush, & Earls, 1997). In Chapter 6, Herrenkohl discusses the implications of collective efficacy with regard to the resilience of youth in the face of repetitive exposure to violence. While consensus is emerging regarding the role and impact that structural characteristics of neighborhoods with regards to violence and violent behavior, issues persist on how to define neighborhoods. Also, further research is needed to establish reliable and valid measures across neighborhoods that are also reliably and validly defined. Neighborhood indicators for children need to tap explicit aspects of inequality such as disparities in the racial, social and economic composition of the residents, disproportionate exposure to violence, and differential access to resources (Coulton & Korbin, 2007).

DIVERGENT SCHOOLS OF THOUGHT

As noted in the area of community violence, adherence to a universal definition of *violence* has distinct benefits. One school of thought advocates that a clear, unambiguous definition of *violence* can advance the assessment of the prevalence of violence, measurement of its impact, and evaluation of the effectiveness of policies and treatment programs aimed at reducing violence and its negative consequences across settings and populations. A uniform and comprehensive definition of *violence* can promote a nuanced understanding, examination, and treatment of violence as well as promote and support an integrated, multilevel, multivariable, and multidisciplinary approach to the prevention of violence. Also, the development and use of a clear and inclusive definition of violence may facilitate a deepened understanding of the etiology of violence as well as the identification, differentiation, and systematic assessment of the full range of violent actions and behaviors and develop policies that address salient risk factors of violence in comprehensive rather than fragmentary and ineffective ways. Furthermore, such a definition can help to facilitate coordinated efforts in partnership to address risk factors of violence and the disproportionate representation of people of color in the criminal justice and child welfare systems and to promote the well-being of individuals, families, and communities.Without a standard definition, systematic efforts to reduce violence at multiple levels and to intervene with those exposed to lessen the deleterious consequences of exposure and to prevent the possibility of further victimization will be diminished (Luthar & Goldstein, 2004). Also, efforts to develop a more integrative approach or model of the origins, effects, and adaptive responses to violence of all forms will be hampered.

Another school of thought, however, posits that such a broad and universal definition is not really possible or useful. According to this perspective, no single factor can adequately explain or define violence since violence is a multidimensional and global reality. Operationalizing various definitions that take into account the presenting context, specific form of violence being examined, and community-specific meanings is deemed to be most effective and feasible. Both schools of thought make significantly contributions to the conceptualization and understanding of violence and warrant further study.

CONCLUSION

Violence wounds and destroys life. Also, it engenders distance, mistrust, and fear in the lives of individuals, families, and communities. In some ways, the study and treatment of violence mirror the divisive consequences of violence. To date, no acceptable, comprehensive understanding of violence holds the field (Krauss, 2005).

To address definitional issues of violence, it is crucial to clarify who makes the determination and on what basis such a determination is made (Krauss, 2006). How violence is defined and who defines it have significant impacts and repercussions with regard to the study of violence, law enforcement, criminal justice and juvenile justice responses to violence, in particular youth and family violence, as well as the planning, development, implementation, and evaluation of violence prevention and intervention programs across the life span. Rather than gloss over this crucial issue of definition, researchers, practitioners, and policy makers need to specifically define those behaviors that constitute each form or typology of violence but, importantly, they must also seek a broader, more systemic conceptualization of violence and a more comprehensive and interdisciplinary approach to address violence.

DEFINITIONS USED THROUGHOUT THE BOOK

Our intent in this chapter is to raise awareness of the ways in which definitions of *violence* differ and how the differences influence research and practice, as well as to point out how current definitions might be broadened to become more inclusive of various aspects of violence. The chapters that follow will address several topic areas, including youth violence, family violence, and prevention. In these chapters, the authors take a broad view of violence that extends to intentional use of physical force or power that involves individuals, groups, and communities (Dahlberg & Krug, 2002). Subsequent chapters have the primary responsibility to summarize the empirical evidence concerning violence, risk factors across diverse and vulnerable populations, and the social and environmental factors that protect children and adolescents from adverse consequences related to exposure to violence. As a result, definitions of *violence* used in these other chapters vary with respect to emphasis placed on issues raised in the discussion presented in Chapter 2.

In Chapters 3 and 4, Williams and colleagues provide a review of research on youth and community violence. *Community violence,* as defined in those chapters, includes behaviors that cause harm and injury to others in settings outside the home, including neighborhoods and schools. Youth violence is an age-based subcategory of community violence that specifically focuses on juveniles, adolescents, and young adults (Mercy et al., 2002) and includes aggressive behaviors such as verbal abuse, bullying, hitting, slapping, or fist fighting. It also includes serious violent and delinquent acts such as aggravated assault, robbery, rape, and homicide. Herrenkohl, in Chapters 5 and 6, focuses mainly on family violence, which includes child maltreatment (abuse and neglect), and domestic violence exposure in children, which includes a child experiencing violence perpetrated by one caregiver toward another. Violence in the home context can involve a range of physically violent behaviors such as hitting, kicking, and burning, as well as threats of physical, sexual, and emotional abuse. Jenson and colleagues, in Chapters 7 and 8, carry forward these definitions in their review of prevention research focused on the contexts of family, school, and community.

REFERENCES

Aisenberg, E., Ayón, C., & Orozco-Figueroa, A. (2008). The role of young adolescents' perception in understanding severity of impact of exposure to community violence. *Journal of Interpersonal Violence, 23,* 1555–1578.

Aisenberg, E., & Ell, K. (2005). Contextualizing community violence and its effects: an ecological model of parent-child interdependent coping. *Journal of Interpersonal Violence, 20,* 855–871.

Browning, C. R., Burrington, L. A., Leventhal, T., & Brooks-Gunn, J. (2008). Neighborhood structural inequality, collective efficacy, and sexual risk behavior among urban youth. *Journal of Health and Social Behavior, 49,* 269–285.

California Policy Council on Violence Prevention. (1995). *Violence prevention, a vision of hope: Final report.* Sacramento: Crime and Violence Prevention Center, California Attorney General's Office.

Centers for Disease Control and Prevention. (1996). *Monthly Vital Statistics Report, 44*(7), Supplement, February 29.

Cooley-Quille, M., Boyd, R. C., Frantz, E., & Walsh, J. (2001). Emotional and behavioral impact of exposure to community violence in inner-city adolescents. *Journal of Clinical Child Psychology, 30,* 199–206.

Coulton, C. J., & Korbin, J. (2007). Indicators of child well-being through a neighborhood lens. *Social Indicators Research, 84,* 349–361.

Dahlberg, L. L., & Krug, E. G. (2002). Violence: A global public health problem. In E. G. Krug, L. L. Dahlberg, J. A. Mercy, A. B. Zwi, & R. Lozano (Eds.), *World report on violence and health* (pp. 1–21). Geneva: World Health Organization.

DeKeseredy, W. S., & Perry, B. (Eds.). (2006). *Advancing critical criminology.* Lanham, MD: Lexington Books.

Derber, C. (1996). *The wilding of America: How greed and violence are eroding our nation's character.* New York: St. Martin's.

Evans-Campbell, T. & Walters, K. L. (2006). Indigenist practice competencies in child welfare practice: A decolonization framework to address family violence and substance abuse, and historical trauma among First Nations peoples. In R. Fong, R. McRoy, & C. Ortiz Hendricks (Eds.). *Intersecting child welfare, substance abuse, and family violence: Culturally competent approaches.* Washington, DC: CSWE Press.

Guterman, N. B., Cameron, M., & Staller K. (2000). Definitional and measurement issues in the study of community violence among children and youths. *Journal of Community Psychology, 28,* 571–587.

Horn, J. L., & Trickett, P. K. (1998). Community violence and child development: A review of research. In P. K. Trickett & C. Schellenbach (Eds.), *Violence against children in the family and community* (pp. 103–138). Washington, DC: APA Books.

Iadicola, P., & Shupe, A. D. (2003). *Violence, inequality, and human freedom* (2nd ed.). Lanham, MD: Rowman & Littlefield.

Jackman, M. R. (2002). Violence in social life. *Annual Review of Sociology,* 387–411.

Krauss, H. H. (2005). Conceptualizing violence. In F. Demark, H. H. Krauss, R. W. Wesner, E. Midlarsky, & U. P. Gielen (Eds.), *Violence in the schools: Cross-national and cross-cultural perspectives* (pp. 11–35). New York: Springer.

Krauss, H. H. (2006). Perspectives on violence. *Annals of the New York Academy of Sciences, 1087,* 4–21.

Linares, L. O., Heeren, T., Bronfman, E., Zuckerman, B., Augustyn, M., & Tronick, E. (2001). A mediational model for the impact of exposure to community violence on early child behavior problems. *Child Development, 72,* 639–652.

Luthar, S., & Goldstein, S. (2004). Children's exposure to community violence: Implications for understanding risk and resilience. *Journal of Clinical Child and Adolescent Psychology, 33,* 499–505.

Mercy, J. A., Rosenberg, M. L., Powell, K. E., Broome, C. V., & Roper, W. L. (1993). Public health policy for preventing violence. *Health Affairs, 12,* 7–29.

Olweus, D. (1999). Sweden. In P. K. Smith, Y. Morita, J. Junger-Tas, D. Olweus, R. Catalano, & P. Slee (Eds.), *The nature of school bullying: A cross-national perspective* (pp. 28–48). London: Routledge.

Overstreet, S. (2000). Exposure to community violence: Defining the problem and understanding the consequences. *Journal of Child and Family Studies, 9,* 7–25.

Raine, A., & Scerbo, A. (1991). Biological theories of violence. In J. S. Milner (Ed.). *Neuropsychology of aggression* (pp. 1–26). Boston: Kluwer Academic.

Reiss, A. J., & Roth, J. A. (Eds.). (1993). *Understanding and preventing violence* (pp. 31–41). Washington, DC: National Academies Press.

Rosenberg, M. L. (1994). *Violence prevention: Integrating public health and criminal justice.* Presentation at the U.S. Attorney's Conference, Washington, DC.

Sampson, R. J., Raudenbush, S. W., & Earls, F. (1997). Neighborhoods and violent crime: A multilevel study of collective efficacy. *Science, 227,* 918–924.

Saul, J., Duffy, J., Noonan, R., Lubell, K., Wandersman, A., Flasphler, P., Stillman, L., Blachman, M., & Dunville, R. (2008). Bridging science and prevention in violence prevention: Addressing ten key challenges. *American Journal of Community Psychology, 41,* 197–205.

Tolan, P. H. (2007). Understanding violence. In D. J. Flannery, A. T. Vazsonyi, & I. D. Waldman (Eds.). *The Cambridge handbook of violent behavior and aggression* (pp. 5–18). New York: Cambridge University Press.

Trickett, P. K., Durán, L., & Horn, J. L. (2003). Community violence as it affects child development: Issues of definition. *Clinical Child and Family Psychology Review, 6,* 223–236.

Underwood, M. K. (2003). *Social aggression among girls.* New York: The Guilford Press.

Volavka, J. (1999). The neurobiology of violence: An update. *The Journal of Neuropsychiatry and Clinical Neurosciences, 11,* 307–314.

Walters, K. (2003). *Microaggressions in urban American Indian populations.* Atlanta, GA: Centers for Disease Control and Prevention.

World Health Organization. (1999). *Injury: A leading cause of the global burden of disease.* Geneva: World Health Organization.

Zoucha, R. (2006). Considering cultural in understanding interpersonal violence. *Journal of Forensic Nursing, 2,* 195–196.

II

RISK AND PROTECTIVE FACTORS FOR YOUTH VIOLENCE

Variations by Race, Ethnicity, and Gender

3

RACIAL AND ETHNIC DIFFERENCES IN RISK AND PROTECTIVE FACTORS ASSOCIATED WITH YOUTH VIOLENCE

JAMES HERBERT WILLIAMS, CHARLOTTE LYN BRIGHT, & GRANGER PETERSEN

As noted in the Introduction (Chapter 1), there are clear and consistent patterns in official and self report data that show African American males are at higher risk for violence than other groups in the U.S. population. The first chapter of this section, Chapter 3, focuses on the ways in which African American youth differ from white youth with respect to risk and protective factors, arrests for violence, and involvement in the juvenile justice system. Specifically, we review and discuss research that shows African Americans are at higher risk than whites to be arrested for delinquent and violent crimes. They are also more likely to enter the juvenile justice system and to be treated differently once they enter the system. We review several theories that help explain some of the racial disparities reflected in this research, including those focused on deep social and economic disadvantages faced by African American families. We note the need for more research on hypotheses of discrimination and systems biases that further disadvantage youth of color by making them more vulnerable to arrest and severe sentencing for violent crimes once an arrest has been made. Chapter 3 concludes with implications for future research and prevention programs that have potential to address the complex risk environments of youth of color.

Chapter 4 explores research findings and theory on gender differences in violence, noting that there is some evidence that rates of arrests appear to be changing differently for boys and girls. In the chapter, we discuss several leading theories on gender and violence, including those that focus on social norms and the ways in which girls are socialized differently than boys to the uses of violence. We also consider the overlap in gender, ethnicity, and social disadvantage. From our discussion of theory, we draw implications for practice focused on gender and call for more research that targets disproportionate contacts in the juvenile justice system.

While researchers, practitioners, policy makers, and service providers ask increasingly for solutions to the enduring problems of youth violence, key issues have gone unaddressed. For example, questions remain about the disparity in the prevalence of violence for African American adolescents. It is unclear whether risk and protective factors for violent behavior differ for youth of color compared with white youth, although several theories suggest that African American youth may be socialized differently to the use and outcomes of violence. To the extent that differences in violence and associated variables are understood, researchers and practitioners will be positioned to more fully meet the needs of particularly vulnerable and marginalized groups. The purpose of this chapter is to distill key race differences in violence, as well as the many risk and protective factors found in the literature. Theories that position race in the etiology of violence are important to understand as we investigate this phenomenon. In this chapter, we will examine differences in the prevalence of violence, as well as variations in risk and protective factors for violence across race/ethnic groups, and we will discuss a few theoretical concepts that propose to explain race/ethnic differences.

JUVENILE VIOLENT OFFENDING: PREVALENCE AND TRENDS

According to the Uniform Crime Report, there were 1.64 million youth arrests in 2007 (Federal Bureau of Investigation, 2008). The 2007 U.S. population estimates for youth aged 10 to 19 were approximately 41 million. The racial and ethnic composition of these youths was 78% white, 17% African American, 5% Asian/Pacific Islander, and 1% Native American. Overall, youth arrest rates have declined since peaking in 1994 and 1995 (Figure 3.1). The 2007 youth arrest rates represent a decrease from 2006

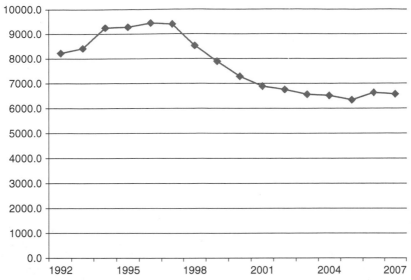

Figure 3.1. Juvenile arrest rates (1990–2007) (arrests of persons aged 10 17/ 100,000 persons aged 10–17).
(From National Center for Juvenile Justice, 2008.)

(Puzzanchera, 2009). A weakness of these data on youth arrests is that Hispanics/Latinos are not disaggregated as a separate category. These data combine Hispanic/Latino youth with whites, limiting the extent to which disproportionality in arrests on the basis of race and ethnicity can be accurately determined.

Chapters 1 and 2 refer to the challenges of defining and measuring violence to emphasize how behaviors are influenced by context. Definitions introduced in Chapter 2 with respect to youth and community violence provide a working framework for this chapter. This chapter will review differences in patterns and predictors of violent behavior for African American and white youth. To understand race differences, it is important to examine official arrest data as well as data on juvenile justice systems involvement of youth, which appear to show notable disparities in the number of white and ethnic minority youths in the system.

Arrest data consist of three discrete categories. The most serious of the three categories is violent index crimes. Violent crimes include forcible rape, robbery, aggravated assault, murder, and non-negligent manslaughter. The youth arrest rates for violent crimes followed a pattern much like that of the overall youth arrest rates; similar to the overall rates, there was decline in youth violent crimes arrest from 2006 to 2007, although murders increased by 3% (Federal Bureau of Invetigation, 2008). Youth accounted for 16% of all violent crime arrests in 2007 (Puzzanchera, 2009). Those under age 15 accounted for 28% of youth violent arrests that were recorded in that year (Figure 3.2).

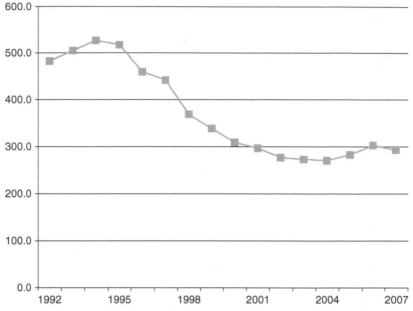

Figure 3.2.   Juvenile violent crime arrest rates (1990 – 2007) (arrests of persons aged 10–17/100,000 persons aged 10–17).
(From National Center for Juvenile Justice, 2008.)

As previously noted, in these arrest data Hispanic/Latino youth are included with whites. We focus on these two groups because data indicate that 98% of all young people who come in contact with the juvenile justice system are youth within these two groups. Of the violent crime arrests in 2007, 51% involved African American youth and 47% involved white youth. Approximately, 2% of arrests were of Asian youth and Native American youth (1% for each category). As reflected in these numbers, the prevalence of violence for Asian and Native Americans are very low, whereas the rates of arrests for violent crimes among African American youth are particularly high relative to their overall numbers in the general populations (about 17%). According to recent statistics (Puzzanchera, 2009), African American youth represented 57% of all young people arrested for murder, 37% of those for rape, and 68% of those for robbery. Arrests of African American youth for violent crimes are 5 times higher than those of whites and Native Americans and 16 times higher than those of Asian youth (Puzzanchera, 2009). In the 1980s, the Violent Crime Index arrest rate for African American youth was between 6 and 7 times the rate for whites, although this gap narrowed somewhat during the 1990s, only to increase again between 1999 and 2007 (to a ratio of 5:1 in 2007). Further, whereas arrests for robberies increased 37% in this time period for African American youth, the rate for whites declined by 17%. Arrests for aggravated assault, while falling off in both groups, declined

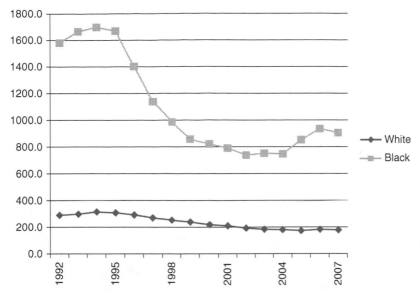

Figure 3.3. Juvenile violent crime arrest rates by race (1990 – 2007) (arrests of persons aged 10–17/100,000 persons aged 10–17).
(From National Center for Juvenile Justice, 2008.)

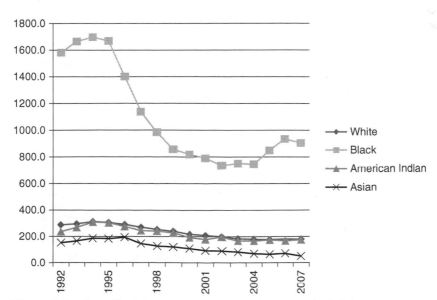

Figure 3.4. Juvenile violent crime arrest rates by race and ethnicity (1990–2007) (arrests of persons aged 10–17/100,000 persons aged 10–17).
(From National Center for Juvenile Justice, 2008.)

less for African American youth (12% overall reduction) compared with whites (27% overall reduction). Collectively, these statistics show that African American youth are at much higher risk of being arrested for violence. There is a need for continued exploration of the reasons underlying this trend. We investigate several relevant hypotheses next.

Not only are African American youth more likely than whites to be arrested for violence, but they are also more likely to enter the juvenile justice system. Data also show that African American youth are treated differently than whites once they enter the system. Between 1985 and 2000, the number of juvenile court cases involving white youth increased 36%, while cases involving African American youth increased a staggering 61% (Puzzanchera, Stahl, Finnegan, Tierney, & Snyder, 2004). Disparities in court processing are even more evident in youth residential placements. Although African Americans were involved in 28% of all delinquency cases processed in 2000, they represented 35% of all detained cases. Between 1985 and 2000, the use of detention was notably higher for delinquency cases involving African American youth compared with cases involving white youth. Delinquency cases that involved African American youth were more likely to be petitioned than those involving whites. Each year, between 1985 and 2000, more delinquency cases involving African American youth were waived from juvenile court to adult court for processing. When this happens, African American youth are denied the protections of juvenile jurisdictions and more likely to receive more severe sentencing.

Another indication of the ways in which African Americans are treated differently than whites is the type of placements youth receive after sentencing. Between 1985 and 2000, African American youth, adjudicated delinquents, were more likely than whites to receive out-of home placements. African American youth were also more likely than whites to have their delinquency cases handled formally (petitioned). Comparatively, more whites were diverted to prevention and treatment programs. These data suggest that racial disparities are systemic and that the treatment of African American youth is particularly severe and highly punitive.

EXPLAINING DISPARITIES IN ARRESTS AND SYSTEMS INVOLVEMENT FOR AFRICAN AMERICAN YOUTH

There are several explanations for the disparities in arrests and processing of youth. One explanation is that African Americans are arrested and handled more severely in the juvenile justice system because they are more violent (Wilbanks, 1987). Some studies show that African Americans initiate violence earlier and are at higher risk than are other groups for serious violence during their adolescent years (Ayers et al., 1999; Williams, Ayers, Abbott, Hawkins, & Catalano, 1999; Williams, Hovmand, & Bright, 2007). However, differences in patterns of violent behavior leading to arrest do not fully explain why cases are handled as differently as they are after contact with the system is made.

Some believe that African American youth are routinely and intentionally targeted for arrests and harsher treatment at entry to the juvenile justice system (Blalock, 1972; Leiber, 2002; Leiber, & Stairs, 1999; Williams, Ayers, Outlaw, Abbott, & Hawkins, 2001). From this perspective, social-structural or context characteristics (e.g., size of African American populations, poverty, and urbanization) lead to more intense monitoring by police and harsher sentencing by the court after formal arrests are made (Cook & Laub, 1998; Engen, Steen, & Bridges, 2002; Hawkins, Laub, & Lauritsen, 1998). While this is a plausible hypothesis, further study of these dynamics is needed. The challenge is in applying a rigorous research design that adequately accounts for the various ways in cases differ beyond the race of the youth involved (e.g., nature of the offense, history of prior offenses, alternatives for treatment, etc.). Next, we turn to theories on the etiology of violence and reasons why African American youth appear to be at higher risk of serious violent behavior.

THEORY, POLICY, AND VIOLENT OFFENDING

For many years, there has been much concern among researchers, practitioners, and policy makers about the overrepresentation of African Americans among violent youth offenders (Puzzanchera, 2009; Williams, Pierce, Young, & Van Dorn, 2001). However, few, if any, current theories of the development of violence account for the range of factors that likely contribute to higher rates of violent conduct among African American youth (Hawkins et al., 1998). One perspective, the biocriminal perspective, suggests that violence is biologically determined; that is, African Americans are more violent because they are biologically predisposed to aggression (Ellis & Walsh, 1997; Herrnstein & Murray, 1994; Wilson & Herrnstein, 1985). While some scholars continue to focus on differences in biology as a basis for variability in rates of offending, most in the field have determined this view to be somewhat shortsighted. With increasing knowledge of the range of social and structural determinants of violence, narrow biological perspectives on violence have received less and less attention (we return to the topic of risk and protective factors later in this chapter).

Biocriminal theories are, perhaps, slightly more advanced in that they at least acknowledge that violence is a product of biological *and* social factors. The emphasis, however, remains on individual constitutional factors, downplaying the role of ecology and environmental risks. Unfortunately, writings by several scholars, such as Wilson and Herrnstein in 1985, continued to attribute race/ethnic differences in violence and crime to constitutional or biological factors primarily.

Perspectives more in keeping with the broader view of this book focus on a range of social, environmental, and cultural determinants of violence

(Engen, Steen, & Bridges, 2002; Hagan & Peterson, 1995; Moynihan, 1965; Sampson, 1987; Wolfgang & Ferracuti, 1967). One is the subculture of violence perspective. This perspective holds that African American youth have fewer opportunities to learn conventional norms and values that deter the use of violence. They are, instead, socialized to the use of violence in certain contexts (Auletta, 1982; Hawkins, 1985; Moynihan, 1965; Wolfgang & Ferracuti, 1967). The belief is that African Americans are more likely to use violence in their day-to-day interactions to settle disputes and are less inclined to develop and use prosocial skills of conflict resolution. The obvious weakness of this perspective is that it, too, fails to account for structural and environmental influences, including many predictors of violence documented in empirical research (Farrington & West, 1993; Hawkins, Abbott, Catalano, & Gillmore, 1991; Hawkins, Catalano, & Miller, 1992; Loeber & Hay, 1997).

Perhaps better aligned with current research is a structural perspective on race and violence. According to scholars of this theory, violence rates are higher for African Americans because they experience more poverty, unemployment, and fewer materials resources than others in the general population (Blau & Blau, 1982; Hagan & Peterson, 1995; Sampson, 1987). Inequality, deprivation, and segregation have, according to structural theorists, led over time to an imbalance in resources and opportunities in society to which all people aspire. Violence is considered a reaction to being disadvantaged. That is, with few opportunities to achieve conventional goals through legitimate means, African Americans, and others in similar conditions, turn to violence as an alternative (Agnew, 1992; Bursik, 1988; Bursik & Grasmick, 1993). This particular perspective has become one of several dominate models in criminology.

Recent research on neighborhood factors adds to what is known about violence at a community level, and relates also to questions about race disparities. Most notable is the work by Sampson and colleagues (Sampson, Raudenbush, & Earls, 1997) mentioned at several points throughout this book. Sampson and colleagues have studied the interaction of structural and social processes related to violence at the neighborhood level and are particularly interested in the ways residents interact to informally control the use of violence within urban communities. They have focused on inner-city neighborhoods of Chicago, which are often occupied by African Americans. What they have found is that several key factors relate to violence within these communities. For example, Sampson et al.'s (1997) study showed that high mobility and low social cohesion among residents predicted more violence within neighborhoods, whereas more cohesion and lower residential turnover predicted lower violence rates. Thus, with respect to race/ethnic differences in offending, it could be that where youth reside, and how residents around them interact to control violence, are particularly pivotal factors. In their recent review of research, Aisenberg and Herrenkohl (2008) reported that neighborhood disadvantage has the added effect of limiting the quantity and quality of positive relationships youth encounter outside their families. Related work by Haynie and colleagues showed that more involvement of residents in groups and organizations lowers youth participation in violence (Haynie, Silver, & Teasdale, 2006).

Social developmental perspectives, which bring together person and environment characteristics, are also useful for understanding race/ethnic differences in offending. For example, the Social Development Model (SDM) of Catalano and Hawkins (1996) is an integrated theory that combines elements from social control (Hirschi, 1969), social learning theories (Bandura, 1977), and differential association theory (Matsueda, 1982, 1988; Sutherland, 1973). The SDM assumes that the prosocial or antisocial behaviors of youth are related to the behaviors, norms, and values of the person(s) to whom a youth is most strongly bonded (e.g., parents or neighborhood adults). The extent to which youth are bonded to others who are themselves prosocial or antisocial will determine the type of behavior in which they, too, will engage (Hawkins, Catalano, Morrison, O'Donnell, Abbott, & Day, 1992; Hawkins, Catalano, & Wells, 1986; Hawkins & Weis, 1985). In the SDM, bonds are hypothesized to moderate the effects of broad social norms on behaviors, such as violence. The SDM has shown utility for predicting violence within diverse populations and can thus help understand racial disparities by isolating variables that are most predictive of violence across various groups (Williams et al., 1996).

RISK AND PROTECTION

While several of the above theories help explain the differences shown in rates and patterns of offending, it is important to examine what research shows about the empirical causes and correlates of violence in youth. A comprehensive risk and protective framework can be used to study and prevent youth violence. We summarize findings of this approach because they provide malleable targets for prevention programs for youth of all ethnicities, including African Americans. This risk and protective factor framework is revisited in subsequent chapters of this book, including Chapters 7 and 8 by Jenson and colleagues, who review promising and rigorously evaluated prevention programs. Next, we highlight some of the findings that have emerged from research on race/ethnic differences in risk and protection. This discussion is continued in Chapter 4.

As noted earlier, risk factors are variables that increase the likelihood of an outcome like violence, whereas protective factors reduce a certain risk factor, or buffer an individual from the cumulative effect of multiple risk factors in the surrounding environment. Risk and protective factors for violence are known to exist in all domains of a youth's life, including family, school, community, and peer groups. Risks are also associated with individuals themselves (Farrington & West, 1993; Hawkins et al., 1991, 1992; Loeber & Hay, 1997; Williams et al., 1996; Williams, & Van Dorn, 1999).

There are several excellent comprehensive reviews of risk factors for violence published in the criminology literature. Readers interested in this topic should see books by Fraser (2004; *Risk and resilience in childhood: An ecological perspective*), Jenson and Howard (1999; *Youth violence: Current research and recent practice innovation*), Loeber and Farrington (1998; *Serious & violent juvenile offenders: Risk factors and successful interventions*), and Loeber and Farrington (2001; *Child delinquents: Development, intervention, and service needs*).

However, there have been only a limited number of studies that have investigated race/ethnic differences in risk and protective factors, also termed "predictors" of violence. And findings of these studies are generally mixed. For example, Rowe, Vazsonyim and Flannery (1994) concluded that developmental processes (e.g., intelligence, attainment, and social adjustment) were the same for both African American and white youth. Yet, McLoed, Kruttschnitt, and Dornfeld (1994) found significant differences in risk processes for African American and whites, including risks of living in poverty, living with a mother who never married, having a large number of siblings, and experiencing physical discipline—all of which are hypothesized predictors of violent offending. Elsewhere, Deater-Deckard and colleagues (1996) found physical discipline to be more strongly associated with antisocial behaviors for whites than for African American youth, concluding that physical discipline in African American households may not be an indicator of lack of warmth but a component of caring and concern (Kelley, Power, & Wimbush, 1992).

Also indicative of possible race/ethnic differences, researchers have found a number of risk factors that correlate with antisocial behaviors for whites but not for African Americans (Deater-Deckard, Dodge, Bates, & Pettit, 1996; Gottfredson & Koper, 1996). One conclusion drawn from these findings is that African American youth experience more risk factors that white youth but react differently to the risks they experience; that is, the risks themselves are greater in number for African American youth but less powerful in their effect on youth outcomes (Deater-Deckard et al., 1996; Gottfredson & Koper, 1996; Farrington, Loeber, Stouthamer-Loeber, 2003).

Studies that have focused particularly on risk factors for African American youth find that violent offending is associated with youths' having a lower school attainment, coming from single-parent family, living in high-crime communities, and having poor parent supervision (Farrington, Loeber, & Stouthamer-Loeber, 2003; Williams, Stiffman, & O'Neal, 1998; Williams, Van Dorn, Bright, Jonson-Reid, & Nebbitt, 2010). Additionally, risk factors such as living in a disorganized neighborhood, residing with a family on public assistance, living in poverty, and having an antisocial father have been found to predict violent offending for African Americans. Interestingly, having a young mother was determined in one study to be more predictive of violence for white youth than for black youth (Farrington et al., 2003).

Risk factors for violence are also well documented at the community level. Data show that approximately 50% of at-risk African American youth reside in disorganized neighborhoods, which are characterized by high levels of crime, low median income, high unemployment, high poverty, high concentrations of youth, and single-parent, female-headed households. Only 2% of white youth live in such neighborhoods (Farrington, Loeber, & Stouthamer-Loeber, 2003). Some scholars have suggested that environmental stressors of African Americans are generally more severe than those of whites, exposing youth to more extreme poverty and more risks within the family (Farrington, Loeber, Stouthamer-Loeber, 2003; Gibson, Morris, & Beaver, 2009; Sampson, Morenoff, & Raudenbush, 2005; Sampson, Raudenbush, & Earls, 1997). The fact that the nature of risk factors themselves may differ by race/ethnicity suggests researchers may need to provide more specificity in definition of risk factors in their data.

Another area in which predictors of violence appear to differ for African Americans and whites is in the domain of school. Williams and colleagues (1996) found that youths' level of commitment to school was more significant in reducing later violence for African-Americans compared with whites. That study also showed that the relationships among school, academic skills, and family relationships were stronger for whites than for African Americans, suggesting more alignment of predictors across domains of risk and protection. In another study, Maguin and Loeber (1996) reported that poor academic performance was a stronger predictor of violence for whites than for African-Americans.

In conclusion, studies have not been consistent in distinguishing African American from white youth on the basis of violence predictors. But, it is well established that, when holding risk factors constant, African American youth (especially males) are more at risk of violence. We are left with a challenge of determining why. It may be that the most compelling answers lie in differences of the structural and social environments of African Americans and whites.

There is also research literature that focuses on what keeps some high-risk individuals from engaging in antisocial behavior. This literature focuses on what is known as protective factors. Research data from various longitudinal youth studies (i.e., Denver, Pittsburgh, Rochester, and Seattle) indicate that risk factors for antisocial behaviors are not simply additive. They interact to produce higher levels of risk burden. It is also posited that risk factors are moderated by protective factors in the family or youth environment and internal resiliency factors or processes (Thornberry et al., 1994, 1995; Williams et al., 1999; Williams & Van Dorn, 1999)

There are several established protective factors that reduce the chances of youth at risk for violence. These factors include female gender, strong attachment to parents, resilient or positive temperament or disposition, ability to adjust and recover, strong external support system that reinforces children's coping efforts, healthy beliefs, prosocial orientation (easy-going disposition and enjoyment of social interaction), and social problem-solving skills (Hawkins et al., 1992; Hawkins, Catalano, & Brewer, 1995). Within the family domain, research from various longitudinal studies has identified five major types of protective family factors: supportive parent-child relationships and family environment, positive discipline techniques, monitoring and supervision, family advocacy for their children, and parents seeking information and support for the benefit of their children (Catalano et al., 1993; Brook, 1993; Williams et al., 1999). Family researchers have associated distinct factors among African American families that serve as protective mechanism for youth. Factors such as a strong economic base, a strong achievement orientation, strong spiritual values, racial pride, extended family bonds, and community involvement and commitment to family (Gonzales, Cauce, Friedman, & Mason, 1996; Williams et al., 1999).

In addition to a growing body of literature on protective factors, there has been an increasing focus on positive youth development. The research conducted by The Search Institute on the influence of developmental assets on youth behaviors has expanded on the resiliency and protective factor knowledge base (Benson et al., 1998; Leffert et al., 1998; Scale et al., 2000). These assets are both internal and external in nature and seem to protect youths against involvement in antisocial behavior (Leffert et al., 1998). External assets are more environmental (e.g., support, empowerment, boundaries and expectations, constructive use of time), while internal assets are more interpersonal/behavioral (e.g., commitment to learning, positive values, social competencies, positive identity) (Benson et al., 1998). It is important to note that while the developmental assets approach provides an additional method of conceptualizing and defining resiliency and protective factors, additional research is needed on nationally representative samples.

IMPLICATIONS AND FUTURE DIRECTIONS: INTERSECTION OF RACE, RISK, AND VIOLENCE

There is no doubt that African American youth, males particularly, are more likely than white youth to be arrested for violent offenses. This is well established. However, the relationship between race and arrest for violent offenses is not as strong when controlling for self-reported violence. The discrepancy between self-reports of violence and actual arrests for violence has several implications. Although it may be that African American youth engage in more violence, a recent meta-analysis of 65 studies found that, after controlling for prior offenses, disparities in arrest rates persisted across studies (Engen et al., 2002). Inequities in the system, systematic discrimination against African American youth at the time of arrest, and juvenile justice processing in all probability account for these observed differences.

SUMMARY

This chapter provides a brief overview of what is known about risk factors, race, and youth violence. This review shows that there is extensive research detailing the various levels of involvement in antisocial behaviors by the youth in this country. There are data on the prevalence of violent offenses as measured by both official data sources and self-report. Longitudinal studies on youth antisocial behaviors, and the annual data compiled by various official law enforcement sources, provide a comprehensive overview of the state of juvenile crime in this country. There are extensive parallel research studies that help us better understand the causes, correlates, policy context, and theoretical undergirding of juvenile crime. In many instances, there has been remarkable advancement in our understanding of the when, where, and why youth become involved in delinquency and violence. However, we must realize the spectrum is very broad and often quite complex. Even with sizeable body of research findings, there remain several gaps in our knowledge about specific populations, particularly related to youth of color. Specifically, there continues to be limited knowledge on the etiology of violence for African Americans, how violence develops, and whether developmental processes leading to the onset of violence are similar or different from white youth. It is apparent that research investigating the intersection of race and violence continues to grow in both scope and content. Indeed, it seems we are a long way from having an across-the-board understanding of the race disparities in adolescent violence. The data show these disparities to be entrenched in our history. It is important to note that although they have fluctuated over the years, rates of disparities are still quite prominent in official statistics. The continuing lack of knowledge in this area has slowed the development of promising programs to address adolescent violence in African American communities.

Many studies have identified risk factors that are considered universal; that is, they are thought to generalize to all youth of all populations. However, studies show inconsistent findings with respect to this issue of generalizabilty. Because much of the research on risk and protective factors for youth violence has been conducted on samples without adequate race/ethnic diversity, and without attempts at detailed information on African American families, comparisons across groups are oversimplified and inadequate. Understanding and studying multiple layers of risk and protection for African American youth and families should help shed light on the actual experiences and environments of these youth. Studies must also consider issues of neighborhood context, discrimination, and social control specific to African American communities.

African American youth often live and learn in physically separate environments. Thus, attending to the intersections of home and school environments for African American youth is another important goal. Further, the experiences of African American youth are primarily in societal institutions (e.g., schools, religious, human services) with other African Americans. Only recent studies have begun to tease out how these experiences shape the socialization of African American youth in possibly different ways from other groups (Drake & Rank, 2009; Coulton & Korbin, 2007; Fauth, Leventhal, & Brooks-Gunn, 2007; Gardner & Brooks-Gunn, 2009; Gibson, Morris, & Beaver, 2009; Kirk, 2008; Nicotera, 2008; Sampson et al., 1997, 2005).

In addition to noted disparities in youths' experience in the juvenile justice system, it is important to acknowledge that disparities exist in other systems that also serve African American young people (e.g., education and child welfare systems). African American children and youth are overrepresented in special education. They are more likely to be identified as children as having emotional and behavioral disorders, as well as attention-deficient/hyperactivity disorder (Gingerich, Turnock, Litfin, & Rosen, 1998; Leigh & Wheatley, 2009). Additionally, African Americans more often come in contact with the child welfare system, which also responds differently to white youth and youth of color (Snyder & Sickmund, 2006).

Finally, within the juvenile justice system, African American youth are not only seen in higher numbers, they are also served less well by the system. Policies are very explicit about the health, social, and psychological needs of youths entering the juvenile justice system. Yet, services rarely attend to the multiple needs of often very disadvantaged children and youth (Abram, Choe, Washburn, Romero, & Teplin, 2009). Services for youth transitioning from the system are also poor or nonexistent. Research on the psychological and social functionality of post incarcerated adolescents found that a significant percentage of these youth continued to require a very high level of care (Abram et al., 2009), possibly African American youth most of all (Abram et al., 2009). In short, a large-scale overhaul of the multiple systems serving youth of color is likely necessary.

Compounding the problems of African American youth, many interventions currently being used in schools and communities are still untested or lack replication to determine their "fit" with the needs of African American youth (see Chapters 7 and 8). Indeed, interventions have seldom been replicated or evaluated for different race/ethnic groups and are only assumed generalizable to different youth populations. And, few programs fall in the category of primary prevention, thereby overlooking many of the early risks that bring African American youth into the juvenile justice system. Risks experienced by youth of color are often addressed too late and with too few resources. We call on researchers, policymakers, and practitioners to increase their awareness of disparate treatment and relative oppression of the environments and programs that serve African American youth. It is important to make continued strides toward understanding and addressing the complex risk environments and needs of youth of color.

REFERENCES

Abrams, K. M., Choe, J. Y., Washburn, J. J., Romero, E. G., & Teplin, L. A. (2009). Functional impairment in youth three years after detention. *Journal of Adolescent Health, 44,* 528–535.

Agnew, R. (1992). Foundation for a general strain theory of crime and delinquency. *Criminology, 30,* 47–87.

Aisenberg, E., & Herrenkohl, T. (2008). Community violence in context: Risk and resilience in children and families. *Journal of Interpersonal Violence, 33,* 296–315.

Auletta, K. (1982). *The underclass.* New York, Random House.

Ayers, C. D., Williams, J. H., Hawkins, D. J., Peterson, P. L., & Abbott, R. D. (1999). Assessing correlates of onset, escalation, deescalation, and desistance of delinquent behavior. *Journal of Quantitative Criminology, 15,* 277–306.

Bandura, A. (1977). *Social learning theory.* New York: General Learning Press.

Blalock, H. M. (1967). Status inconsistency and interaction: Some alternative models. *American Journal of Sociology, 73,* 305–315.

Blau, J. R., & Blau, P. M. (1982). The cost of inequality: Metropolitan structure and violent crime. *American Sociological Review, 47,* 114–129.

Benson, P. L., Leffert, N., Scales, P. C., & Blyth, D. A. (1998). Beyond the "village" rhetoric: Creating healthy communities for children and adolescents. *Applied Developmental Science, 2,* 138–159.

Bridges, G. S., Conley, D. J., Engen, R. L., Price-Spratlen, T. (1995). Racial disparities in the confinement of juveniles: Effects of crime and community social structure on punishment. In K. K. Leonard, C. E. Pope, & W. Feyerherm (Eds.), *Minorities in juvenile justice* (pp. 128–152). Thousand Oaks, CA: Sage Publications.

Brook, J. S. (1993). Interactional theory: Its utility in explaining drug use behavior among African-American and Puerto Rican youth. In M. R. De La Rosa & J.-L. R. Adrados (Eds.) *Drug abuse among minority youth: Advances in research methodology* (pp. 79–101). National Institute on Drug Abuse Research Monograph 130. NIH Pub. No. 93-3479. Washington, DC: U.S. Government Printing Office.

Brook, J. S., Brook, D. W., Gordon, A. S., whiteman, M., & Cohen, P. (1990). The psychosocial etiology of adolescent drug use: A family interactional approach. *Genetic, Social and General Psychology Monographs, 116,* 111–267.

Bursik, R. J. (1988). Social disorganization and theories of crime and delinquency: Problems and prospects. *Criminology, 26,* 519–551.

Bursik, R. J., & Grasmick, H. G. (1993). The use of multiple indicators to estimate crime trends in American cities. *Journal of Criminal Justice, 21,* 509–516.

Catalano, R. F., Hawkins, J. D., Krenz, C., Gillmore, M., Morrison, D., Wells, E., & Abbott, R. (1993). Using research to guide culturally appropriated drug abuse prevention. *Journal of Consulting and Clinical Psychology, 61,* 804–811.

Chapin Hall Center for Children. (2008). *Understanding racial and ethnic disparity in child welfare and juvenile justice.* Chicago: Chapin Hall Center for Children at the University of Chicago.

Coulton, C. J., & Korbin, J. E. (2007). Indicators of child well-being though a neighborhood lens. *Social Indicators Research, 84,* 349–361.

Cook, P. J., & Laub, J. H. (1998). The unprecedented epidemic in youth violence. *Crime and Justice, 24*, 27–64.

Curry, G. D., & Decker, S. H. (1998). *Confronting gangs: Crime and community.* Cary, NC, Roxbury Publishing Company.

Deater-Deckard, K., Dodge, K. A., Bates, J. E., & Pettit, G. S. (1996). Physical discipline among African American and European American mothers: Links to children's externalizing behaviors. *Developmental Psychology, 32*, 1065–1072.

Drake, B., & Rank, M. R. (2009). The racial divide among American children in poverty: Reassessing the importance of neighborhood. *Children and Youth Services Review, 31*, 1264–1271.

Ellis, L., & Walsh, A. (1997). Gene-based evolutionary theories in criminology. *Criminology, 35*, 229–276.

Elliot, D. S. (1994). Serious violent offenders: Onset, developmental course, and termination-the American society of criminology presidential address. *Criminology, 32*, 1–21.

Engen, R. L., Steen, S., & Bridges, G. S. (2002). Racial disparities in the punishment of youth: A theoretical and empirical assessment of the literature. *Social Problems, 49*, 194–220.

Fagan, J. (1996). Gangs, drugs, and neighborhood change. In R. Huff (Ed.), *Gangs in America* (pp. 39–74). Thousand Oaks, CA: Sage Publications.

Farrington, D. P. (1989). Early predictors of adolescent aggression and adult violence. *Violence and Victims, 4*, 79–100.

Farrington, D. P. (1991). Psychological contributions to the explanation of offending. *Issues in Criminological and Legal Psychology, 1*, 7–19.

Farrington, D. P., Loeber, R., & Stouthamer-Loeber, M. (2003). How can the relationship between race and violence be explained? In D. F. Hawkins (Ed.), *Violent crime: Assessing race & ethnic differences* (pp. 213–237). New York: Cambridge University Press.

Farrington, D. P., & West, D. J. (1993). Criminal, penal and life histories of chronic offenders: Risk and protective factors and early identification. *Criminal Behaviour and Mental Health, 3*, 492–523.

Fauth, R. C., Leventhal, T., & Brooks-Gunn, J. (2007). Welcome to the neighborhood? Long-term impacts of moving to low-poverty neighborhoods on poor children's adolescents' outcomes. *Journal of Research on Adolescence, 17*, 249–284.

Federal Bureau of Investigation (2008). *Crime in the United States 2007.* Retrieved May 29, 2009, from http://www.fbi.gov/ucr/cius2007/data/table_38.html

Finley, M., & Schindler, M. (1999). Punitive juvenile justice policies and the impact on minority youth. *Federal Probation, 63*, 11–15.

Fraser, M. W. (2004). *Risk and resilience in childhood: An ecological perspective* (2nd ed.). Washington, DC: NASW Press

Gardner, M., & Brooks-Gunn, J. (2009). Adolescents' exposure to community violence: Are neighborhood youth organizations protective? *Journal of Community Psychology, 37*, 505–525.

Gibson, C. L., Morris, S. Z., & Beaver, K. M. (2009) Secondary exposure to violence during childhood and adolescence: Does neighborhood context matter? *Justice Quarterly, 26*, 30–57.

Gingerich, K. J., Turnock, P., Litfin, J. K., & Rosen, L. A. (1998). Diversity and attention deficit hyperactivity disorder. *Journal of Clinical Psychology, 54*, 415–426.

Gonzales, N., Cauce, A. M., Friedman, R. J., & Mason, C. A. (1996). Family, peer, and neighborhood influences on academic achievement among African-American adolescents: One-year prospective effects. *American Journal of Community Psychology, 24*(3), 365–387.

Gottfredson, D. C., & Koper, C. S. (1996). Race and sex differences in the prediction of drug use. *Journal of Consulting and Clinical Psychology, 64,* 305–313.

Griffin, K. W., Botvin, G. J., Scheier, L. M., Doyle, M. M., & Williams, C. (2003). Common predictors of cigarette smoking, alcohol use, aggression, and delinquency among inner-city minority youth. *Addictive Behaviors, 28,* 1141–1148.

Hagan, J., & Peterson, R. D. (1995). *Crime and Inequality.* Stanford, CA: Stanford University Press.

Haskett, M. E., & Willoughby, M. (2006). Paths to child social adjustment: Parenting quality and children's processing of social information. *Child: Care, Health and Development, 33,* 67–77.

Hawkins, D. F. (1985). Black homicide: The adequacy of existing research for devising prevention strategies. *Crime and Delinquency, 31,* 81–101.

Hawkins, D. F., Laub, J. H., & Lauritsen, J. L. (1998). Race, ethnicity, and serious juvenile offending. In R. Loeber & D. P. Farrington (Eds.), *Serious and violent juvenile offenders: Risk factors and successful interventions* (pp. 30–46). Thousand Oaks, CA: Sage Publications.

Hawkins, J. D., Abbott, R., Catalano, R. F., & Gillmore, M. R. (1991). Assessing effectiveness of drug abuse prevention: Implementation issues relevant to long-term effects and replication. In C. G. Leukefeld & W. J. Bukoski (Eds.), *Drug abuse prevention intervention research: Methodological issues* (pp. 195–212). Rockville, MD: US Dept of Health and Human Services.

Hawkins, J. D., Catalano, R. F., & Brewer, D. D. (1995). Preventing serious, violent, and chronic juvenile offending: Effective strategies from conception to age 6. In J. C. Howell, B. Krisberg, J. D. Hawkins, & J. J. Wilson (Eds.), *Sourcebook on serious, violent, and chronic juvenile offenders* (pp. 47–61). Thousand Oaks, CA: Sage Publications.

Hawkins, J. D., Catalano, R. F., & Miller, J. Y. (1992). Risk and protective factors for alcohol and other drug problems in adolescence and early adulthood: Implications for substance abuse prevention. *Psychological Bulletin, 112,* 64–105.

Hawkins, J. D., & Weis, J. G. (1985). The social development model: An integrated approach to delinquency prevention. *Journal of Primary Prevention, 6,* 73–97.

Hawkins, J. D., Catalano, R. F., & Wells, E. A. (1986). Measuring effects of a skills training intervention for drug abusers. *Journal of Consulting and Clinical Psychology, 54,* 661–664.

Hawkins, J. D., Catalano, R. F., Morrison, D. M., O'Donnell, J., Abbott, R. D., & Day, L. E. (1992). The Seattle Social Development Project: Effects of the first four years on protective factors and problem behaviors. In J. McCord & R. E. Tremblay (Eds.), *Preventing antisocial behavior: Interventions from birth through adolescence* (pp. 139–161). New York: Guilford Press.

Haynie, D. L., Silver, E., & Teasdale, B. (2006). Neighborhood characteristics, peer networks, and adolescent violence. *Journal of Quantitative Criminology, 22,* 147–169.

Herrenkohl, T. I., Maguin, E., Hill, K. G., Hawkins, J. D., Abbott, R. D., & Catalano, R. F. (2000). Developmental risk factors for youth violence. *Journal of Adolescent Health, 26,* 176–186.

Herrnstein, R. J., & Murray, C. (1994). *The bell curve: Intelligence and class structure in American life.* New York, Free Press.

Hill, K. G., Howell, J. C., Hawkins, J. D., & Battin-Pearson, S. R. (1999). Childhood risk factors for adolescent gang membership: Results from the Seattle Social Development Project. *Journal of Research in Crime and Delinquency, 36,* 300–322.

Hindelang, M. J. (1973). Causes of delinquency: A partial replication and extension. *Social Problems. 20,* 471–487.

Hirschi, T. (1969). *Causes of Delinquency.* Berkeley, CA: University of California Press.

Hogh, E., & Wolf, P. (1983). Violent crime in a birth cohort Copenhagen 1953–1977. In K. T. Van Dusen & S. A. Mednick (Eds.), *Prospective studies of crime and delinquency* (pp. 249–267). Hingham, MA: Kluwer-Nijhoff Publishing.

Hundleby, J. D., & Mercer, G. W. (1987). Family and friends as social environments and their relationship to young adolescents' use of alcohol, tobacco, and marijuana. *Journal of Marriage and the Family, 49,* 151–164.

Jenson, J. M., & Howard, M. O. (1999). *Youth violence: Current research and recent practice innovations.* Washington, DC: NASW Press.

Jonson-Reid, M., Williams, J. H., & Webster, D. (2001). Severe emotional disturbance and violent offending among incarcerated adolescents. *Social Work Research, 25,* 213–222.

Kandel, D. B., & Andrews, K. (1987). Processes of adolescent socialization by parents and peers. *International Journal of the Addictions, 22,* 319–342.

Kelley, M. L., Power, T. G., & Wimbush, D. D. (1992). Determinants of disciplinary practices in low-income black mothers. *Child Development, 63,* 573–582.

Kempf-Leonard, K. (2007). Minority youths and juvenile justice: Disproportionate minority contact after nearly 20 years of reform efforts. *Youth Violence and Juvenile Justice, 5,* 71–87.

Kirk, D. S. (2008). The neighborhood context of racial and ethnic disparities in arrest. *Demography, 45,* 55–77.

Krivo, L. J., & Peterson, R. D. (1996). Extremely disadvantaged neighborhoods and urban crime. *Social Forces, 75,* 619–650.

Leffert, N., Benson, P. L., Scales, P. C., Sharma, A., Drake, D., & Blyth, D. A. (1998). Developmental assets: Measurement and prediction of risk behaviors among adolescents. *Applied Developmental Science, 2*(4), 209–230.

Leiber, M. J. (2002). Disproportionate minority confinement (DMC) of youth: An analysis of state and federal efforts to address the issue. *Crime and Delinquency, 48,* 3–45.

Leiber, M. J., & Stairs, J. M. (1999). Race, contexts, and the use of intake diversion. *Journal of Research in Crime and Delinquency, 36,* 56–86.

Leigh, W. A., & Wheatlley, A. L. (2009). *Trends in child health 1997–2006: Assessing racial/ethnic disparities in diagnoses of ADHD/ADD and of learning disability.* Washington, DC: Joint Center for Political and Economic Studies.

Loeber, R. (1990). Disruptive and antisocial behavior in childhood and adolescence: Development and risk factors. In K. Hurrelmann & F. Lösel (Eds.),

Health Hazards in Adolescence (pp. 233–257), Oxford, England: Walter De Gruyter.

Loeber, R. (1991). Development and risk factors of juvenile antisocial behavior and delinquency. *Clinical Psychology Review, 10,* 1–41.

Loeber, R. (1996). Developmental continuity, change, and pathways in male juvenile problem behaviors and delinquency. In D. J. Hawkins (Ed.), *Delinquency and Crime: Current Theories* (pp. 1–27), New York, NY, US: Cambridge University Press.

Loeber, R., & Hay, D. (1997). Key issues in the development of aggression and violence from childhood to early adulthood. *Annual Review of Psychology, 48,* 371–410.

Loeber, R., & Farrington, D. P. (1998). *Serious and violent juvenile offenders: Risk factors and successful interventions.* Thousand Oaks, CA: Sage Publications.

Loeber, R., & Farrington, D. P. (2001). *Child delinquent: Development, intervention, and service needs.* Thousand Oaks, CA: Sage Publications.

Loeber, R., & Stouthamer-Loeber, M. (1986). Family factors as correlates and predictors of juvenile conduct problems and delinquency. In M. Tonry & N. Morris (Eds.), *Crime and justice* (pp. 29–149), Chicago: University of Chicago Press.

Lynch, M., & Cicchetti, D. (2002). Links between community violence and the family system: Evidence from children's feelings of relatedness and perceptions of parent behaviors. *Family Process, 41,* 519–532.

Maguin, E., & Loeber, R. (1996). Academic performance and delinquency. In Michael Tonry (Ed.), *Crime and justice* (pp. 145–264). Chicago: University of Chicago Press.

Martinez, R., Stowell, J. I., & Cancino, J. M. (2008). A tale of two border cities: Community context, ethnicity, and homicide. *Social Science Quarterly, 89,* 1–16.

Matsueda, R. L. (1982). Testing control theory and differential association: A causal modeling approach. *American Sociological Review, 47,* 489–504.

Matsueda, R. L. (1988). The current state of differential association theory. *Crime and Delinquency, 34,* 277–306.

McCord, J., & Ensminger, M. E. (1997). Multiple risks and comorbidity in an African-American population. *Criminal Behaviour and Mental Health, 7,* 339–352.

McLeod, J. D., Kruttschnitt, C., & Dornfeld, M. (1994). Does parenting explain the effects of structural conditions on children's antisocial behaviors? A comparison of blacks and whites. *Social Forces, 73,* 575–604.

Morenoff, J. D., Sampson, R. J., & Raudenbush, S. (2001). Neighborhood inequality, collective efficacy, and the special dynamics of urban violence. *Criminology, 39,* 517–560.

Moynihan, D. P. (1965). The Negro family: The case for national action. Retrieved May 20, 2009, from http://www.dol.gov/oasam/programs/history/webid-meynihan.htm

National Center for Juvenile Justice (2008). *Juvenile arrest rates by offense, sex, and race.* Retrieved May 20, 2009, from http://ojjdp.ncjrs.org/ojstatbb/crime/excel/JAR_2008.xls

Nicotera, N. (2008). Children speak about neighborhoods: Using mixed methods to measure the construct neighborhood. *Journal of Community Psychology, 36,* 333–351.

Patterson, G. R., & Stouthamer-Loeber, M. (1984). The correlation of family management practices and delinquency. *Child Development, 55,* 1299–1307.

Puzzanchera, C. (2009, April). Juvenile arrests 2007. *Juvenile Justice Bulletin.* Retrieved May 19, 2009, from http://www.ncjrs.gov/pdffiles1/ojjdp/225344.pdf.

Puzzanchera, C., Stahl, A. L., Finnegan, T. A., Tierney, N., & Snyder, H. N. (2004). *Juvenile court statistics 2000.* Pittsburgh, PA: National Center for Juvenile Justice.

Rowe, D. C., Vazsonyi, A. T., & Flannery, D. J. (1994). No more than skin deep: Ethnic and racial similarity in developmental process. *Psychological Review, 101,* 396–413.

Rutter, M. (1985). Family and school influences on behavioural development. *Journal of Child Psychology and Psychiatry, 26,* 349–368.

Salzinger, S., Rosario, M., & Feldman, R. S. (2007). Physical child abuse and adolescent violent delinquency: The mediating and moderating roles of personal relationships. *Child Maltreatment, 12,* 208–219.

Sampson, R. J. (1987). Urban black violence: The effect of male joblessness and family disruption. *American Journal of Sociology, 93,* 348–382.

Sampson, R. J., & Bartusch, D. J. (1998). Legal cynicism and (subcultural?) tolerance of deviance: The neighborhood context of racial differences. *Law and Society Review, 32,* 777–804.

Sampson, R. J., & Laub, J. H. (1994). Urban poverty and the family context of delinquency: A new look at structure and process in a classic study. *Child Development, 65,* 523–540.

Sampson, R. J., Morenoff, J. D., & Gannon-Rowley, T. (2002). Assessing "neighborhood effects": Social processes and new directions in social research. *Annual Review of Sociology, 28,* 443–478.

Sampson, R. J., Morenoff, J. D., & Raudenbush, S. (2005). Social anatomy of racial and ethnic disparities in violence. *American Journal of Public Health, 95,* 224–232.

Sampson, R. J., Raudenbush, S. W., & Earls, F. (1997). Neighborhoods and violent crime: A multilevel study of collective efficacy. *Science, 277,* 918–924.

Scales, P. C., Benson, P. L., Leffert, N., & Blyth, D. A. (2000). Contribution of developmental assets to the prediction of thriving among adolescents. *Applied Developmental Science,* 27–46.

Smith, D. A., & Jarjoura, G. R. (1988). Social structure and criminal victimization. *Journal of Research in Crime and Delinquency, 25,* 27–51.

Shedler, J., & Block, J. (1990). Adolescent drug use and psychological health: a longitudinal inquiry. *American Psychologist, 45,* 612–630.

Smith, D. A., & Jarjoura, G. R. (1988). Social structure and criminal victimization. *Journal of Research in Crime and Delinquency, 25,* 27–52.

Smith, C., & Thornberry, T. P. (1995). The relationship between childhood maltreatment and adolescent involvement in delinquency. *Criminology, 33,* 451–481.

Snyder, H. N., & Sickmund, M. (2006). *Juvenile offenders and victims: 2006 National report.* Washington, DC: U.S. Department of Justice, Office of Justice Programs, Office of Juvenile Justice and Delinquency Prevention.

Stattin, H., & Magnusson, D. (1989). The role of early aggressive behavior in the frequency, seriousness, and types of later crime. *Journal of Consulting and Clinical Psychology, 57,* 710–718.

Stouthamer-Loeber, M., Wei, E. H., Homish, D. L., & Loeber, Ro. (2002). Which family and demographic factors are related to both maltreatment and persistent serious juvenile delinquency? *Children's Services: Social Policy, Research, and Practice, 5*, 261–272.

Sutherland, E. (1973). *On analyzing crime.* Chicago: University of Chicago Press.

Swenson, C. C., Brown, E. J., & Sheidow, A. (2003). Medical, legal, and mental health service utilization by physically abused children and their caregivers. *Child Maltreatment, 8*, 138–144.

Thornberry, T. P., Huizinga, D., & Loeber, R. (1995). Prevention of serious delinquency and violence: Implications from the program of research on the causes and correlates of delinquency. In J. C. Howell, B. Krisberg, J. D. Hawkins, & J. J. Wilson (Eds.), *Sourcebook on serious, violent, and chronic juvenile offenders* (pp. 213–237). Thousand Oaks, CA: Sage Publications.

Thornberry, T. P., Lizotte, A. J., Krohn, M. D., Farnworth, M., & Jang, S. J. (1994). Delinquent peers, beliefs, and delinquent behavior: A longitudinal test of interactional theory. *Criminology, 32*, 47–83.

Tolan, P. H., & Thomas, P. (1995). The implications of age of onset for delinquency risk. II: Longitudinal data. *Journal of Abnormal Child Psychology, 23*, 157–181.

Tremblay, R. E. (1988). Aggressive behavior. In S. J. Apter & A. P. Goldstein (Eds.), *Youth violence: Program and prospects,* Oxford: Pergamon Press.

Widom, C. S. (1989). *The intergenerational transmission of violence.* New York: Harry Frank Guggenheim Foundation.

Wilbanks, W. (1987). *The myth of a racist criminal justice system.* Belmont, CA: Wadsworth Publishing.

Williams, J. H., Ayers, C. D., Abbott, R. D., Hawkins, J. D., & Catalano, R. F. (1999). Racial differences in risk factors for delinquency and substance use among adolescents. *Social Work Research, 23*, 241–257.

Williams, J. H., Ayers, C. D., Abbott, R. D., Hawkins, J. D., & Catalano, R. F. (1996). Structural equivalence of involvement in problem behavior across racial groups using multiple group confirmatory factor analysis. *Social Work Research, 20*, 168–179.

Williams, J. H., Ayers, C. D., Outlaw, W. S., Abbott, R. D., & Hawkins, J. D. (2001). The effects of race in the juvenile justice system: Investigating early stage processes. *Journal for Juvenile Justice and Detention Services, 16*, 77–91.

Williams, J. H., & Van Dorn, R. A. (1999). Delinquency, gangs, and youth violence. In J. M. Jenson & M. O. Howard (Eds.), *Prevention and treatment of violence in children and youth: Etiology, assessment, and recent practice innovations* (pp. 199–225). Washington, DC: NASW Press.

Williams, J. H., Van Dorn, R. A., Bright, C. L., Jonson-Reid, M., & Nebbitt, V. E. (2010). Child maltreatment and delinquency onset among African American adolescent males. *Research on Social Work Practice, 20*, 253–259.

Williams, J. H., Stiffman, A. R., & O'Neal, J. L. (1998). Violence among urban African American youths: An analysis of environmental and behavioral risk factors. *Social Work Research, 22*, 3–13.

Williams, J. H., Pierce, R., Young, N. S., & Van Dorn, R. A. (2001). Service utilization in high-*crime* communities: Consumer views on supports and barriers. *Families in Society, 82*, 409–417.

Williams, J. H., Hovmand, P. S., & Bright, C. L. (2007). Overrepresentation of African Americans incarcerated for delinquency offenses in juvenile institutions. In D. W. Springer & A. R. Roberts (Eds.), *Handbook of forensic mental health with victims and offenders: Assessment, treatment, and research* (pp. 363–381). New York: Springer Publishing.

Wilson, J. Q., & Herrnstein, R. J. (1985). *Crime and human nature.* New York: Simon & Schuster, 1985.

Wolfgang, M. E., & Ferracuti, F. (1967). *Subculture of violence: Towards an integrated theory in criminology.* London: Tavistock Publications.

Zingraff, M. T., Leiter, J., Myers, K. A., & Johnson, M. C. (1993). Child maltreatment and youthful problem behavior. *Criminology, 31,* 173–202.

4

GENDER DIFFERENCES IN RISK AND PROTECTIVE FACTORS ASSOCIATED WITH YOUTH VIOLENCE

Charlotte Lyn Bright, James Herbert Williams, & Granger Petersen

It has been posited that the juvenile justice system was designed around the needs of boys, who traditionally have constituted the majority juvenile court–involved population (Zahn, Hawkins, Chiancone, & Whitworth, 2008). As girls have become a larger and better understood minority in this system, however, scholarship has begun to recognize their specific pathways and needs (Cauffman, 2008). This chapter will focus on gender and violent offending, emphasizing the most recent empirical and theoretical scholarship on similarities and differences in boys' and girls' violent behavior. We seek to shed light on the following questions: What proportion of violent crimes do male and female youth commit? Are boys and girls becoming more or less violent? Why do youth behave violently in the first place, and why do girls seem to be less violent than boys? What can protect boys and girls from committing violent behavior? How do race, ethnicity, and gender impact violence and the juvenile justice system's response to it? What are the potential young adult outcomes of violence among girls? Finally, what can we do about boys' and girls' violence, and what do we still need to learn in order to respond to appropriately?

JUVENILE VIOLENT OFFENDING: PREVALENCE AND TRENDS

The Federal Bureau of Investigation (FBI; n.d.) publishes an annual report, *Crime in the United States,* which describes the demographic characteristics of arrests each year. The data describe the number of people arrested, with the most serious charge being noted for incidents where multiple charges are issued. In 2007, the most recent year for which complete data are available, just over 1.1 million arrests made were of males under age 18, while slightly under 500,000 arrests were of females under age 18. Females thus constituted about 30% of all juvenile arrests. Girls still represent a minority of juvenile arrests, but this proportion is growing. In 1995, according to the FBI, girls constituted 25% of juvenile arrests. In the 10-year period from 1998 to 2007, the agency notes that arrests among boys have decreased by 23%, while arrests of girls have decreased 13.5%, a smaller change. FBI data indicate that, while arrests in most categories of offenses among boys have decreased since the late 1990s, arrests for girls in a number of categories have increased during the same time period or have decreased much less (Figure 4.1).

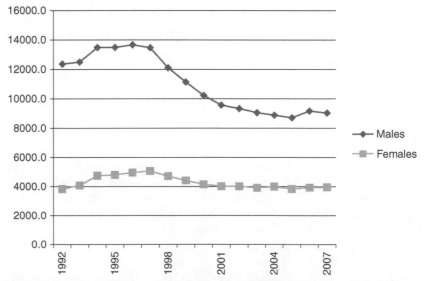

Figure 4.1. Juvenile arrest rates by gender (1990–2007) (arrests of persons aged 10–17/100,000 persons aged 10–17).
(National Center for Juvenile Justice, 2008).

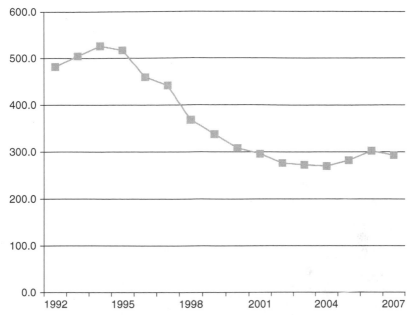

Figure 4.2. Juvenile violent crime arrest rates (1990–2007) (arrests of persons aged 10–17/100,000 persons aged 10–17).
(National Center for Juvenile Justice, 2008).

Overall, juveniles constitute about 16% of all arrests for violent crime (Puzzanchera, 2009) (Figure 4.2). The statistics on violent crime reflect an increase in girls' arrests compared with earlier numbers and the proportion of all current arrests for violent crime. Arrests for assault have decreased in the past 10 years, but this decline has been greater for boys than for girls (Puzzanchera, 2009). Between 1998 and 2007, boys' arrests for murder, manslaughter, forcible rape, robbery, and assault decreased 8.0%, while girls' arrests for these offenses *increased* 5.3%. Girls constituted about 8.8% of all juvenile arrests for murder, forcible rape, and robbery and approximately 31.7% of all arrests for aggravated and nonaggravated assaults in 2007 (FBI, n. d.). Still, the gender discrepancy for violent crime arrests is larger than for other (property, public order, and status) arrests. These gender differences are similar for juveniles and for adults in the criminal justice system (Puzzanchera, 2009) (seeFigure 4.3).

Another measure of violent crime is the National Crime Victimization Survey (NCVS), administered annually by the Bureau of Justice Statistics to U.S. residents ages 12 and over. The survey is designed to include information on all crime victimizations, including those not reported to the police (National Archive of Criminal Justice Data, n.d.). According to the NCVS, reports of violent crime in the United States have diminished substantially since the early 1990s (Bureau of Justice Statistics, 2009). In the time period 1993 to 2003, nonlethal violent offending (i.e., violent

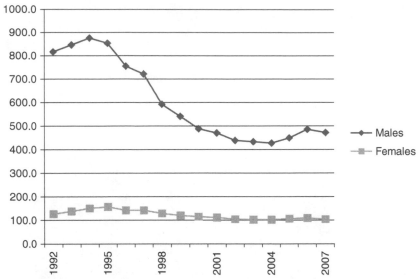

Figure 4.3. Juvenile violent crime arrest rates by gender (1990–2007) (arrests of persons aged 10–17/100,000 persons aged 10–17).
(National Center for Juvenile Justice, 2008).

offenses other than homicide) remained relatively stable among male and female adolescents; about one-fourth of these crimes were perpetrated by females. Homicides perpetrated by both genders decreased substantially in that same time period (Baum, 2005).

These different sources of information present a somewhat puzzling picture about violent offending and gender. One key question is, "If victims' incident reports are relatively stable over time for both male and female youth, why are arrest rates changing in different ways for boys and girls?"

The answer to this question requires an understanding of the policy context of police decision making and that of possible cultural and social shifts. In their analysis of 20 years of arrest trends, Snyder and Sickmund (2006) found that arrests of girls for violent crime have increased considerably in that time period, concomitant with decreases in violent crime arrests for boys. The authors suggest that these arrests relate more to police practices regarding domestic violence than to actual changes in girls' behavior; more girls than boys commit violent acts against family members, and police are now more likely to make an arrest based on an incident of domestic violence than they were in the past. Some of the increase in girls' violent crime arrests may even result from re-labeling, with girls being charged with committing domestic violence following family conflicts, rather than with running away, as in the past (Chesney-Lind & Belknap, 2004). This re-labeling of status offenses as violent crimes is posited to disproportionately impact girls of color, who, like males of color, are overrepresented at all stages of juvenile justice processing (American Bar Association, 2001).

Beyond police and juvenile justice system–level decision making, broader social and cultural changes may also be impacting the change in girls'arrests for violent crime. It has been suggested that there is now a greater recognition of fights among girls, along with a decrease in protective, tolerant views on violence perpetrated by females (Steffensmeier, Schwartz, Zhong, & Ackerman, 2005). These societal changes may result, in part, from increased media attention to girls' violent acts and the interpretation in television and print news sources that girls' behavior has changed in dangerous and frightening ways (Irwin & Chesney-Lind, 2008; Luke, 2008).

Relational Aggression

While this chapter, and most others in this book, focuses on physical violence, a more inclusive examination of girls' violence requires mention of relational aggression. Relational aggression is not physical in nature but involves such behaviors as exclusion, manipulation, and criticism intended to damage the victim's relationships or social standing (Crick & Grotpeter, 1995). Relational aggression has been recognized as the predominant form of aggression among girls, more common than physical or sexual violence or threats (Underwood, Galen, & Paquette, 2001). Relational aggression may be related to commission of interpersonal violence, but this association has been found to be weaker among boys than among girls (Zimmer-Gembeck, Geiger, & Crick, 2005). Such behavior has problematic implications for social development and future relationships, above and beyond the issues youth experience due to physically aggressive behavior (Crick, 1996).

THEORY, GENDER, AND VIOLENT OFFENDING

As noted earlier, much traditional scholarship in juvenile justice has focused on the needs and experiences of boys. Because of the different experiences of boys and girls in this system, however, a "one-size-fits-all" theory is limited in its applicability to both genders. While certain theoretical constructs and propositions have the potential to explain offending in both boys and girls, presumably the mechanisms by which causal relationships occur will differ. A comprehensive discussion of traditional criminologic theories and their advantages and disadvantages in explaining violent behavior in both genders is beyond the scope of this chapter. Rather, our intention is to critically examine and apply some potentially causal constructs, with a focus on how boys' and girls' experiences may differ. Our presentation of theory will therefore follow Steffensmeier and Allan (1996) in taking a "gendered" approach. In essence, this perspective involves assessing the contributions existing theory can make in explaining not only juvenile violent offending behavior itself but also the reasons why females commit fewer violent offenses than males. Additionally, a gendered perspective takes into account the differences in male and female experiences, promoting an understanding of separate pathways to delinquency. Two interrelated and cross-cutting concepts guiding our review of theory are the role of trauma and the disparate socialization of boys and girls.

As noted by Aisenberg and colleagues in Chapter 2 and by Herrenkohl in Chapters 5 and 6, the experience of witnessing and being victimized by violence can lead to a range of problems for children and youth, including their own use of violence against others. The mechanisms for better understanding how early experiences in and exposure to violence affects later behavior are addressed in several social and psychological theories, including cognitive and social learning perspectives. Cognitive theories assert that the trauma that extends from witnessing violence affects children's development by creating problematic assumptions about the ways individuals interact with one another and the role of violence in relationships (Baer & Maschi, 2003). A social learning perspective suggests that criminal behavior can be learned in the home or neighborhood, through modeling and imitation. In terms of violent behavior, witnessing or being subjected to aggression and receiving reinforcement for aggressive behavior are posited as causal mechanisms for the development of violence (Bandura, 2007). Regardless of how trauma results in later violence, it is important to note that greater exposure to community and family violence may put urban youth in impoverished, higher-crime neighborhoods at disproportionate risk (see related discussion by Herrenkohl in Chapter 5).

The processes by which a child victim of violence becomes a perpetrator of violence are at central to the "cycle of violence" hypothesis, which posits that victims of maltreatment learn to use violence in their own relationships and that violence becomes a preferred method to solve problems and handle conflict (Brezina, 1998; Jonson-Reid, 1998). As discussed by Herrenkohl in Chapter 6, an important caveat to these assertions is that many maltreated children do not display violent behavior later in their development; that is, they avoid becoming perpetrators of violence despite the violence they experienced as children.

A gendered understanding of the role of maltreatment needs to account for differences in experience of and reactions to traumatic events. In several mixed-gender studies, it appears that maltreatment is more predictive of delinquent behavior for girls compared with boys (e.g., Bright & Jonson-Reid, 2008; McCormack, Janus, & Burgess, 1986; Widom & Maxfield, 2001), although, as noted in Chapter 5, findings overall on gender differences and maltreatment are inconsistent. Additionally findings on gender may be complicated by the use of inconsistent definitions of violence and violence exposure, severity of the behaviors in question, and varying individual responses to these traumatic events (see Chapters 2 and 5 for more discussion of these issues).

Various theorists have connected trauma and victimization to gender-based differences in socialization and opportunity. Irwin and Chesney-Lind (2008) explain violent behavior in the context of two types of inequality: inequality of victimization, in which girls are disproportionately traumatized (particularly sexually), and inequality of opportunity, in which boys are accorded greater value. On this topic, Schaffner (2007) stated, "Whereas for boys, abuse goes against what they are taught to expect from their gender position of superiority, abuse of girls confirms their place in the gender hierarchy" (p. 1231). In other words, victim status may come as more of a surprise to boys than to girls.

Social learning theory allows for the consideration of gender in learned behavior. Early proponents of social learning theory suggest that gender differences in behavior may be attributable to differential role modeling and reinforcement (Bandura & Walters, 1963; Minuchin, 1969). In particular, aggression may be positively reinforced in boys, while dependence is reinforced in girls (Akers, 1973; Bandura & Walters). More recent work (e.g., Jensen, 2003) has promoted a cognitive component of social learning, intimating that reinforcement of behavior helps shape gender identity and that girls are therefore less likely than boys to behave aggressively because of pressure to conform to a loving, nurturing identity. As Heimer and De Coster (1999) note, "[G]irls' violence is reduced by learning traditional definitions of gender, whereas these have little effect on boys' violence" (p. 303). Violence among girls, therefore, may be a byproduct of more severe dysfunction in the home, as it requires an extreme challenge to the gender identity girls are pressured to develop. In boys, by contrast, violent behavior is considered a socially acceptable behavior in certain contexts as well as a sanctioned response to threats or acts of violence perpetrated by others (Maschi & Bradley, 2008).

Interestingly, young girls are more likely than young boys to promote stereotyped gender roles (Albert & Porter, 1988), and this internalized sexism has been conceptualized to explain why girls most often victimize other girls; in a society in which girls are marginalized, it is safer and more socially acceptable for them to turn against one another than to direct aggression toward males (Irwin & Chesney-Lind, 2008). Dougherty (1998) comments that the differences between sexes are valued differently, with "feminine" traits being devalued within the patriarchy of society; this leads women and girls, as well as men and boys, to consider females inferior to males. Of course, the expectation that youth will adhere to gender roles is also damaging to boys, particularly in that they can internalize the notion that violence is the way to resolve conflict (Levant, 1996). The argument can be made that boys are essentially forced into violent roles to uphold a social order of male privilege (Pettersson, 2005).

Gilligan (1993a, 1993b) stresses the importance of developmental theory in explaining both male and female behavior. She describes girls as growing to value relationships and connectedness, and boys as emphasizing individuality and competition. This perspective offers some insight into gender differences in violent behavior. Timing of developmental stages is also a salient issue; antisocial behavior in males is often identifiable in early elementary school, while girls' behavior problems tend to begin later, in middle school (Chamberlain, 2006). Therefore, theorists considering trajectories and development in their explanation of aggression must take gender into account.

Social control theories assert that the pertinent question is not why some people offend and others do not; to the contrary, the important dynamic to understand is what constrains some individuals from offending. Again, gender socialization can be interpreted as playing a key role in this process. Steffensmeier and Allan (1996) propose that differences in how girls and boys are raised result in increased supervision for girls and the promotion of nurturing and dependent characteristics, which are generally incompatible with criminal behavior. Singer and Levine (1988) found that maternal control is more evident toward girls than boys. In other words, mothers exert more control over their daughters than over their sons, meaning that a within-family source of social control is applied differently by gender. They hypothesize that this may account for the some of the difference in delinquency rates between male and female youth. Finally, girls have been found to espouse conventional values more frequently than boys, which may explain some gender differences in violent offending (Liu & Kaplan, 1999).

Hagan, McCarthy, and Holly (2002) amend social control theories to include a dimension of gender inequality. In their power-control theory, they note that patriarchal families encourage risk-taking behavior of males and discourage it among females; they also supervise and monitor girls' behavior more than they do boys' behavior. This preferential treatment of males is reflected in the greater society through male employment and ownership advantages. One criticism of Hagan and colleagues' work is that research does not support the notion that more egalitarian families produce a smaller gender gap in delinquent behavior, as implied in the patriarchal family explanation of gender differences offered by power-control theory (Brannigan, 1997). Also, this theory was not developed to explain violent behavior but rather other kinds of deviance (Hagan, Gillis, & Simpson, 1985).

An integrated theoretical perspective on girls' violence should take into account both environmental determinants of behavior and development as a process. The model depicted in Figure 4.4 is adapted from Szapocznik and Coatsworth (1999) and Zayas and colleagues (2005). It displays factors within the family, neighborhood, community, and society as salient for female development. The circles representing development, neighborhood and family functioning, and environment are nested within one another to indicate that they operate at micro, meso, and macro levels, respectively, and that these factors influence psychosocial functioning both independently (where the circles do not overlap) and conjointly

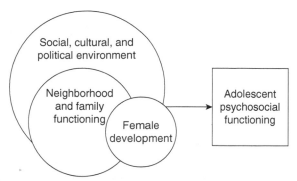

Figure 4.4. Developmental-ecological model of female violence, as a component of adolescent psychosocial functioning.

(where the circles do overlap). In many ways, this model is consistent with the ecologic perspective mentioned in Chapter 1.

RISK AND PROTECTION

To determine which youth are more likely to commit violent offenses, researchers have begun analyzing risk factors and protective factors. Unfortunately, findings on risk and protection do not map neatly onto the broad theoretical perspectives discussed above. Consequently, empirical findings on risk and protective factors are considered separately.

Broadly defined, risk factors are any influences that may lead to problem behaviors or conditions (Fraser, Kirby, & Smokowski, 2004). Risk factors can be conceptualized as either causes or correlates of offending, the former requiring temporal ordering among variables (DeMatteo & Marczyk, 2005). The presence of one or more risk factors is believed to increase the chance of offending, while protective factors are presumed to interact with risk factors to reduce the likelihood of offending behavior (Howell, 2003; Williams, Ayers, Van Dorn, & Arthur, 2004). Risk factors can be distal (i.e., occurring years before the onset of violent offending) or proximal to the measured outcome of violence (Smokowski, Mann, Reynolds, & Fraser, 2003). Next, we review empirical findings on risk and protection as they relate to violence in male and female youth.

Risk, Protection, and Male Violent Behavior

Risk factors are predictive of an increased probability of a subsequent undesirable outcome, such as violence or substance use (Farrington, Loeber, Stouthamer-Loeber, Van Kammen, & Schmidt, Laura, 1996; Hawkins, Catalano, & Miller, 1992). Risk factors for violent behaviors are found in several domains (i.e., individual, family, peer, school, and community). At the level of the individual children, risk factors for violence include a range of factors, from genetic and physiologic characteristics to hyperactivity and early oppositional and aggressive behavior. Research shows that children who exhibit aggressive behavior in early childhood are at higher risk of violence and other problems in adolescence (Cairns & Cairns, 1991) and convictions for violent offenses by age 32 (Farrington, 1991b).

Research indicates that youth who associate with violent peers are more likely to perpetrate violence in the community (Cairns, Leung, Buchanan, Cairns, 1995; Farrington, 1991a; Hawkins et al., 1992; Williams et al., 1998). Studies indicate that, within groups of delinquent peers and gangs, violence is often reinforced and encouraged, leading the offending behaviors of some youth to increase notably (Cairns et al., 1995; Thornberry et al., 1994). Attitudes and beliefs favorable toward deviance as well as impulsive behaviors are considered to be risk factors for violent offending behavior (Elliott, 1994; Van Dorn & Williams, 2003).

Within the family domain, risk factor such as family conflict and parents' inappropriate modeling behavior, poor family management practices are related to youth violence. Youth exposed to poor family management practices are at higher risk of engaging in violent behavior (Farrington, 1991a; Thornberry, 1994). Additionally, parental conflict and coercive family interaction create a situation that reinforces aggressiveness and that domestic violence increases the likelihood of a youth's involvement in violent behavior (Loeber & Dishion, 1984; Patterson & Dishion, 1985).

As previously noted, and also discussed in later chapters, child maltreatment is a salient predictor of violence in youth (see Herrrenkohl's review and discussion in Chapter 5). In etiologic studies, child maltreatment and related constructs of inconsistent discipline, harsh punishment, and authoritarian parenting have all been shown to predict conduct problems in children of various forms, which can progress to violent offending if not addressed early (Patterson & Stouthamer-Loeber, 1984).

Finally, as noted in Chapter 1 and elsewhere in the book, research has identified various structural and social processes of communities that appear to increase risk for violence among youth (Garbarino et al., 1992; Williams, Stiffman, & O'Neal, 1998). For example, community poverty and social disorganization are salient risk factors for youth violence (Simcha-Fagan & Schwartz, 1986). Work by Sampson and colleagues on collective efficacy and social control is also important from the standpoint of understanding community risks, although details of their work are provided in other chapters of the book (see Chapters 3 and 5). While living in high-crime, low-income neighborhoods has been identified in ethnographic research as contributing to violent behavior among girls (Ness, 2004), this connection has not yet been well established in quantitative scholarship (Chauhan & Reppucci, 2009). Because this question has not been examined in many large-scale studies, more research is needed to determine if and how community and neighborhood risk factors result in violent behavior in female youth particularly.

Risk, Protection, and Female Violent Behavior

While the literature on delinquent behavior among female youth has expanded considerably in the past several years, empirical literature specific to girls' violence and violence prevention remains extremely limited (Odgers, Moretti, & Reppucci, 2005). Much of the scholarly literature is retrospective and descriptive; for example, some studies conduct surveys or interviews of girls charged with violent offenses and inquire about their histories, rather than following samples across multiple time points and investigating which girls initiate violent behavior. Existing literature on girls and violence is therefore summarized here, supplemented with some information on adult women and general delinquency (not limited to violent offending) among girls. It is hoped that future research will provide a clearer, more complete picture of juvenile violent offending among girls.

Victimization is the most commonly reported risk factor for girls' violence. Victimization can involve being physically and sexual abused by a family member (Artz, 1998; Acoca, 1999; Herrera & McCloskey, 2001; Holsinger & Holsinger, 2005; Trickett & Gordis, 2004), being beaten, shot, or stabbed (Shaffer & Ruback, 2002), or even being harassed, labeled, or ignored by peers (Schaffner, 2007; Zahn et al., 2008). Being the victim of violence can lead some girls to become violent themselves out of fear and for self-protection. In this sense, violence can serve a number of functions, including responses to present or past threats and promotion of an image of toughness (Irwin & Chesney-Lind, 2008), as well as protection of friends or family members (Ness, 2004). For adult women, being the victim of intimate partner violence is associated with the perpetration of violence (Weitzmann-Henelius, Viemerö, & Eronen, 2004); this may also be the case with adolescent females, although no known literature has yet documented this specific connection.

Substance use is associated with violence in girls (Holsinger & Holsinger, 2005; Lanctôt, Émond, & Le Blanc, 2004), and both substance use and mental health problems have been documented in adult women perpetrators of violence (Weitzmann Henelius, Viemerö, & Eronen, 2004). Mental health problems have been noted to be more frequent in girls than in boys with juvenile justice system involvement, and substance abuse is a noted risk factor for both boys and girls (Calhoun, 2001; Dixon, Howie, & Starling, 2005; Goldstein et al., 2003; Gover, 2004; Lederman, Dakof, Larrea, & Li, 2004; McCabe, Lansing, Garland, & Hough, 2002; Timmons-Mitchell et al., 1997; Wasserman et al., 2005). The impact of substance use on serious property and violent offenses may be more marked in boys than in girls, however (Huizinga, Loeber, Thornberry, & Cothern, 2000). As most of this literature does not examine violent offending separately from other offenses, the relationships among mental health, substance use, and violence in girls remains unclear.

Research is very limited from the standpoint of documented protective factors for girls, although one study found that positive parenting can be protective against girls' perpetration of violence (Holsinger & Holsinger, 2005). Other studies have examined protective factors for female delinquency in general, noting that family monitoring, attachment, relationships, and support (Crosnoe, Erickson, & Dornbusch, 2002; Griffin et al., 2000; Silverman & Caldwell, 2005) can protect some girls from engaging in violence. School-related protective factors include liking school, being bonded to school, and expecting to complete high school or earn a GED (Chapple, McQuillian, & Berdahl, 2005; Galbavy, 2003; Lederman, Dakof, Larrea, & Li, 2004). Receiving in-home child welfare services may be protective for some, particularly for girls of color (Jonson-Reid, 2002; Jonson-Reid & Barth, 2000). Finally, living by conventional values and having prosocial beliefs can be protective for youth, both girls and boys (Chapple, McQuillian, & Berdahl, 2004; Piquero, Gover, MacDonald, & Piquero, 2005).

INTERSECTION OF ETHNICITY, GENDER, AND VIOLENCE

As discussed in Chapter 3, both boys and girls of color are disproportionately represented in the juvenile justice system, and this disparity is most distinct with respect to violent offending (Williams, Hovmand, & Bright, 2007). African American youth, in particular, are more likely than white youth to enter detention facilities, to be formally petitioned for offenses, and to be transferred to the adult criminal justice system (American Bar Association and National Bar Association, 2001). While behavioral differences between African American and white youth have been reported, a meta-analysis of 65 studies addressed the question of differential offending and found that these differences were not of sufficient magnitude to explain the inequities in the system (Engen, Steen, & Bridges, 2002).

Little research on violence disaggregates African American and white youth by gender, and even less considers boys and girls of other ethnicities. Existing scholarship suggests, however, that risk factors and situational appraisals leading to violence may differ between white and African American boys and between white and African American girls (Daley & Onwuegbuzie, 2004; Holsinger & Holsinger, 2005). It has also been noted that girls of color face the multiple disadvantages of sexism, racism, and often classism in the juvenile justice system (Chesney-Lind & Pasko, 2003) and that media portrayals of violent behavior among girls focus attention on the stereotyped image of the aggressive African American female (Irwin & Chesney-Lind, 2008).

IMPLICATIONS AND FUTURE DIRECTIONS

What of the longer-term impact of girls' violence? Like juvenile offenders, adult female offenders often present with mental and physical health needs and substance abuse, lack educational and vocational skills, come from impoverished backgrounds, and have histories of early pregnancy (Aderibigbe, Arboleda-Florez, & Crisante, 1996; Green, Miranda, Daroowalla, & Siddique, 2005; Sacks, 2004). A recent study of juvenile court–involved girls found that having multiple offenses in the juvenile system predicts adult criminal justice system involvement during early adulthood (Bright & Jonson-Reid, 2010). In an earlier study, violent behavior in adolescence has been found to be relatively stable from adolescence into the young adult years, with violent juvenile females accounting for a more disproportionate share of adult violent crime than their male counterparts (Kempf-Leonard, Tracy, & Howell, 2001). Because of the considerable implications to these young women in terms of the impact of criminal justice system involvement and the costs to victims and communities, it is essential to prevent or disrupt violent crime among girls as early as possible.

As discussed in Chapters 7 and 8 by Jenson and colleagues, promising prevention programs focus on known risk and protective. Prevention programs can target risk and protective factors for youth who have not yet engaged in violence, as well as those already perpetrating violence. The goal of prevention focused on violent and delinquent youth is to prevent future violence. Although research has been slower to identify protective factors, it is important to incorporate what is known about protective influences into strengths-based models of prevention.

The most robust predictor of adolescent violence is early conduct problems. The types of childhood behaviors that constitute early conduct behaviors (physical aggression, disruptive behaviors, covert behaviors, oppositional and defiant behaviors, conduct disorders) should be considered risk factors or early developmental precursors for later problem behaviors. We know that risk factors are found all across the social ecology of childhood, and the greater the number of risks in an individual's life, the greater is the probability of involvement in antisocial behaviors (Institute of Medicine, 1994). Thus, to be most effective, prevention and treatment interventions must focus on a comprehensive approach that addresses risk factors across a social ecologic framework. The more common approach to program development emphasizes the reduction of risk factors and, at the same time, enhances identified protective factors using universal, indicated, and selective preventive interventions. The prevention and intervention literature clearly posits that reducing youth violence requires a multifaceted, coordinated approach in which early intervention and prevention form a critical step. While violence prevention strategies focus on all social domains (i.e., individual, peer cluster, family, school settings, and community), these strategies primarily focus on individual and family risk factors.

A number of authors have advocated that girls and boys in the juvenile justice system should be treated differently, receiving services designed to meet their specific needs (Acoca, 1999; Bloom, Owen, Rosenbaum, & Deschenes, 2003; Greene, Peters, & Associates, 1998; Holsinger, 2000;

Okamoto & Chesney-Lind, 2004). The evidence base for gender-specific services is in its infancy, so recommendations for gendered service provision with violent boys and girls remain largely conceptual. Nevertheless, as gender differences in development, socialization, and risk and protection persist, it is important to take gender into account when designing and implementing interventions. Additionally, as Aisenberg and colleagues note in Chapter 2, the juvenile justice system must shift its focus from the individual to the environmental level to adequately respond to the multiple systems that impact risk and protection. Juvenile justice professionals must be flexible enough to respond to youth situations and needs based on their individual experiences, and identifying risk and protective factors can enable appropriate matching of youth to services. Based on the literature reviewed here, violent girls will often need services dealing with trauma and victimization, mental health, and substance use needs. Often similar services are required for boys. It is important to note that the onset of antisocial behaviors is earlier for boys than for girls and thus the implementation of prevention programming should be implemented earlier for boys than for girls.

The increase in female arrests for violent crimes likely has its roots in policy decisions such as the increase in domestic violence arrests. Boys and girls of color may be more at risk for arrest based on zero-tolerance policies in schools (Advancement Project, 2005; Skiba, Michael, Nardo, & Peterson, 2002). While policy must change and adapt to the changing nature of society, it is essential that policy makers and analysts consider the populations that may be harmed or treated differently as a result of policy changes. The juvenile justice system encounters youth with multiple vulnerabilities and disadvantages. To address system needs for girls, policy makers should develop a vision and related policy goals and build coalitions and alliances. Effective juvenile justice intervention must be implemented at the policy level. Communities and policy makers must leverage monetary resources and effective programming to address the needs of girls in the juvenile justice system. We urge policy makers to consider supporting prevention efforts rather than pursuing what are in essence net-widening approaches to dealing with youth behavior.

Much more research is needed to more fully describe the complex circumstances that lead to violent behavior and to investigate effective prevention and intervention strategies. It is important that research focus on boys' and girls' similarities and differences. Prospective, longitudinal studies yield unmatched riches in the data they produce, but they are time consuming and expensive to undertake. Qualitative and cross-sectional designs can provide important information on young people's lives, and their perspectives are invaluable. Remaining challenges for researchers include developing a more comprehensive understanding of risk and protection for violent behavior in both genders, uncovering policy and practice strategies to decrease disproportionate minority contact in the juvenile justice system (particularly with respect to violent offenses), and identifying the essential, active ingredients that will allow for implementation of appropriate intervention and prevention measures.

Information on youth violence comes from many places—crime statistics, the media, anecdotes, scholars, juvenile justice and law enforcement professionals, and youth and families themselves. Critical analysis and evaluation of these oftentimes conflicting sources are challenging but essential. Reactions to youth violence must be as informed as possible to be appropriately targeted and effective, and recognition of gender differences and similarities is a step toward a more comprehensive understanding of the phenomenon of youth violence. While much work is yet to be done, a gendered framework can be an appropriate lens for interpreting information and making decisions.

REFERENCES

Acoca, L. (1999). Investing in girls: A 21st century strategy. *Journal of the Office of Juvenile Justice and Delinquency Prevention, 6,* 3–13.

Aderibigbe, Y. A., Arboleda-Florez, J., & Crisante, A. (1996). Reflections on the sociodemographic and medicolegal profiles of female criminal defendants. *International Journal of Offender Therapy and Comparative Criminology, 40,* 74–84.

Advancement Project. (2005). *Education on lockdown: The schoolhouse to jailhouse track.* Retrieved May 21, 2009, from http://www.advancementproject.org/reports/FINALEOLrep.pdf

Akers, R. L. (1973). *Deviant behavior: A social learning approach.* Belmont, CA: Wadsworth Publishing Company.

Albert, A. A., & Porter, J. R. (1988). Children's gender-role stereotypes: A sociological investigation of psychological models. *Sociological Forum, 3,* 184–210.

American Bar Association and National Bar Association. (2001). *Justice by gender: The lack of appropriate prevention, diversion and treatment alternatives for girls in the justice system.* Retrieved June 9, 2009, from http://www.abanet.org/crimjust/juvjus/justicebygenderweb.pdf

Artz, S. (1998). Where have all the school girls gone? Violent girls in the school yard. *Child and Youth Care Forum, 27,* 77–109.

Baer, J., & Maschi, T. (2003). Random acts of delinquency: Trauma and self-destructiveness in juvenile offenders. *Child and Adolescent Social Work Journal, 20,* 85–98.

Bandura, A. (2007). Social learning theory of aggression. In J. F. Knutson (Ed.), *The control of aggression* (pp. 201–250). Piscataway, NJ: Transaction.

Baum, K. (2005). *Juvenile victimization and offending, 1993–2003.* Bureau of Justice Statistics Special Report No. NCJ 209468. Retrieved May 18, 2009, from http://www.ojp.usdoj.gov/bjs/pub/pdf/jvo03.pdf

Bloom, B., Owen, B., Deschenes, E. P., & Rosenbaum, J. (2002). Moving toward justice for female juvenile offenders in the new millennium: Modeling gender-specific policies and programs. *Journal of Contemporary Criminal Justice, 18,* 37–56.

Brannigan, A. (1997). Self control, social control and evolutionary psychology: Towards an integrated perspective on crime. *Canadian Journal of Criminology, 39,* 403–431.

Brezina, T. (1998). Adolescent maltreatment and delinquency: The question of the intervening process. *Journal of Research and Crime in Delinquency, 35,* 71–99.

Bright, C. L., & Jonson-Reid, M. (2008). Onset of juvenile court involvement: Exploring gender-specific associations with maltreatment and poverty. *Child and Youth Services Review, 30,* 914–927.

Bright, C. L., & Jonson-Reid, M. (2010). Young adult outcomes of juvenile court involved girls. *Journal of Social Service Research, 36,* 94–106.

Bureau of Justice Statistics. (2009). *Crime characteristics.* Retrieved May 18, 2009, from http://www.ojp.gov/bjs/cvict_c.htm#violent

Calhoun, G. (2001). Differences between male and female juvenile offenders as measured by the BASC. *Journal of Offender Rehabilitation, 33,* 87–96.

Cauffman, E. (2008). Understanding the female offender. *Future of Children, 18,* 119–142.

Cairns, R. B., & Cairns, B. D. (1991). Social cognition and social networks: A developmental perspective. In D. J. Pepler, & K. H. Rubin (Eds.). *The development and treatment of childhood aggression* (pp. 249–278). Hillsdale, NJ: Lawrence Erlbaum Associates.

Cairns, R. B., Leung, M. C., Buchanan, L., & Cairns, B. D. (1995). Friendships and social networks in childhood and adolescence: Fluidity, reliability, and interrelations. *Child Development, 66,* 1330–1345.

Chamberlain, P. (2006). *Parent management training in child welfare and juvenile justice settings.* Presented at a seminar of the George Warren Brown Center for Mental Health Services Research, Saint Louis, MO.

Chapple, C. L., McQuillan, J. A., & Berdahl, T. A. (2005). Gender, social bonds, and delinquency: A comparison of boys' and girls' models. *Social Science Research, 34,* 357–383.

Chauhan, P., & Reppucci, N. D. (2009). The impact of neighborhood disadvantage and exposure to violence on self-report of antisocial behavior among girls in the juvenile justice system. *Journal of Youth and Adolescence, 38,* 401–416.

Chesney-Lind, M., & Belknap, J. (2004). Trends in delinquent girls' aggression and violent behavior: A review of the evidence. In M. Putallaz & K. L. Bierman (Eds.), *Aggression, antisocial behavior, and violence among girls: A developmental perspective* (pp. 203–220). New York: Guilford Publications.

Chesney-Lind, M., & Pasko, L. (2003). *The female offender: Girls, women, and crime* (2nd ed.). Thousand Oaks, CA: Sage.

Crick, N. R. (1996). The role of overt aggression, relational aggression, and prosocial behavior in the prediction of children's future social adjustment. *Child Development, 67,* 2317–2327.

Crick, N. R., & Grotpeter, J. K. (1995). Relational aggression, gender, and social-psychological adjustment. *Child Development, 66,* 710–722.

Crosnoe, R., Erikson, K. G., & Dornbusch, S. M. (2002). Protective functions of family relationships and school factors on the deviant behavior of adolescent boys and girls: reducing the impact of risky friendships. *Youth and Society. 33,* 515–544.

Daley, C. E., & Onwuegbuzie, A. J. (2004). Attributions toward violence of male juvenile delinquents: A concurrent mixed-methodological analysis. *Journal of Social Psychology, 144,* 549–570.

DeMatteo, D., & Marczyk, G. (2005). Risk factors, protective factors, and the prevention of antisocial behavior among juveniles. In N. E. S. Goldstein, &

R. E. Redding (Eds.), *Juvenile delinquency: Prevention, assessment, and intervention.* New York: Oxford University Press.

Dixon, A., Howie, S., & Starling, J. (2005). Trauma exposure, posttraumatic stress, and psychiatric comorbidity in female juvenile offenders. *Journal of American Academy of Child and Adolescent Psychology, 44,* 798–806.

Dougherty, J. (1998). Power-belief theory: Female criminality and the dynamics of oppression. In R. T. Zaplin (Ed.), *Female offenders: Critical perspectives and effective interventions* (pp. 133–159). Gaithersburg, MD: Aspen.

Elliott, D. S. (1994a). *Youth violence: An overview.* Boulder: University of Colorado, Center for the Study and Prevention of Violence.

Engen, R. L., Steen, S., & Bridges, G. S. (2002). Racial disparities in the punishment of youth: A theoretical and empirical assessment of the literature. *Social Problems, 49,* 194–220.

Farrington, D. P. (1991a). Childhood aggression and adult violence: Early precursors and later-life outcomes. In D. J. Pepler, & K. H. Rubin (Eds.), *The development and treatment of childhood aggression* (pp. 5–29). Hillsdale, NJ: Lawrence Erlbaum Associates.

Farrington, D. P. (1991b). Psychological contributions to the explanation of offending. *Issues in Criminological and Legal Psychology, 1,* 7–19.

Farrington, D. P., Loeber, R., Stouthamer-Loeber, M., Van Kammen, W. B., & Schmidt, L. (1996). Self-reported delinquency and a combined delinquency seriousness scale based on boys, mothers, and teachers: Concurrent and predictive validity for African-Americans and Caucasians. *Criminology, 34,* 493–517.

Federal Bureau of Investigation. (n.d.). *Crime in the United States 2007.* Retrieved January 21, 2009, from http://www.fbi.gov/ucr/cius2007/index.html

Fraser, M. W., Kirby, L. D., & Smokowski, P. R. (2004). *Risk and resilience in childhood.* In M. W. Fraser (Ed.). *Risk and resilience in childhood: An ecological perspective* (2nd ed., pp. 13–66). Washington, DC: NASW.

Galbavy, R. J. (2003). Juvenile delinquency: Peer influences, gender differences and prevention. *Journal of Prevention & Intervention in the Community, 25,* 65–78.

Garbino, J., Dubrow, N., Kostelny, K., & Pardo, C. (1992). *Children in danger: Coping with the consequences of community violence.* San Francisco, CA: Jossey-Bass.

Gilligan, C. (1993a). In a different voice: Psychological theory and women's development. In A. Dobrin (Ed.), *Being good and doing right: Readings in moral development* (pp. 37–54). Lanham, MD: University Press of America.

Gilligan, C. (1993b). Joining the resistance: Psychology, politics, girls, and women. In L. Weis & M. Fine (Eds.), *Beyond silenced voices: Class, race, and gender in United States schools* (pp. 143–168). Albany, NY: State University of New York Press.

Goldstein, N. E., Arnold, D. H., Weil, J., Mesiark, C. M., Peuschold, D., Grisso, T., & Osman, D. (2003). Comorbid symptom patterns in female juvenile offenders. *International Journal of Law and Psychiatry, 26,* 565–582.

Gover, A. R. (2004). Childhood sexual abuse, gender, and depression among incarcerated youth. *International Journal of Offender Therapy and Comparative Criminology, 48,* 683–696.

Green, B. J., Miranda, J., Daroowalla, A., & Siddique, J. (2005). Trauma exposure, mental health functioning, and program needs of women in jail. *Crime and Delinquency, 51,* 133–151.

Greene, Peters, and Associates. (1998). *Guiding principles for promising female programming: An inventory of best practices.* Washington, DC: Office of Juvenile Justice and Delinquency Prevention.

Griffin, K. W., Botvin, G. J., Scheier, L. M., Diaz, T., & Miller, N. L. (2000). Parenting practices as predictors of substance use, delinquency, and aggression among urban minority youth: Moderating effects of family structure and gender. *Psychology of Addictive Behaviors, 14,* 174–184.

Hagan, J., Gillis, A. R., & Simpson, J. (1985). The class structure of gender and delinquency: Toward a power–control theory of common delinquent behavior. *American Journal of Sociology, 90,* 1151–1178.

Hagan, J., McCarthy, B., & Foster, H. (2002). A gendered theory of delinquency and despair in the life course. *Acta Sociologica, 45,* 37–46.

Hawkins, J. D., Catalano, R. F., & Miller, J. Y. (1992). Risk and protective factors for alcohol and other drug problems in adolescence and early adulthood: Implications for substance abuse prevention. *Psychological Bulletin, 112,* 64–105.

Heimer, K., & De Coster, S. (1999). The gendering of violent delinquency. *Criminology, 37,* 277–318.

Herrera, V. M., & McCloskey, L. A. (2001). Gender differences in the risk for delinquency among youth exposed to family violence. *Child Abuse and Neglect, 25,* 1037–1051.

Holsinger, K. (2000). Feminist perspectives on female offending: Examining real girls' lives. *Women and Criminal Justice, 12,* 23–51.

Holsinger, K., & Holsinger, A. M. (2005). Differential pathways to violence and self-injurious behavior: African American and white girls in the juvenile justice system. *Journal of Research in Crime and Delinquency, 42,* 211–242.

Howell, J. C. (2003). Diffusing research into practice using the comprehensive strategy for serious, violent, and chronic juvenile offenders. *Youth Violence and Juvenile Justice, 1,* 219–245.

Huizinga, D., Loeber, R., Thornberry, T. P., & Cothern, L. (2000). Co-occurrence of delinquency and other problem behaviors. *Juvenile Justice Bulletin.* Retrieved May 21, 2009, from http://www.ncjrs.gov/pdffiles1/ojjdp/182211.pdf

Institute of Medicine (1994). *Reducing risks for mental disorders: Frontiers for preventive intervention research.* Washington, DC: The National Academie Press.

Irwin, K., & Chesney-Lind, M. (2008). Girls' violence: Beyond dangerous masculinity. *Sociology Compass, 2/3,* 83–855.

Jensen, G. F. (2003). Gender variation in delinquency: Self-images, beliefs, and peers as mediating mechanisms. In G. F. Jensen (Ed.), *Social learning theory and the explanation of crime* (pp. 151–177). New Brunswick, NJ: Transaction.

Jenson, J. M. (2006). Advances and challenges in preventing childhood and adolescent problem behavior. *Social Work Research, 30,* 131–134.

Jonson-Reid, M. (1998). Youth violence and exposure to violence in childhood: An ecological view. *Aggression and Violent Behavior, 3,* 159–179.

Jonson-Reid, M. (2002). Exploring the relationship between child welfare intervention and juvenile corrections involvement. *American Journal of Orthopsychiatry, 72,* 559–576.

Jonson-Reid, M., & Barth, R. P. (2000). From placement to prison: the path to adolescent incarceration from child welfare supervised foster or group care. *Children and Youth Services Review, 22*, 493–516.

Kempf-Leonard, K., Tracy, P. E., & Howell, J. C. (2001). Serious, violent, and chronic juvenile offenders: The relationship of delinquency career types to adult criminality. *Justice Quarterly, 18*(3), 449–478.

Lanctôt, N., Émond, C., & Le Blanc, M. (2004). Adjudicated females' participation in violence from adolescence to adulthood: Results from a longitudinal study. In M. M. Moretti, C. L. Odgers, & M. A. Jackson (Eds.), *Girls and aggression: Contributing factors and intervention principles*. New York: Kluwer Academic.

Lederman, C. S., Dakof, G. A., Larrera, M. A., & Li, H. (2004). Characteristics of adolescent females in juvenile detention. *International Journal of Law and Psychiatry, 27*, 321–337.

Levant, R. F. (1996). The new psychology of men. *Professional Psychology: Research and Practice, 27*, 259–265.

Liu, X., & Kaplan, H. B. (1999). Explaining transgenerational continuity in antisocial behavior during early adolescence. In C. Slomkowski, C., & L. N. Robins (Eds.), *Historical and geographical influences on psychopathology.* (pp. 163–191). Mahwah, NJ: Lawrence Erlbaum Associates.

Loeber, R., & Dishion, T. J. (1984). Boys who fight at home and school: Family conditions influencing cross-setting consistency. *Journal of Consulting and Clinical Psychology, 52*, 759–768.

Luke, K. P. (2008). Are girls really becoming more violent? A critical analysis. *Affilia, 23*, 38–50.

Maschi, T., & Bradley, C. (2008). Exploring the moderating influences of delinquent peers on the link between trauma, anger, and violence among male youth: Implications for social work practice. *Child and Adolescent Social Work Journal, 25*, 125–138.

McCabe, K. M., Lansing, A. E., Garland, A., & Hough, R. (2002). Gender differences in psychopathology, functional impairment, and familial risk factors among adjudicated delinquents. *Journal of the American Academy of Child & Adolescent Psychiatry, 41*, 860–867.

McCormack, A., Janus, M. D., & Burgess, A. W. (1986). Runaway youths and sexual victimization: Gender differences in an adolescent runaway population. *Child Abuse and Neglect, 10*, 387–395.

National Archive of Criminal Justice Data. (no date). *National Crime Victimization Survey resource guide*. Retrieved June 9, 2009, from http://www.icpsr.umich.edu/NACJD/NCVS/.

National Center for Juvenile Justice. (2008). *Juvenile arrest rates by offense, sex, and race*. Online. Retrieved May 20, 2009, from http://ojjdp.ncjrs.org/ojstatbb/crime/excel/JAR_2008.xls

Ness, C. D. (2004). Why girls fight: Female youth violence in the inner city. *Annals of the American Academy of Political and Social Science, 595*, 32–48.

Odgers, C. L., Moretti, M. M., & Reppucci, N. D. (2005). Examining the science and practice of violence risk assessment with female adolescents. *Law and Human Behavior, 29*, 7–27.

Okamoto, M., & Chesney-Lind, S. K. (2001). Gender matters: Patterns in girls' delinquency and gender responsive programming. *Journal of Forensic Psychology Practice, 1*, 1–28.

Patterson, G. R., & Dishion, T. J. (1985). Contributions of families and peers to delinquency. *Criminology, 23,* 63–79.

Patterson, G. R., & Stouthamer-Loeber, M. (1984). The correlation of family management practices and delinquency. *Child Development, 55,* 1299–1307.

Pettersson, T. (2005). Gendering delinquent networks: A gendered analysis of violent crimes and the structure of boys' and girls' co-offending networks. *Young, 13,* 247–267.

Piquero, N. L., Gover, A. R., MacDonald, J. M., & Piquero, A. R. (2005). The influence of delinquent peers on delinquency: Does gender matter? *Youth & Society, 36,* 251–275.

Puzzanchera, C. (2009, April). Juvenile arrests 2007. *Juvenile Justice Bulletin.* Retrieved May 19, 2009, from http://www.ncjrs.gov/pdffiles1/ojjdp/225344.pdf

Sacks, J. Y. (2004). Women with co-occurring substance use and mental disorders (COD) in the criminal justice system: A research review. *Behavioral Sciences and the Law, 22,* 449–466.

Schaffner, L. (2007). Violence against girls provokes girls' violence: From private injury to public harm. *Violence against Women, 13,* 1229–1248.

Shaffer, J. N., & Ruback, R. B. (2002, December). Violent victimization as a risk factor for violent offending among juveniles. *Juvenile Justice Bulletin.* Retrieved May 20, 2009, from http://www.ncjrs.gov/pdffiles1/ojjdp/195737.pdf

Silverman, J. R., & Caldwell, R. M. (2005). The influence of parental emotional support and monitoring on self-reported delinquent impulsive behavior and noncompliance among juvenile offenders: An examination of gender differences. *International Journal of Forensic Mental Health, 4,* 159–174.

Simcha-Fagan, O., & Schwartz, J. E. (1986). Neighborhoods and delinquency: An assessment of contextual effects. *Criminology, 24,* 667–703.

Singer, S. I., & Levine, M. (1988). Power-control theory, gender, and delinquency: A partial replication with additional evidence on the effects of peers. *Criminology, 26,* 627–647.

Skiba, R. J., Michael, R. S., Nardo, A. C., & Peterson, R. L. (2002). The color of discipline: Sources of racial and gender disproportionality in school punishment. *Urban Review, 34,* 317–342.

Smith, C., & Thornberry, T. P. (1995). The relationship between childhood maltreatment and adolescent involvement in delinquency. *Criminology, 33,* 451–481.

Smokowski, P. R., Mann, E. R., Reynolds, A. J., & Fraser, M. W. (2004). Childhood risk and protective factors and late adolescent adjustment in inner city minority youth. *Children and Youth Services Review, 26,* 63–91.

Snyder, H. N., & Sickmund, M. (2006). *Juvenile offenders and victims: 2006 National report.* Pittsburgh, PA: Office of Juvenile Justice and Delinquency Prevention.

Steffensmeier, D., & Allen, E. (1996). Gender and crime: Towards a gendered theory of female offending. *Annual Review of Sociology, 22,* 459–480.

Steffensmeier, D., Schwartz, J. Zhong, H., & Ackerman, J. (2005). An assessment of recent trends in girls' violence using longitudinal sources: Is the gender gap closing? *Criminology, 43,* 355–406.

Szapocznik, J., & Coatsworth, J. D. (1999). An ecodevelopmental framework for organizing the influences of drug abuse: A developmental model of risk and protection. In M. Glantz & C. R. Hartel (Eds.), *Drug abuse: Origins and interventions* (pp. 331–366). Washington, DC: American Psychological Association.

Thornberry, T. P. (1994). *Violent families and youth violence*. Washington, DC: Office of Juvenile Justice and Delinquency Prevention.

Thornberry, T. P., Lizotte, A. J., Krohn, M. D., Farnsworth, M., & Sung, J. J. (1994). Delinquent peers, beliefs and delinquent behaviors: A longitudinal test of interactional theory. *Criminology, 32*, 47–83.

Timmons-Mitchell, J., Brown, C., Schulz, C. S., Webster, S. E., Underwood, L. A., & Semple, W. E. (1997). Comparing the mental health needs of female and male incarcerated juvenile delinquents. *Behavioral Sciences & the Law, 15*, 195–202.

Trickett, P. K., & Gordis, E. B. (2004). Aggression and antisocial behavior in sexually abused females. In M. Putallaz & K. L. Bierman (Eds.), *Aggression, antisocial behavior, and violence among girls: A developmental perspective* (pp. 162–185). New York: Guilford Press.

Underwood, M. K., Galen, B. R., & Paquette, J. A. (2001). Top ten challenges for understanding gender and aggression in children: Why can't we all just get along? *Social Development, 10*, 248–266.

Van Dorn, R. A., & Williams, J. H. (2003). Correlates associated with escalation of delinquent behavior in incarcerated youth. *Social Work, 48*, 523–531.

Weitzmann-Henelius, G., Viemerö, V., & Eronen, M. (2004). Psychological risk markers in violent female behavior. *International Journal of Forensic Mental Health, 3*, 185–196.

Wasserman, G. A., McReynolds, L. S., Ko, S. J., Katz, L. M., & Carpenter, J. R. (2005). Gender differences in psychiatric disorders at juvenile probation intake. *American Journal of Public Health, 9*, 131–137.

Widom, C. S. (1991). The role of placement experiences in mediating the criminal consequences of early childhood victimization. *American Journal of Orthopsychiatry, 61*, 195–209.

Widom, C. S. (1998). Child victims: Searching for opportunities to break the cycle of violence. *Applied and Preventive Psychology, 7*, 225–234.

Widom, C. S., & Maxfield, M. G. (2001). *An update on the "cycle of violence."* Washington, DC: National Institute of Justice.

Williams, J. H., Ayers, C. D., Van Dorn, R. A., & Arthur, M. W. (2004). Risk and protective factors in the development of delinquency and conduct disorder. In M. W. Fraser (Ed.), *Risk and resiliency in childhood: An ecological perspective* (2nd ed., pp. 209–249). Washington, DC: NASW.

Williams, J. H., Hovmand, P. S., & Bright, C. L. (2007). Overrepresentation of African Americans incarcerated for delinquency offenses in juvenile institutions. In D. W. Springer & A. R. Roberts (Eds.), *Handbook of forensic mental health with victims and offenders: Assessment, treatment, and research* (pp. 363–381). New York: Springer Publishing.

Williams, J. H., Stiffman, A. R., & O'Neal, J. L. (1998). Violence among urban African American youths: An analysis of environmental and behavioral risk factors. *Social Work Research, 22*, 3–13.

Yoshikawa, H. (1994). Prevention as cumulative protection: Effects of early family support and education on chronic delinquency and its risks. *Psychological Bulletin, 115*, 28–54.

Zahn, M. A., Hawkins, S. R., Chiancone, J., & Whitworth, A. (2008). *The Girls Study Group – Charting the way to delinquency prevention for girls*. Retrieved May 21, 2009, from http://www.ncjrs.gov/pdffiles1/ojjdp/223434.pdf

Zayas, L. H., Lester, R. J., Cabassa, L. J., & Fortuna, L. R. (2005). Why do so many Latina teens attempt suicide? A conceptual model for research. *American Journal of Orthopsychiatry, 75*, 275–287.

Zimmer-Gembeck, M. J., Geiger, T. C., & Crick, N. R. (2005). Relational and physical aggression, prosocial behavior, and peer relations: Gender moderation and bidirectional associations. *Journal of Early Adolescence, 25*, 421–452.

III

THE CONTEXT OF FAMILY VIOLENCE AND CO-OCCURRING RISKS FOR CHILDREN

Implications for Prevention

5

FAMILY VIOLENCE AND CO-OCCURRING RISK FACTORS FOR CHILDREN EXPOSED TO VIOLENCE

TODD I. HERRENKOHL

Prior chapters of this book examined patterns and predictors of youth violence. In this section, we turn to violence exposure in children, environmental risks, and outcomes over the life course for vulnerable children. Additionally, we examine the topic of resilience and the ways in which children exposed to violence cope with trauma developmentally.

Highlights of Chapter 5 include an examination of the overlap in physical child abuse and domestic violence exposure (dual exposure) for children and developmental consequences following that exposure. We also investigate themes introduced earlier, including the "cycle of violence" phenomenon introduced by Bright and colleagues in Chapter 4. As in the preceding chapters, we examine race, ethnicity, and gender as important demographic variables that help define groups at higher and lower risk of violence and its effects.

Chapter 6 offers a critical analysis and review of resilience research. We examine conceptualizations and measurement approaches and review current evidence on resilience in children exposed to violence. Research highlights the many ways that children can emerge from sometimes horrific experiences (e.g., chronic childhood abuse) to lead productive and satisfying lives. We conclude both chapters with implications for practice and policy development.

In this section of the book, we carry forward several of the definitions introduced by Aisenberg and colleagues in Chapter 2. We examine research on child maltreatment and physical child abuse, which includes nonaccidental acts of physical punishment by a parent or other caregiver that may or may not result in observable injuries to the child. Findings on sexual abuse and molestation are also included in our review. Further, we consider childhood exposure to domestic and community violence, both of which can include a child's directly witnessing violence perpetrated by one adult to another, or a child's hearing violent acts within and outside the home.

Failure to account for overlapping forms of violence and risk within and across settings has contributed to an incomplete and possibly inaccurate understanding of the risk environments in which many vulnerable children reside. In this chapter, we examine the intersection of violence across key settings and the impact of violence exposure on children's development. The summary overview of research includes a discussion of possible race/ethnic and gender differences in rates of exposure, developmental processes, and outcomes of violence exposure in children.

PREVALENCE OF CHILDHOOD EXPOSURE TO VIOLENCE

There are major discrepancies in estimates of child abuse, children's exposure to domestic violence, and community violence due primarily to differences in criteria used to define exposure, as well as measurement approaches (Buka, Stichick, Birdthistle, & Earls, 2001; Margolin & Gordis, 2000; Osofsky, 1999) (see a related discussion in Chapter 2 by Aisenberg and colleagues). Official record estimates apply a legal definition of what constitutes child abuse and domestic violence exposure in children, which are not uniform and can vary by state according to state laws and regulations (Goldman, Salus, Wolcott, & Kennedy, 2003). Yet, most definitions used in official surveillance and recording of abuse require there is some evidence of physical injury to a child (e.g., bruises, fractures, etc.), thereby limiting estimates to severe acts of violence perpetrated by a parent or other primary caregiver (Goldman et al., 2003). Rates of domestic violence exposure in children are particularly difficult to record because so few acts of violence are actually reported and because it is often unclear whether or how a child was involved. Yet, evidence from various sources suggests that children are often present at the time of domestic violence incidents (Fusco & Fantuzzo, 2009). It is estimated that up to 10 million children are exposed to domestic violence annually (Fusco & Fantuzzo, 2009; Moylan et al., in press).

As discussed in Chapter 2, definitions of violence and violence exposure can differ quite markedly. Indeed, legal definitions of child abuse vary from those used in survey research, which tend to be more broadly inclusive and not limited to acts that end in physical injury to a child (Herrenkohl & Herrenkohl, in press; Herrenkohl, Sousa, Tajima, Herrenkohl, & Moylan, 2008). Survey researchers also tend to define domestic violence exposure in children more broadly than do legal experts because they consider how the child could be impacted emotionally or psychologically.

Yet, definitions, and corresponding rates of violence exposure, vary even across research studies. Consequently, the job of compiling and synthesizing research findings is particularly challenging. As noted by Aisenberg and his colleagues in Chapter 2, even subtle variations in definitions and inclusion criteria can make for sizeable differences in estimated rates of abuse or exposure to violence. For domestic violence exposure, some researchers may accept a child's hearing or knowing of violence in the home (sensory exposure) but not necessarily witnessing the violence directly, whereas others limit exposure to incidents where the child actually observed the violence unfold (Fusco & Fantuzzo, 2009; Gewirtz & Edleson, 2007). Using less or more restrictive criteria for domestic violence exposure results in widely varying estimates of the actual number of children exposed to this form of violence. Estimates also vary by research sampling methods, differences in sample composition (e.g., clinical versus community samples), and data sources used to compile information (Fusco & Fantuzzo, 2009). Those who study community violence speak of similar challenges.

While there is very little consensus in definitions of violence and violence exposure in children, it cannot be disputed that violence is widespread. It is also known that violence exposures (e.g., child abuse, domestic violence, community violence) often co-occur (Herrenkohl et al., 2008). While there are few solid investigations of the overlap in violence exposures across settings, the co-occurrence of child abuse and children's exposure to domestic violence is well documented (Appel & Holden, 1998; Fantuzzo, Boruch, Beriama, Atkins, & Marcus, 1997; McCloskey, Figueredo, & Koss, 1995; Moffitt & Caspi, 2003; Straus, 1990). Dong et al.'s (2004) analyses of data from the Adverse Childhood Experiences (ACE) study show this to be the case. In that study, 57.5% of adults who reported earlier domestic violence exposure had also been abused, compared with 21.7% of those who reported no prior domestic violence exposure. Other studies and reviews of literature similarly document high degree of overlap in these forms of violence (Edleson, 2001; Gewirtz & Edleson, 2007; McCloskey & Lichter, 2003; Osofsky, 1999; Tajima, 2000).

In their often cited review of studies involving battered women, Appel and Holden (1998) found a median rate of co-occurrence between child abuse and domestic violence of 41%, although in some studies included in that review, rates of overlap were even higher. In a more recent examination of retrospective data on child abuse and exposure to intimate partner violence for a sample of welfare families, Renner and Slack (2006) reported a correlation of 0.52, within the range of the earlier Appel and Holden review.

As noted by Bright and her colleagues in Chapter 4, children living in poverty and disadvantaged communities—often children of color—are at higher risk for violence exposure (Fang & Corso, 2007; Garbarino, Hammon, Mercy, & Yung, 2004; Middlebrooks & Audage, 2008), although children of all backgrounds come in contact with violence (Evans, Davies, & DiLillo, 2008). In fact, national statistics suggest that physical violence affects nearly 50% of all U.S. families (Fagan & Browne, 1994). Thus, while rates of exposure to violence vary across demographic and socioeconomic groups, no group is fully shielded from violence or its effects.

Adding to the vulnerability of some children, those exposed to violence can, and often do, encounter additional risk factors in their families and communities (Fang & Corso, 2007; Fantuzzo et al., 1997; Haugaard & Feerick, 2002). For example, parents of abused children are typically younger and have less education than other parents, which translates into fewer employment opportunities for these parents and less earning potential for the family. Parents who abusively discipline their children are also more likely to have been victims of abuse themselves and, by extension, to have poor impulse control and to suffer from mental health and substance use problems (Goldman et al., 2003; Haugaard & Feerick, 2002; World Health Organization [WHO], 2006). Sadly, these same children often encounter even more risks in the surrounding environment, including community-level poverty and weak social support networks (Aisenberg & Herrenkohl, 2008; Drake, Lee, & Jonson-Reid, 2009; Freisthler & Crampton, 2009; Herrenkohl et al., 2008; Margolin & Gordis, 2000). Thus, the burden of risk experienced by some children and their families is so great that without planned interventions (see Chapters 7 and 8), the children will remain more vulnerable than others to a range of problems, including health risk behaviors, poor health, and substance use problems (Herrenkohl et al., 2008; Rutter, 2001; Steinberg & Avenevoli, 2000).

Ethnicity

In Chapters 3 and 4, Williams, Bright, and their colleagues refer to persistent race and ethnic disparities in youth violent offending, arrests, and juvenile justice system involvement. Research shows there are also disparities in documented cases of abuse and neglect (Drake et al., 2009). According to child protective services data in 2005, children and families of color were more likely than were others to enter the child protection system following abuse disclosure. For African Americans, there were nearly 1,950 officially recorded maltreatment victims per 100,000 children in the population, 1,650 victims per 100,000 children for Native Americans and Alaska Natives, and 1,610 victims per 100,000 children for Pacific Islanders (compared with just over 1,200 per 100,000 children overall) (Centers for Disease Control and Prevention [CDC], 2007a). Asians were least likely to be processed for child maltreatment in 2005 (CDC, 2007a).

Disparities in child maltreatment are less evident according to other data sources. For example, in a 1996 U.S. Department of Health and Human Services National Incidence Study (NIS-3), based on data from child protective service agencies and other community service providers, researchers found there were no race differences in child maltreatment incidence or maltreatment-related injuries (Sedlak & Broadhurst, 1996). Similarly, Drake et al. (2009) found no evidence of disproportionality in child welfare reports for the state of Missouri. These inconsistent findings appear to show that official action based on reports of maltreatment may be influenced not just by the type or severity of abuse recorded but also by the ways in which cases are investigated and handled by those who come to the aid of abused children (Harden & Nzinga-Johnson, 2006). As with findings on juvenile justice involvement discussed earlier, those related to child welfare suggest the need for careful scrutiny of current policies and procedures, as well as better training of those who investigate child abuse reports.

Numbers regarding race and ethnicity derived from surveys and crime records for domestic violence cases are also inconsistent. A 1995 special report of the Bureau of Justice Statistics (BJS), based on a nationally representative survey of households in the National Crime Victimization Survey, found that race was not associated with violence perpetrated against women by an intimate partner (Bachman & Saltzman, 1995). In another BJS report, non-Hispanic whites were found to represent nearly 75% of all family violence victims, a slightly higher number than is reflected in their corresponding proportion of the U.S. population (Durose et al., 2005). Yet, other sources find higher prevalence and incidence rates of intimate partner violence among blacks and Hispanics compared with whites (Caetano, Field, Ramisetty-Mikler, & McGrath, 2005; Fusco & Fantuzzo, 2009), suggesting the need for a closer look at selection and measurement differences in these studies.

As previously noted (Chapters 1, 3, and 4), race and ethnicity are consistently tied to youth and community violence, regardless of data sources and/or measures of violence that are used. Statistics compiled by the CDC show that homicides remain the leading cause of death for African Americans between the ages of 10 and 24 and is the second leading cause of death for Hispanics of this age (CDC, 2007b). Other ethnic minority groups (Native Americans, Alaska Natives, and Asian/Pacific Islanders) also are at higher risk than are non-Hispanic whites for homicide deaths. More youth witness serious violence within disadvantaged neighborhoods (e.g., shootings or armed robberies) than are directly victimized (Stein, Jaycox, Katoka, Rhodes, & Vestal, 2003), indicating that estimates, based on official crime statistics, capture just a fraction of all ethnic minority youth who are impacted by violence in some way.

Explanations for why race and ethnic disparities in violence and violence exposure persist at the community level focus on concentrated poverty, racism, and economic disadvantages experienced by African Americans and other groups (Hampton & Oliver, 2006). Scholars have, for many years, emphasized the link between violence and the marginalization of ethnic minority groups, as well as the lack of opportunities afforded youth and adults of color in the way of schooling and employment (Hampton & Oliver, 2006). These and other related themes are discussed by Williams and colleagues in Chapter 3 and by Bright and colleagues in Chapter 4. Evidence also suggests that chronic stress and structural factors of residential turnover and low social cohesion add to the stress and social vulnerability of children who grow up poor in inner-city communities (Sampson, Morenoff, & Gannon-Rowley, 2002; Sampson, Raudenbush, & Earls, 1997). Importantly, advances in etiologic studies of community risk and prevention have helped increase awareness of these issues and emphasized the ways in which community mobilization can be used to enhance protection from violence risk factors (see Chapters 7 and 8).

ADVERSE OUTCOMES OF CHILDREN'S EXPOSURE TO VIOLENCE

All forms of violence exposure appear potentially harmful to children (Goldman et al., 2003). However, most is known about the developmental consequences of physical child abuse, which has been the focus of intense investigation in both prospective and retrospective, cross-sectional survey studies (Herrenkohl et al., 2008). While it is beginning to appear that the effects of violence exposure are similar across exposure categories (e.g., child abuse and domestic violence exposure), evidence shows that child outcomes can vary by the severity and duration of the exposure itself and by the age of the child at the point of exposure. Differences have also been hypothesized according to the relationship of the abused to the abuser (CDC, 2006; Felitti et al., 1998; Kitzmann, Gaylord, Holt, & Kenny, 2003; Sternberg, Baradaran, Abbott, Lamb, & Guterman, 2006).

Additionally, there is some research that has found differences between those who witness an event and those who are directly victimized (see further discussion in Chapter 2), although studies are few in number and somewhat inconsistent in their findings (Sternberg et al., 2006; Trickett, Duran, & Horn, 2003). In one study by Sternberg et al. (1993) of 110 Israeli children (aged 8 to 12 years), results showed that children who either were abused or exposed to spouse abuse were at higher risk than nonexposed youth for internalizing and externalizing problems. However, children who were abused (whether or not they were also exposed to spouse abuse) appeared most at risk for adverse outcomes, including clinical depression.

A range of trauma symptoms are known to occur in children exposed to violence (Margolin & Gordis, 2000). In particularly severe cases, children can manifest symptoms of posttraumatic stress disorder (PTSD). Symptoms of PTSD include difficulty concentrating, sleep problems, severe emotional distress, and frequent upsetting thoughts and memories of the events that were experienced (Lynch, 2003). Young children exposed to violence can also report somatic complaints and describe fears of being left alone. These symptoms can persist well beyond the point of exposure, continuing for some into adulthood. Moderate and long-term psychological, emotional, and conduct problems, such as low self-esteem, depression, anxiety, physical aggression, peer rejection, school failure, and substance use, are more common in children who were exposed to violence compared with those who were not exposed (Edleson, 1999; Fantuzzo et al., 1997; Graham Bermann, 1998; Hughes, 1988; Lichter & McCloskey, 2004; Litrownik, Newton, Hunter, English, & Everson, 2003; McCloskey, Figueredo, & Koss, 1995; McCloskey & Lichter, 2003; Moffitt & Caspi, 2003; Sudermann & Jaffe, 1997). Links between child abuse and poor mental and physical health later in life including heart and lung diseases, cancer, and liver disease have also been documented retrospectively, although findings require replication in prospective studies. Health impairments and health risks extending from early violence exposure include lower immune functioning, higher rates of smoking, more alcohol use, and overeating and obesity (Felitti et al., 1998; Goldman et al., 2003).

Attention has turned recently to the developmental effects of overlapping forms of violence exposure (Herrenkohl et al., 2008; Middlebrooks & Audage, 2008). Here, the assumption is that children exposed to two or more forms of violence (e.g., child abuse and domestic violence exposure) will have worse outcomes than will those who experience only a single form. Several studies have investigated the effects on children of being doubly exposed to child abuse and domestic violence (Hughes, Parkinson, & Vargo, 1989; McCloskey, Figueredo, & Koss, 1995; Wolfe, Crooks, Lee, McIntyre-Smith, & Jaffe, 2003). In one study of children residing in a battered women's shelter, Hughes and colleagues (1989) found that those who had been abused *and* witnessed violence were at higher risk of internalizing and externalizing symptoms than were those who had only witnessed violence. McClosky et al. (1995) arrived at a similar conclusion. Felitti et al.'s (1998) cross-sectional study of adults found that the number of serious health risk indicators for individuals increased linearly with the number of their childhood exposures to violence (including domestic violence and direct abuse). Edwards and colleagues (2003) described a dose-response relation between the number of types of maltreatment and mental health scores. In another cross-sectional study by Graham-Bermann and Seng (2005), analyses showed that childhood exposure to abuse and domestic violence predicted child health problems above and beyond several demographic variables, including a child's sex, socioeconomic status, and maternal substance use. Further, Cunningham's (2003) analysis of data from the 1985 National Family Violence Survey showed a compounding effect on later risk of perpetrating abuse of an individual's having been physically punished and having witnessed interparental violence. Heyman and Slep's (2002) analysis of these data examined the effect of an individual's childhood exposure to family violence (direct abuse and exposure to interparental violence) and his or her current use of violence as an adult partner and caregiver to children. For fathers and mothers both, there was an association between having experienced violence as a child and their later abuse of their own children. However, only for women was there a further elevation in risk of current abuse from their having been exposed to multiple versus a single form of violence. Similar findings were shown with current partner violence as an outcome. Finally, Appleyard, Egeland, van Dulman, and Sroufe (2005) determined that children with an increasing number of risk factors—including abuse and exposure to domestic violence—exhibited more externalizing problems than did children with fewer risks overall. In that study, 171 youth respondents at high risk due to poverty were followed from 12 months to age 16 (94 males and 74 females; 68% white, 10% African American, and 10% mixed race/ethnicity; parents for 59% of the sample were single at the time of their birth). Analyses used summed indexes of dichotomized risk scores (for child maltreatment, interparental violence, family disruption, low socioeconomic status, and high maternal stress) to measure cumulative risk in early childhood (younger than 64 months) and middle childhood. They also used an overall risk index that combined the two risk composites. Results of the study showed a linear effect (contrasted to a threshold effect) of risks on outcomes in which more risks was correlated with more problems in the child. Risk effects in early childhood were maintained even after accounting for risks in middle childhood.

GENDER DIFFERENCES IN OUTCOMES OF VIOLENCE EXPOSURE

In Chapter 4, Bright and colleagues examined issues of gender differences in the perpetration of violence. Here, we examine the ways in which gender intersects with rates and outcomes of violence exposure. Interestingly, evidence shows that girls are somewhat more likely than boys to be represented among substantiated child abuse cases and are notably more likely to be sexually abused and sexually assaulted (CDC, 2007a; Sedlak & Broadhurst, 1996). Boys, however, are more likely than girls to suffer serious physical injuries from abuse (Sedlak & Broadhurst, 1996). While there is no hard evidence that boys and girls differ in their responses to abuse and other exposures to violence, there is some research that suggests they do (Sternberg et al., 2006). Boys who are abused and/or exposed to domestic violence appear at particularly high risk for externalizing behaviors, including aggression, impulsivity, and defiance, whereas girls appear more vulnerable to internalizing problems of depression, low self-confidence, and social withdrawal (Graham Bermann & Hughes, 2003;

Widom, 1998). Yet Sternberg and colleagues (1993) found girls to be at higher risk for both internalizing and externalizing behaviors, due possibly to girls' greater tendency to identify with the victim of violence (in the case of spouse abuse) or "to develop a devalued and victim-like identity" (p. 92). Feiring, Taska, and Lewis (1999) also found girls to be more vulnerable. Results showed that sexually abused girls were more likely to report feelings of shame following the abuse and to report more intrusive thoughts and hyperarousal (probable indicators of PTSD). Girls also experienced more personal vulnerability and perceived the world as a more dangerous place, which, according to the authors, may be due to their greater tendency to "focus on their emotional state and inhibiting actions that might distract them from their negative mood" (Feiring et al., 1999, p. 123).

Further complicating the picture of these gender differences are several studies that show no moderation effects. For example, Kitzman et al.'s (2003) meta-analysis of 118 studies of psychosocial outcomes of children's exposure to interparental violence found comparable effect sizes for boys and girls and no evidence of gender-by-outcome interactions. Wolfe et al.'s (2003) meta-analysis of 41 studies on the effects of children's exposure to domestic violence arrived at a similar conclusion.

Clearly, the question of whether outcomes of violence exposure differ by gender is incomplete. And, some research suggests that a particular focus on gender differences in violence exposure and outcomes will not address what is perhaps a more fundamental question about why individuals differ at all in their reactions to violence. Steinberg and colleagues (2000) offer that gender moderation is better understood when framed as a question of biology and individual dispositions. They argue that, whereas common stressors (risk factors) carry a "universal threat potential" (the ability to cause problems when experienced by all children), how those threats are experienced and manifested in behavior has more to do with psychological, biological, and physiologic processes (e.g., regulation and arousal) than with gender or gendered socialization.

RACE/ETHNIC DIFFERENCES IN OUTCOMES OF VIOLENCE EXPOSURE

Similar questions have been asked about differences in exposure on the basis of race and ethnicity. Unfortunately, there have been relatively few studies on the topic and findings overall are relatively inconsistent (Elliott & Urquiza, 2006; Margolin & Gordis, 2000). In their review of research, Elliott and Urquiza (2006) note that there are a number of problems that have slowed progress on the race/ethnicity question. These include a tendency to use different definitions of exposure, different methods of study, and to apply overly broad ethnic group labels (e.g., minority versus white), which ignores possible within-group variation in exposure, developmental processes, and outcomes of exposure. Williams and colleagues (Chapter 3) also refer to the limitations of current analysis approaches in the study of race and ethnic differences. They and others call for an increasing focus on ethnic variation in both epidemiologic and etiologic research on violence exposure (and perpetration) in children and youth.

MECHANISMS LINKING VIOLENCE EXPOSURE TO ADVERSE OUTCOMES

There are several hypotheses about the ways in which violence exposure leads to long-term, developmental consequences, some of which focus on psychobiological processes and the brain (Lynch, 2003; Margolin & Gordis, 2000). In fact, studies have documented important changes in patterns of arousal, stress response, and stress regulation (e.g., lower threshold for stress), as well as changes in cortisol production, functioning of the sympathetic nervous system, autonomic arousal (related to heart rate, blood pressure, and startle response), and immune functioning among children who have been abused (Margolin & Gordis, 2000; McEwen & Seeman, 1999; Middlebrooks & Audage, 2008). Children's exposure to low-level violence and conflict in the home (e.g., arguments, yelling, threats) also can promote distress in young children, leading to elevated cortisol reactivity (Davies, Sturge-Apple, Cicchetti, & Cummings, 2008). A compelling study by Davies and colleagues (2008) found that a particularly strong association between distress and cortisol reactivity emerged for children who became highly involved in the perceived conflict of their parents, thus illustrating how damage can be inflicted on children when they strongly identify with a victimized parent or try to control a conflict out of desperation for it to stop. Research on biology and trauma has shown effects as well on the timing and onset of puberty and early sexual behavior, a link, perhaps, to another documented outcome of physical abuse: teen pregnancy (McGloin & Widom, 2001). Indeed, research in this area hints at important advances in the study of violence exposure and its effects.

Hypotheses from social developmental perspectives emphasize the impact of violence exposure on children's outlook and future orientation with respect to relationships, schooling, and employment. The effects of violence exposure on relationships and relationship quality are documented in several sources (Herrenkohl, Mason, Kosterman, Lengua, & Hawkins, 2004; Lynch & Cicchetti, 2003). For example, social learning models suggest that children exposed to violence learn to use violence, in subtle and more direct and ways, to control and dominate others. These patterns of control can become evident in the ways abused children approach and negotiate relationships with peers and, later, their intimate partners (Herrenkohl et al., 2008).

Attachment theory suggests that children exposed to violence and/or directly victimized by violence in the home are impacted primarily by the lack of warmth, nurturance, and close relationship ties that young children need to thrive. Lynch and Cicchetti (2003) suggest that violence exposure outside the home may cause significant stress in the parent-child relationship or lead to high levels of parental distress, which, in turn, affects children's behavior and escalates conflict. The researchers studied 127 children between the ages of 7 and 13 living in an urban setting and examined the association between community violence exposure and various aspects of family functioning. Results of the study showed that child-reported exposure to high levels of community violence was associated with children's feeling less secure with their caregivers, experiencing less positive affect when they were with their caregivers, and reporting less satisfaction with the closeness to their caregivers. Children also experienced more separation anxiety and reported more negative maternal behavior. The researchers examined gender differences and found that that girls, but not boys, who experienced high levels of community violence exposure reported significantly lower levels of positive affect toward maternal caregivers. Sternberg and colleagues (2006) report that children exposed to violence, particularly those in abusive and violent homes, may not experience or develop the capacity to trust and show affection toward others. Research also suggests that children who witness violence show less empathy and have more difficulty identifying and responding to the emotions of others (Owen et al., 2008).

Another way by which violence exposure impacts children is by interfering with parents' ability to "parent." For example, evidence suggests that violence affects the well-being of children when parents become less available as caregivers—physically and/or emotionally (Kohen, Dahinten, Lenventhal, & McIntosh, 2008; Margolin & Gordis, 2000). Parents under considerable stress due to threats and intimidation by a partner can be less emotionally responsive to the needs of their children and unable to monitor their children's social activities and behavior (Kohen et al., 2008; Margolin, Gordis, Medina, & Oliver, 2003). Additionally, there is a tendency for parents to adjust their parenting to the conditions of the surrounding environment. In this regard, parents may be less or more responsive depending on the surrounding context and level of threat from outside sources. For example, parents who perceive the surrounding neighborhood as unsafe may try to limit their children's activities outside the home by monitoring their children's social interactions and limiting with whom their children can spend time (Hill & Herman-Stahl, 2002). Out of fear for children's safety, or simply overburdened by the challenges of trying to parent in a highly stressful environment, parents of children in dangerous neighborhoods can, in extreme conditions, become moderately or even highly punitive in their disciplining (Kohen et al., 2008; Margolin & Gordis, 2000), thereby risking additional trauma to a the child (Huth-Bocks & Hughes, 2008). In an illustrative study, Kohen and colleagues (2008) examined the effects of neighborhood disadvantage on family process and child outcomes. Their research showed that neighborhood disadvantage was associated with maternal depression and family dysfunction.

These factors were, in turn, associated with less consistent and more punitive parenting, leading eventually to child behavior problems and lower
child verbal abilities.

The experience of being in an abusive intimate relationship can also
lessen a parent's ability to parent and increase that parent's use of punitive
discipline. In Margolin et al.'s (2003) study of the effects of husband-to-
wife and family of origin aggression, results showed that the experience of
being in a relationship with an abusive partner was positively related to
mothers' use of power and control tactics, as well as physical punishment
of children and frequent yelling. Fathers in violent relationships were also
more inclined to use physical punishment with their children.

Further evidence of a link between parenting stress and outcomes of
children exposed to violence is documented in a study by Huth-Bocks and
Hughes (2008). They studied 190 mother-child pairs in a predominantly
African American sample of battered women. Results showed that parenting stress increased behavior and emotional problems in children aged 4
to 12. However, parenting stress did not appear to impact child outcomes
by changing the parenting practices used in the family. Huth-Bocks and
Hughes call for further examination of stress-mediation models using
broader samples and more refined measures of parenting stress (e.g., tran-
sitory versus chronic stress) and parent (maternal) functioning.

High levels of social support experienced by children and even adult
victims may buffer the effects of violence exposure (see further discussion
of this topic in Chapter 6). Conversely, low levels of support can instead
increase internalizing and externalizing behaviors in children who have
been exposed to violence (Owen et al., 2008). In their review of research
on neighborhood safety and social involvement, Hill and colleagues
(2002) note that although children in more well-off areas benefit from a
collective investment in parenting from neighborhood residents, those in
disadvantaged areas often experience low support and social isolation.
Consequently, children may not have access to protective factors that
could otherwise help them overcome the effects of various risk factors
(including violence exposure). Williams and colleagues (Chapter 3)
also discuss these dynamics in relation to youth violence perpetration and
prevention.

Social support can play an important, buffering role in the lives of
children exposed to interparental violence. In a study of 148 African
American children aged 8 to 12, Owen et al. (2008) investigated the association between intimate partner conflict and child outcomes of internalizing and externalizing behaviors, with perceived social support by children
and mothers hypothesized as potential mediators. Results of the analyses
showed that perceived social support significantly mediated the effect of
conflict on both outcomes. For mothers, social support mediated the
effect of parental conflict on child internalizing, but not externalizing,
behaviors. The investigators conclude that perceived (low) social support
is a risk factor for emotional and behavioral problems in African American

children and, thus, possibly an explanatory variable that links domestic violence exposure to later problems in children.

IMPLICATIONS FOR FURTHER RESEARCH AND PRACTICE

Existing research on overlapping forms of violence suggests the following with respect to further research and practice: Because violence exposure of the forms discussed in this review (child abuse, domestic violence, and community violence exposure) do appear to co-occur, there is a pressing need to look more directly at the nature and extent of overlapping stressors. For example, it is important to know whether certain forms of violence exposure occur more often together than with others and, if so, why? It is also important to know the combined and unique effects of each form of violence exposure on children's development and to use that information to guide prevention and intervention programs. A majority of studies reviewed for this chapter examined only one form of violence exposure in children, making it very difficult to determine whether that one form is masking or encompassing the effects of another. It is also important to study violence exposure of multiple forms in the context of other known risk factors and indicators of family adversity, such as parental substance use and psychopathology (Gewirtz & Edleson, 2007; Herrenkohl & Herrenkohl, 2007; Herrenkohl et al., 2008; Middlebrooks & Audage, 2008). Understanding the full extent of risk factors experienced by children impacted by violence will help answer questions about etiology and promote a stronger foundation from which to plan and deliver targeted prevention and intervention programs. Additionally, research is needed to determine the possible additive and/or cumulative effects of violence exposure and other known risk factors for children at differing ages, to assess and document the developmental salience of particular risk factors in relation to others. Although several studies have examined questions about the child gender and age at the time of violence exposure, and effects that follow, findings are mixed and inconclusive. Thus, more research on gender as a predictor of violence exposure, and moderator of risks on outcomes for youth, is desperately needed.

Conceptual and definitional differences for variables used in the study of violence exposure should also be considered, as should the varied methods used to study exposure and outcomes. Attention to each and all aspects of research is needed—sampling, research design (e.g., cross-sectional versus longitudinal panel studies), and construct measurement. Use of consistent definitions and more rigorous research designs should help bring results closer together and allow more complete and accurate syntheses of study results. Working toward universal typologies of abuse and violence exposure is also key to aligning studies and deriving implications. All tasks are necessary to inform and advance practice and policy (Herrenkohl & Herrenkohl, in press).

There have been some, although relatively few, attempts to investigate, and incorporate into theory, the ways in which gender and race/ethnicity interact with exposure (and related risks) in predicting later outcomes for children and youth. Further alignment of studies focused on gender and race/ethnic differences in rates of exposure, processes, and outcomes of exposure should move the field ahead with respect to understanding etiology and will provide much-needed empirical guidance for the development of prevention and intervention programs. Bright et al.'s (Chapter 4) reference to gendered theories and perspectives raises important considerations about conceptualizing and studying the role of gender in studies on violence. In short, the evidence is clear—children of color, African Americans in particular, are more heavily burdened by risks and influenced by violence than are other groups. Thus, careful attention should be given to understanding how to plan and intervene in ways to readily assist children and families of color, particularly those who reside in the most challenging, high-risk settings. The challenge of intervening to lessen multiple, overlapping risks across contexts requires a renewed interest in social interventions and context that extend beyond the individual child or family to the surrounding contexts. In Chapter 6, we continue this discussion, with attention focused particularly on the topic of resilience—how resilience is conceptualized and studied as a developmental process in relation to violence and violence exposure in children. We also discuss the application of resilience in prevention and intervention models as a lead-in to a more comprehensive review of programs by Jenson and colleagues in Chapters 7 and 8.

ACKNOWLEDGMENTS   The author would like to thank Cynthia Sousa, J. Bart Klika, and Lisa Stewart for their help in compiling research for this review and for commenting on earlier drafts of the manuscript.

REFERENCES

Aisenberg, E., & Herrenkohl, T. I. (2008). Community violence in context: Risk and resilience in children and families. *Journal of Interpersonal Violence, 23,* 296–315.

Appel, A. E., & Holden, G. W. (1998). The co-occurrence of spouse and physical child abuse: A review and appraisal. *Journal of Family Psychology, 12*(4), 578–599.

Appleyard, K., Egeland, B., van Dulman, M., & Sroufe, L. A. (2005). When more is not better: The role of cumulative risk in child behavior outcomes. *Journal of Child Psychology and Psychiatry, 46*(3), 235–245.

Bachman, R., & Saltzman, L. E. (1995). *Violence against women: Estimates from the redesigned survey.* Washington, DC: U.S. Department of Justice.

*Buka, S. L., Stichick, T. L., Birdthistle, I., & Earls, F. J. (2001). Youth exposure to violence: Prevalence, risks, and consequences. *American Journal of Orthopsychiatry, 71*(3), 298–310.

Caetano, R., Field, C. A., Ramisetty-Mikler, S., & McGrath, C. (2005). The 5-year course of intimate partner violence among white, black, and Hispanic couples in the United States. *Journal of Interpersonal Violence, 20*(9), 1039–1057.

Centers for Disease Control and Prevention (CDC). (2006). *Intimate partner violence.* Atlanta, GA: CDC, National Center for Injury Prevention and Control.

Centers for Disease Control and Prevention (CDC). (2007a). *Child maltreatment.* Atlanta, GA: CDC, National Center for Injury Prevention and Control.

Centers for Disease Control and Prevention (CDC). (2007b). *Youth violence* Atlanta, GA: CDC, National Center for Injury Prevention and Control.

Cunningham, S. M. (2003). The joint contribution of experiencing and witnessing violence during childhood on child abuse in the parent role. *Violence and Victims, 18*(6), 619–639.

Davies, P. T., Sturge-Apple, M. L., Cicchetti, D., & Cummings, E. M. (2008). Adrenocortical underpinnings of children's psychological reactivity to inter-parental conflict. *Child Development, 79*(6), 1693–1706.

Dong, M., Anda, R. F., Felitti, V. J., Dube, S. R., Williamson, D. F., Thompson, T. J., et al. (2004). The interrelatedness of multiple forms of childhood abuse, neglect, and household dysfunction. *Child Abuse & Neglect, 28,* 771–784.

Drake, B., Lee, S. M., & Jonson-Reid, M. (2009). Race and child maltreatment resporting: Are Blacks overrepresented? *Children and Youth Services Review, 31,* 309–316.

Durose, M. R., Harlow, C. W., Langan, P. A., Motivans, M., Rantala, R. R., & Smith, E. L. (2005). *Family violence statistics.* Washington, DC: U.S. Department of Justice.

Edleson, J. L. (1999). Problems associated with children's witnessing domestic violence. Violence Against Women Online Resources. Retrieved June 9, 2004, from www.vaw.umn.edu

Edleson, J. L. (2001). Studying the co-occurrence of child maltreatment and domestic violence in families. In S. A. Graham-Bermann & J. L. Edleson (Eds.), *Domestic violence in the lives of children: The future of research, inter-vention, and social policy* (pp. 91–110). Washington, DC: American Psychological Association.

Edwards, V., Holden, G. W., Felitti, V. J., & Anda, R. F. (2003). Relationship between multiple forms of childhood maltreatment and adult mental health in community respondents: Results from the Adverse Childhood Experiences Study. *American Journal of Psychiatry, 160*(8), 1453–1461.

Elliott, K., & Urquiza, A. (2006). Ethnicity, culture, and child maltreatment. Journal of social issues, *62*(4), 787–809.

*Evans, S. E., Davies, C., & DiLillo, D. (2008). Exposure to domestic violence: A meta-analysis of child and adolescent outcomes. *Aggression and Violent Behavior, 13,* 131–140.

Fagan, J., & Browne, A. (1994). Violence between spouses and intimates: Physical aggression between women and men in intimate relationships. In J. A. Roth (Ed.), *Understanding and preventing violence* (Vol. 3, pp. 115–292). Washington, DC: National Academies Press.

Fang, X., & Corso, P. S. (2007). Child maltreatment, youth violence, and intimate partner violence: Developmental relationships. *American Journal of Preventive Medicine, 33*(4), 281–290.

*Fantuzzo, J., Boruch, R., Beriama, A., Atkins, M., & Marcus, S. (1997). Domestic violence and children: Prevalence and risk in five major U.S. cities. *Journal of the American Academy of Child and Adolescent Psychiatry, 36*(1), 116–122.

Feiring, C., Taska, L., & Lewis, M. (1999). Age and gender differences in children's and adolescents' adaptation to sexual abuse. *Child Abuse & Neglect, 23*(2), 115–128.

Felitti, V. J., Anda, R. F., Nordenberg, D., Williamson, D. F., Spitz, A. M., Edwards, V., et al. (1998). Relationship of childhood abuse and household dysfunction to many of the leading causes of death in adults: The Adverse Childhood Experiences (ACE) Study. *American Journal of Preventive Medicine, 14*(4), 245–258.

Freisthler, B., & Crampton, D. (2009). Environment and child well-being. *Children and Youth Services Review, 31*, 297–299.

Fusco, R. A., & Fantuzzo, J. W. (2009). Domestic violence crimes and children: A population-based investigation of direct sensory exposure and the nature of involvement. *Children and Youth Services Review, 31*(2), 249–256.

*Garbarino, J., Hammon, W. R., Mercy, J., & Yung, B. R. (2004). Community violence and children: Preventing exposure and reducing harm. In K. I. Maton, C. J. Schellenbach, B. J. Leadbeater & A. L. Solarz (Eds.), *Investing in children, youth, families, and communities: Strengths-Based Research and Policy* (pp. 303–320). Washington, DC: American Psychological Association.

Gewirtz, A. H., & Edleson, J. L. (2007). Young children's exposure to intimate partner violence: Towards a developmental risk and resilience framework for research and intervention. *Journal of Family Violence, 22*(151–163).

*Goldman, J., Salus, M. K., Wolcott, D., & Kennedy, K. Y. (2003). *A coordinated response to child abuse and neglect: The foundation for practice.* Washington, DC: U.S. Department of Health and Human Services.

Graham Bermann, S. A. (1998). The impact of woman abuse on children's social development: Research and theoretical perspectives. In G. W. Holden, R. Geffner & E. N. Jouriles (Eds.), *Children exposed to marital violence: Theory, research, and applied issues* (pp. 21–54). Washington, DC: American Psychological Association.

Graham Bermann, S. A., & Hughes, H. M. (2003). Intervention for children exposed to interparental violence (IPV): Assessment of needs and research priorities. *Clinical Child and Family Psychology Review, 6*(3), 189–204.

Graham Bermann, S. A., & Seng, J. (2005). Violence exposure and traumatic stress symptoms as additional predictors of health problems in high-risk children. *Journal of Pediatrics, 146*(3), 349–354.

Hampton, R. L., & Oliver, W. (2006). Violence in the Black family: What we know, where we go. In R. L. Hampton & T. P. Gullotta (Eds.), *Interpersonal violence in the African-American community* (pp. 1–16). New London, CT: Springer.

Harden, B. J., & Nzinga-Johnson, S. (2006). Young, wounded, and black: The maltreatment of African-American children in the early years. In R. L. Hampton & T. P. Gullotta (Eds.), *Interpersonal violence in the African-American community* (pp. 17–46). New York: Springer.

Haugaard, J. J., & Feerick, M. (2002). Interventions for maltreated children to reduce their likelihood of engaging in juvenile delinquency. *Children's Services: Social Policy, Research, and Practice, 5*(4), 285–297.

Herrenkohl, R. C., & Herrenkohl, T. I. (In press). Assessing a child's experience of multiple maltreatment types: Some unfinished business. *Journal of Family Violence.*

Herrenkohl, T. I., & Herrenkohl, R. C. (2007). Examining the overlap and prediction of multiple forms of child maltreatment, stressors, and socioeconomic status: A longitudinal analysis of youth outcomes. *Journal of Family Violence, 22*, 553–562.

Herrenkohl, T. I., Mason, W. A., Kosterman, R., Lengua, L. J., & Hawkins, J. D. (2004). Pathways from physical child abuse to partner violence in young adulthood. *Violence and Victims, 19*, 123–136.

*Herrenkohl, T. I., Sousa, C., Tajima, E. A., Herrenkohl, R. C., & Moylan, C. A. (2008). Intersection of child abuse and children's exposure to domestic violence. *Trauma, Violence, & Abuse, 9*(2), 84–99.

Heyman, R. E., & Slep, A. M. (2002). Do child abuse and interparental violence lead to adulthood family violence? *Journal of Marriage and Family, 64*, 864–870.

Hill, N. E., & Herman-Stahl, M. A. (2002). Neighborhood safety and social involvement: Associations with parenting behaviors and depressive symptoms among African American and Euro-American mothers. *Journal of Family Psychology, 16*(2), 209–219.

Hughes, H. M. (1988). Psychological and behavioral correlates of family violence in child witnesses and victims. *American Journal of Orthopsychiatry, 58*(1), 77–90.

Hughes, H. M., Parkinson, D., & Vargo, M. (1989). Witnessing spouse abuse and experiencing physical abuse: A "double whammy"? *Journal of Family Violence, 4*(2), 197–209.

Huth-Bocks, A. C., & Hughes, H. M. (2008). Parenting stress, parenting behavior, and children's adjustment in families experiencing intimate partner violence. *Journal of Family Violence, 23*, 243–251.

Kitzmann, K. M., Gaylord, N. K., Holt, A. R., & Kenny, E. D. (2003). Child witnesses to domestic violence: A meta-analytic review. *Journal of Consulting and Clinical Psychology, 71*(2), 339–352.

Kohen, D. E., Dahinten, V. S., Leventhal, T., & McIntosh, C., N. (2008). Neighborhood disadvantage: Pathways for effects for young children. *Child Development, 79*(1), 156–169.

Lichter, E. L., & McCloskey, L. A. (2004). The effects of childhood exposure to marital violence on adolescent gender-role beliefs and dating violence. *Psychology of Women Quarterly, 28*, 344–357.

Litrownik, A. J., Newton, R., Hunter, W. M., English, D., & Everson, M. D. (2003). Exposure to family violence in young at-risk children: A longitudinal look at the effects of victimization and witnessed physical and psychological aggression. *Journal of Family Violence, 18*(1), 59–73.

Lynch, M. (2003). Consequences of children's exposure to community violence. *Clinical Child and Family Psychology Review, 6*(4), 265–274.

Lynch, M., & Cicchetti, D. (2003). Links between community violence and the family system: Evidence from children's feeling's of relatedness and perceptions of parent behavior. *Family Process, 41*(3), 519–532.

Margolin, G., & Gordis, E. B. (2000). The effects of family and community violence on children. *Annual Review of Psychology, 51*, 445–479.

Margolin, G., Gordis, E. B., Medina, A. M., & Oliver, P. H. (2003). The co-occurrence of husband-to-wife aggression, family-of-origin aggression, and child abuse potential in a community sample. *Journal of Interpersonal Violence, 18*(4), 413–440.

*McCloskey, L. A., Figueredo, A. J., & Koss, M. P. (1995). The effects of systemic family violence on children's mental health. *Child Development, 66*(5), 1239–1261.

McCloskey, L. A., & Lichter, E. L. (2003). The contribution of marital violence to adolescent aggression across different relationships. *Journal of Interpersonal Violence, 18*(4), 390–412.

McEwen, B. S., & Seeman, T. (1999). Protective and damaging effects of mediators of stress: Elaborating and testing the concepts of allostasis and allostatic load. *Annals of the New York Academy of Sciences, 896*, 30–47.

McGloin, J. M., & Widom, C. S. (2001). Resilience among abused and neglected children grown up. *Development and Psychopathology, 13*(4), 1021–1038.

Middlebrooks, J. S., & Audage, N. C. (2008). *The effects of childhood stress on health across the lifespan*. Atlanta, GA: Centers for Disease Control and Prevention, National Center for Injury Prevention and Control.

Moffitt, T. E., & Caspi, A. (2003). Preventing the intergenerational continuity of antisocial behaviour: Implications of partner violence. In D. P. Farrington & J. W. Coid (Eds.), *Early prevention of adult antisocial behaviour* (pp. 109–129). Cambridge: Cambridge University Press.

Moylan, C. A., Herrenkohl, T. I., Sousa, C., Tajima, E. A., Herrenkohl, R. C., & Russo, M. J. (in press). The effects of child abuse and exposure to domestic violence on adolescent internalizing and externalizing behavior problems. *Journal of Family Violence*.

Osofsky, J. D. (1999). The impact of violence on children. *Future of Children, 9*(3), 33–49.

Owen, A. E., Thompson, M. P., Mitchell, M. D., Kennebrew, S. Y., Paranjape, A., Reddick, T. L., et al. (2008). Perceived social support as a mediator of the link between intimate partner conflict and child adjustment. *Journal of Family Violence, 23*, 221–230.

Renner, L. M., & Slack, K. S. (2006). Intimate partner violence and child maltreatment: Understanding the intragenerational and intergenerational connections. *Child Abuse & Neglect, 30*, 599–617.

Rutter, M. (2001). Psychosocial adversity: Risk, resilience and recovery. In J. M. Richman & M. W. Fraser (Eds.), *The context of youth violence: Resilience, risk and protection* (pp. 13–42). Westport, CT: Praeger Publishers.

Sampson, R. J., Morenoff, J. D., & Gannon-Rowley, T. (2002). Assessing neighborhood effects: Social processes and new directions in research. *Annual Review of Sociology, 28*, 443–478.

Sampson, R. J., Raudenbush, S. W., & Earls, F. J. (1997). Neighborhoods and violent crime: A multilevel study of collective efficacy. *Science, 277*, 918–924.

Sedlak, A. J., & Broadhurst, D. D. (1996). *Executive summary of the third National Study of Child Abuse and Neglect*. Washington, DC: U.S. Department of Health and Human Services.

Stein, B. D., Jaycox, L., Katoka, S. H., Rhodes, H., & Vestal, K. D. (2003). Prevalence of child and adolescent exposure to community violence. *Clinical Child and Family Psychology Review, 6*, 247–264.

Steinberg, L., & Avenevoli, S. (2000). The role of context in the development of psychopathology: A conceptual framework and some speculative propositions. *Child Development, 71*(1), 66–74.

Sternberg, K. J., Baradaran, L. P., Abbott, C. B., Lamb, M. E., & Guterman, E. (2006). Type of violence, age, and gender differences in the effects of family violence on children's behavior problems: A mega-analysis. *Developmental Review, 26*, 89–112.

Sternberg, K. J., Lamb, M. E., Greenbaum, C., Cicchetti, D., Dawud, S., Cortes, R. M., et al. (1993). Effects of domestic violence on children's behavior problems and depression. *Developmental Psychology, 29*(1), 44–52.

Straus, M. A. (1990). Methodological issues in the study of family violence. In M. A. Straus & R. J. Gelles (Eds.), *Physical violence in American families: Risk factors and adaptations to violence in 8,145 families* (pp. 17–28). New Brunswick, NJ: Transaction Publishers.

Sudermann, M., & Jaffe, P. (1997). Children and youth who witness violence: New directions in intervention and prevention. In D. A. Wolfe, R. J. McMahon & R. D. Peters (Eds.), *Child abuse: New directions in prevention and treatment across the lifespan* (pp. 55–78). Thousand Oaks, CA: Sage.

Tajima, E. A. (2000). The relative importance of wife abuse as a risk factor for violence against children. *Child Abuse & Neglect, 24*(11), 1383–1398.

Trickett, P. K., Duran, L., & Horn, J. L. (2003). Community violence as it affects child development: Issues of definition. *Clinical Child and Family Psychology Review, 6*(223–236).

World Health Organization (WHO). (2006). *Child maltreatment and alcohol.* Geneva, Switzerland: WHO.

Widom, C. S. (1998). Childhood victimization: Early adversity and subsequent psychopathology. In B. P. Dohrenwend (Ed.), *Adversity, stress, and psychopathology* (pp. 81–95). London: Oxford University Press.

Wolfe, D. A., Crooks, C. V., Lee, V., McIntyre-Smith, A., & Jaffe, P. G. (2003). The effects of children's exposure to domestic violence: A meta-analysis and critique. *Clinical Child and Family Psychology Review, 6*(3), 171–187.

6

RESILIENCE AND PROTECTION FROM VIOLENCE EXPOSURE IN CHILDREN
Implications for Prevention and Intervention Programs with Vulnerable Populations

TODD I. HERRENKOHL

As discussed in Chapter 5, there are many high-risk environments that expose children to violence. Research on how children and youth in high-risk environments overcome the odds of negative outcomes is crucial to the development of prevention and intervention efforts. In this chapter, we explore the concepts of resilience and protection with respect to violence exposure in children. Issues of race and gender are again considered. Implications for both targeted and universal prevention and intervention programs are discussed briefly.

CONCEPTUALIZING AND OPERATIONALIZING RESILIENCE

Resilience in the developmental literature is often studied as an end-point determination of an individual's having adjusted well (i.e., achieved positive outcomes or avoided negative outcomes) despite earlier risk exposure

(Cowen et al., 1997; McGloin & Widom, 2001), although resilience among vulnerable children—including those exposed to violence— is perhaps better understood as a pattern of positive adaptation following earlier adversity (Mrazek & Mrazek, 1987; Wright & Masten, 2005). The difference is in viewing resilience less as a static outcome and more a fluid process that changes with development (Cicchetti & Rogosch, 1997; Cicchetti & Toth, 1998; Leadbeater, Schellenbach, Maton, & Dodgen, 2004; Luthar, Cicchetti, & Becker, 2000; Masten, 2001; Masten, Best, & Garmezy, 1990; Masten et al., 1999). Other terms that approximate the concept of resilience include hardiness, mastery, and personal competence, which are used in different disciplines and in different contexts to explain a similar idea of bouncing back or overcoming the odds of negative outcomes in the face of adversity (Kaplan, 2005).

How researchers define *resilience* will, of course, depend on the age and developmental status of those they are studying and the qualities or experiences deemed by them most important as indicators of positive adjustment, competence, or well-being (Masten, 2001). Narrow to very broad definitions of *resilience* are found throughout the research literature; most incorporate indicators of prosocial behavior, emotional stability, well-being, or achievement into at least one life domain (e.g., school, family). For example, O'Donnell and colleagues (2004) examined seven indicators of resilience for youth exposed to community violence: youths' future expectations, self-reliance, interpersonal relations, lower substance use, lower delinquency and school misconduct, lower depression and anxiety, and lower somatization. McGloin and Widom (2001) defined *resilience* in their study of adults with histories of child maltreatment as an individual's having achieved successful employment, having avoided homelessness, having graduated high school, having been involved in social activities, having not developed psychiatric or substance use disorders, having not been arrested, and having not perpetrated violence. Finally, in their groundbreaking study of a birth cohort on the island of Kauai, Werner and Smith (2001) broadly characterized resilient adults as those who were free of learning and behavior problems in childhood and adolescence; who did well in school, in their homes, and in their social lives; who set realistic goals and expectations upon graduation from high school; and who, as they entered adulthood, "developed into competent, confident, and caring persons who expressed a great desire to make use of whatever opportunities came along to improve themselves" (p. 56). In Chapter 2, Aisenberg and colleagues refer to the need for more consistency in definitions of *violence*. There is also a need to develop common definitions of *resilience* that will enhance the exchange of information and comparison of research findings (Heller, Heller, Larrieu, D'Imperio, & Boris, 1999). However, with the range of ideas and topics studied from a resilience perspective, agreed-on definitions and/or thresholds of positive functioning that meet criteria of positive adjustment may be difficult to achieve.

RESILIENCE AND PROTECTIVE FACTORS

Whereas risk factors promote a higher probability of a negative or undesired outcome, protective factors, also termed "resiliency factors," "buffers," or "assets," are innate or learned qualities of an individual, social interactions, or aspects of the environment that increase the likelihood of positive adjustment following earlier adversity (Bogar & Hulse-Killacky, 2006; Katz & Gottman, 1997; Leadbeater et al., 2004; Luthar, 2006; Masten, 2001; Rutter, 2001). According to Cowen and colleagues (1997), the study of protective factors help answer the "how" question with respect to the ways individuals overcome adversity and/or achieve and maintain resilience as they develop. As with risk factors, protective factors typically co-occur and fluctuate in number and intensity with the passage of time, leading to less or more vulnerability and stability over an individual's lifetime. Figure 6.1 from Leadbeater and colleagues (2004) illustrates the developmental process of individual competence as it interacts with risks and protective factors in the social environment. The figure shows a gradual upward trend in competence as levels of protection increase over time. As noted, a gradual lowering of competence and/or resilience (i.e., poorer adjustment) also is possible if an individual's vulnerability from earlier risk exposure is not balanced to some degree by protective influences in the environment. Because individuals who encounter multiple risk factors are least likely to come by protective factors naturally, resilience among individuals of particularly disadvantaged groups (e.g., youth in high poverty, high crime neighborhoods) depends on planned interventions that reduce risks and promote access to resources and networks of social support (Hawkins, Catalano, Kosterman, Abbott, & Hill, 1999; Pollard, Hawkins, & Arthur, 1999). In Chapters 7 and 8, Jenson and colleagues

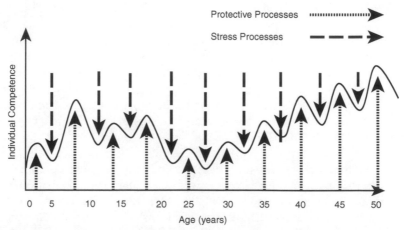

Figure 6.1.   Interaction of risk and protective processes related to individual competence.
(From Leadbeater et al., 2004.)

discuss several programs that have the potential to lessen risk factors and strengthen protection at the community level.

Despite a long-standing interest in resilience and childhood adversity (DiRago & Vaillant, 2007; Gewirtz & Edleson, 2007; Kaufman & Zigler, 1989; Luthar et al., 2000; Masten et al., 1990; Mrazek & Mrazek, 1987; Rutter, 2001; Trickett, Kurtz, & Pizzigati, 2004; Werner & Smith, 1992; Wolin & Wolin, 1993), there are relatively few well-designed (prospective) studies from which to derive information on protective factors related to resilience in children exposed to violence. However, it is important to use what currently is known from the few studies there are to strengthen theory and to accelerate the task of implementing strengths-based models of practice that can reduce violence exposure and promote well-being among vulnerable children. In this next section, we review current findings on protective factors for children exposed to community and family violence. We conclude the chapter with a call for further research and review implications for practice and policy.

RESILIENCE FROM EXPOSURE TO COMMUNITY VIOLENCE

As noted in the previous chapters, community violence affects ethnic minority youth in urban settings disproportionately. Youth living in disadvantaged neighborhoods not only encounter a higher risk of violence exposure, they also experience fewer opportunities for prosocial peer involvement and more opportunities to become involved with antisocial peers who reinforce problem behaviors, such as violence, substance use, and delinquency (Catalano & Hawkins, 1996; Chung & Steinberg, 2006; Dubow, Edwards, & Ippolito, 1997; Sampson, Raudenbush, & Earls, 1997). Poverty and limited resources within very disadvantaged neighborhoods translate to less human capital (e.g., social support, mentoring) to promote positive youth development (Burton & Jarrett, 2000; Ceballo, McLoyd, & Toyokawa, 2004; Furstenberg, 1993; Jencks & Mayer, 1990; Wilson, 1987). However, work by various scholars has shown that, even within disadvantaged neighborhoods, there is variability in social resources and networks of support that can protect children and youth from violence exposure, and the problems that follow. For example, in their study of fourth-, fifth-, and sixth-grade children living in disadvantaged neighborhoods, Dubow et al. (1997) found that higher levels of family support moderated the effect of stressful life events on antisocial behavior. Interestingly, peer support had the opposite effect; it exacerbated the effect of stress on antisocial behavior. Support from peers also added to the risk of antisocial behavior associated with physical aspects of the neighborhood itself (e.g., broken bottles/trash in yards and alleys, drug-selling, gun violence), suggesting, perhaps, the need to account in analyses for peer deviance as well as support (Catalano & Hawkins, 1996; Chung & Steinberg, 2006).

As noted earlier, research by Sampson and colleagues (1997) identified collective efficacy as a pivotal factor related to community violence and protection. Collective efficacy is the degree to which residents share values and are poised to intervene for the common good of the neighborhood. Sampson and colleagues have shown that higher collective efficacy is associated with lower rates of violence and this variable accounts largely for the direct effect of neighborhood structural factors on violent crime. Further, work by Furstenberg and colleagues (1993) showed that collective vigilance, values favoring strong families, and shared responsibility for the parenting of children within disadvantaged areas provide direct benefits to families by reducing stress and lessening social isolation, thereby improving parents' capacity to parent well. Social interaction among families also increases the likelihood that children within the neighborhood will be monitored and kept safe (Hill & Herman-Stahl, 2002). Thus, while children and youth in poor, disadvantaged neighborhoods are more vulnerable to violence exposure and other risk factors, the social organization of neighborhoods can in some cases offer protection and buffer the effects of risk factors on developmental outcomes for these youth.

According to the work of Furstenberg (1993) and others, how well children cope with being exposed to violence in the community appears to hinge on their parents' ability to "parent" under conditions of high stress (DiRago & Vaillant, 2007; Hill & Herman-Stahl, 2002; Kohen, Dahinten, Lenventhal, & McIntosh, 2008; Tolan, Sherrod, Gorman-Smith, & Henry, 2004). Not surprisingly, what qualifies as good parenting depends to some extent on the surrounding context (Tolan et al., 2004). For example, parents of youth living in disadvantaged areas may need to be more vigilant and responsive to negative influences in the environment than would parents of youth living in lower-risk and better-protected areas (Furstenberg, 1993). Yet, in general, consistent, less punitive discipline, more cohesion, warmth, and support among family members has been found to promote positive development in children and to strengthen coping and resilience among those exposed to violence (DiRago & Vaillant, 2007; Kohen et al., 2008).

In a study by Gorman-Smith et al. (2004), the importance of "good" parenting (conceptualized broadly using positive discipline and monitoring practices) was examined as a potential buffer of violence exposure among inner-city youth. The study was of 263 African American and Latino males sampled from fifth- and seventh-grade classrooms in 17 Chicago public schools. Results showed that youth from families with poor parenting and low emotional cohesion were more likely to be exposed to community violence. Community violence exposure was, in turn, linked to the perpetration of violence among youth. However, youth exposed to high levels of violence, but living in families with positive parenting and emotional cohesion, perpetrated less violence than did similarly exposed youth in poorer functioning families.

Evidence from other studies also shows the benefits of positive parenting and family cohesion (Luthar, 2006). In a study by Hammack et al. (2004) of inner-city African American adolescents, several factors related to family cohesion and social support were found to act as protective-stabilizing influences for those who witnessed community violence. Maternal closeness, time spent with one's family, social support (availability and quality of support received from family, friends, and other adults), and daily support (friendliness and helpfulness of those with whom they interact) lessened the risk of anxiety and depressive symptoms for youth. However, at high levels of exposure to violence, these variables appeared less protective from mental health problems, suggesting there may be a limit to how much protection from violence is possible when children encounter enduring stress or particularly high-level risk exposure.

O'Donnell and colleagues (2004) studied the effects of social support in relation to community violence exposure for urban youth in grades 6, 8, and 10. They found that parent, peer, and school support were associated with various indicators of resilience among those youth who had been victimized by violence. Parent support was more strongly associated with resilience indicators of less substance use and abuse, less school misconduct, and lower depression when measured cross-sectionally. Interestingly, support by parents was less of a positive influence two years later. School support, however, became an increasingly stronger buffer when measured longitudinally, predicting less substance abuse and lower school misconduct among youth. Related research by Ozer and Weinstein (2004) showed that social support from family members (mothers, fathers, siblings) and school (teachers) lessened rates of psychological problems (depression and posttraumatic stress disorder [PTSD]) for violence exposed youth. Perceived school safety and fewer barriers to discussing violence (i.e., children feeling freer to talk about violence), also provided some protection from the consequences of community violence.

Indeed, support from extended family can be a crucial factor for children exposed to violence, and, for some children, the involvement of extended family flows naturally from culturally defined patterns and roles already established around parenting (Harden & Nzinga-Johnson, 2006; White, Bruce, Farrell, & Kllewer, 1998). In their study of a primarily African American youth sample, White et al. (1998) investigated whether social support from immediate and extended family moderated the effect of community violence exposure on later-measured anxiety in youth. While there was no interaction of family support and exposure in the prediction of anxiety, family support was negatively associated with anxiety in girls. Interestingly, the research showed pronounced differences between girls and boys in their self-reports of anxiety following community violence exposure, with girls appearing more susceptible to anxiety problems than boys.

RESILIENCE FROM CHILD MALTREATMENT AND VIOLENCE EXPOSURE IN THE FAMILY

As with children exposed to community violence, research on maltreated children suggests that some child victims are resilient; that is, they meet some predetermined threshold of positive functioning at a particular age, despite the adversity they experienced (McGloin & Widom, 2001). McGloin and Widom's (2001) study showed that up to 74% of participants who were abused and neglected as children met at least one criterion of success/resilience when they were later assessed between the ages of 18 and 41 (average age 28.7 years). In fact, 22% of those in their study met an overall threshold of six of eight life successes, a remarkable finding given the strict criteria used in that study to define adult resilience. Others have found equal or even higher rates of resilient functioning among individuals with an abuse history (Bogar & Hulse-Killacky, 2006; Finkelhor, 1990; Werner & Smith, 2001).

Early research on factors predictive of resilience in maltreated children focused mainly on individual qualities and psychological strengths of the child (Masten, 2001). More recent research has extended the focus to social, interpersonal, and environmental resources that are thought to buffer the effects of early adversity (Bogar & Hulse-Killacky, 2006; Dubow et al., 1997; Masten, 2001; Wright & Masten, 2005). For example, there has been increasing attention to the ways in which family, peer, and school supports can strengthen positive functioning among abused children (Herrenkohl, Sousa, Tajima, Herrenkohl, & Moylan, 2008).

Various publications offer reviews of resilience and protective factor research. Werner's (2005) review is one particularly helpful source because the emphasis of that review is on protective factors that have been replicated in two or more longitudinal studies. From that and other comprehensive reports, the following are among the most well-established protective factors. For the child, factors include low distress, low emotionality, high sociability, having an affectionate/engaging temperament, having average or above average intelligence, and having a strong internal locus of control. Resilience in abused children is also associated with a child's capacity to form relationships with others, her or his ability to maintain a positive self-image/self-esteem having an optimistic outlook on the future, using effective coping strategies, and deciding to lead a life different from that of an abusive parent (Bolger & Patterson, 2001; Cicchetti, Toth, & Rogosch, 2000; Herrenkohl, Herrenkohl, & Egolf, 1994; Mrazek & Mrazek, 1987; Trickett et al., 2004). Still other protective factors include maternal competence; a child's having a close bond with a primary caregiver; experiencing sporadic (not chronic) abuse; having an otherwise stable living environment and/or stable caretaking from at least one adult; receiving clear expectations from one or more caregivers about the importance of succeeding in school; and having supportive grandparents, supportive siblings, and competent peer friends (Herrenkohl et al., 1994;

Trickett et al., 2004; Werner, 2005). Finally, research has shown that better outcomes are expected for maltreated children who attend and receive support from community groups and religious organizations, such as churches and synagogues (Leadbeater et al., 2004).

Unfortunately, most of the research on protective factors and resilience in the area of family violence has focused on child abuse apart from domestic violence, although we know the two often co-occur (Gewirtz & Edleson, 2007; Hughes, Graham-Bermann, & Gruber, 2001). However, in a prospective study, Tajima et al. (in press) found that the association between exposure to domestic violence (accounting also for co-occurring child abuse) and adverse youth outcomes differed in some cases according to parenting characteristics and adolescent peer support. For example, among youth whose mothers were highly accepting and responsive to the child (e.g., respect the child's feelings; accept the child for who she/he is), the relationship between exposure to domestic violence and risks of teenage pregnancy and running away from home was reduced significantly. Both peer communication and peer trust moderated the relationship between exposure to violence and adolescent depression and running from home. Peer communication also moderated the effects of domestic violence exposure on later high school dropout.

In another study using the same longitudinal dataset, Sousa and colleagues (in press) investigated the protective role of parent-child attachments for children exposed to both child abuse and domestic violence (dual exposure). While they found effects of dual exposure on various subscales of attachment, the researchers did not find that parent-child attachments moderated the effect of violence exposure (dual *or* single exposure) on outcomes of youth antisocial behavior. As with the White et al. (1998) study mentioned earlier, the non-significant moderation findings of this study could be due to a lack of sensitivity in the measures or to aspects of the exposure context that were not measured (e.g., duration of exposure and factors surrounding the event(s). Yet, in another study by McCloskey et al. (1995) on the role of sibling and parental warmth in relation to family violence exposure and child psychopathology, findings again showed no significant moderation pattern. That is, while there was less sibling and parent warmth in violent families, more warmth did not appear to lessen the risk of problems in the children exposed to violence.

When dynamics of the family are such that children cannot access the support they require of parents or siblings, mentors and social networks of support in the community may become increasingly important. In a study by Silk and colleagues (2004), neighborhood cohesion was examined as a potential buffer of hostile maternal parenting on child outcomes. The small sample of 42 children and their mothers was mostly (64%) African American. The researchers found that children's and mothers' reports of neighborhood involvement-cohesion interacted with maternal hostility (e.g., more severe punishment) in predicting child externalizing behaviors, after accounting for maternal education and family income. Specifically, higher scores on the neighborhood measure predicted less externalizing for those children with more hostile mothers. Thus, while community factors can have a negative impact on children's development when there are chronic stressors and few resources in the environment, research also suggests that neighborhoods can buffer the effects of family violence, particularly if there are opportunities provided children for meaningful engagement with other adults and prosocial peers, who can serve as mentors and sources of social support.

In sum, although studies on protection and resilience from violence exposure are few overall and limited by design weaknesses, available evidence shows that social and interpersonal influences can have profound and measurable impacts on developmental outcomes children who have been exposed to violence. Certain qualities and traits of the child also appear as key predictors and correlates of resilience, including individual intelligence, resourceful thinking, optimism, and an internal locus of control. Children most resilient to the effects of violence exposure are likely those who experience several protective factors in combination, which is consistent with the upward trend in individual competence shown in Figure 6.1 at the beginning of this chapter.

FUTURE RESEARCH: STUDYING THE DYNAMIC QUALITY OF RESILIENCE

As noted at the start of this chapter, *resilience* is a changeable pattern that shifts over time in relation to risks and protective factors in the surrounding environment. There is some research that shows individuals differ in their expression of resilience and that many show success in one or more life domains. Given the range of these successes, some scholars have suggested there is limited utility in general or global measures of resilience (Luthar, 1993; Luthar, Cicchetti, & Becker, 2000). In fact, Luthar and colleagues (1993) have argued against global measures in favor of domain-specific measures that emphasize "spheres" of adjustment: cognitive, social, and emotional. Conceivably, individuals can, at any point in development, function well in one domain or sphere but not another. Our own research from a 30-year prospective study has begun to show this pattern (Herrenkohl et al., 1994, 2008). Predictive modeling, and case studies of participants now in adulthood, illustrate how many children with histories of abuse and domestic violence exposure emerge from very negative early experiences to achieve a variety of life successes in later years. While often quite different in coping mechanisms and life achievements, participants of the study share a common determination to do things differently in their own families, particularly with respect to parenting and rearing of their own children. While not all individuals we have examined in the study would be considered "resilient" according to global definitions (McGloin & Widom, 2001), most show signs of having accomplished remarkable things in their lives despite their trauma histories.

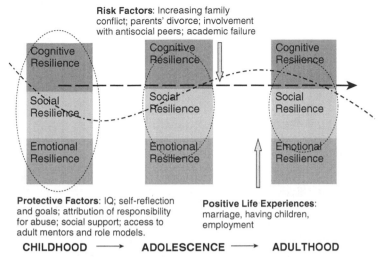

Figure 6.2. Studying resilience as a developmental process.

Figure 6.2 illustrates the patterns in our data mapped on to the three domains described by Luthar and colleagues. The figure shows three measurement points—childhood, adolescence, and adulthood—that reflect the longitudinal design of the study. We have found that, measured over time, what qualifies as resilient is likely to change and that the construct itself takes on different meanings at different life stages. Additionally, while some children show a stable, relatively consistent pattern of positive functioning over time (indicated by the straight line across the top of the Figure 6.2), more often the patterns resemble something closer to the curved line in the middle of the figure; for these individuals, resilience is a far more dynamic, variable process in which levels of functioning change developmentally as a function of individual traits and environmental buffers (Leadbeater, Schellenbach, Maton, & Dodgen, 2004). Life transitions that set an individual on a more positive course (e.g., finding a supportive spouse or having children) are also part of the resilience process that differentiates those who do well in adulthood from those who do less well. These findings are important from the standpoint of intervention planning and also emphasize the undisputed value of longitudinal studies, multimodal measurement, and mixed methods analysis procedures, which include qualitative life histories and case studies. Findings also suggest moving away from simplified, generalized models of resilience based on point-in-time estimates and cross-sectional data, however resilience is defined. Our goal is to use this research to encourage further investigations of the many ways resilience is reflected in the lives of vulnerable children as they navigate the demands of each developmental period into their adult years.

IMPLICATIONS OF RESILIENCE RESEARCH FOR PREVENTION AND INTERVENTION

Lessening violence exposure and outcomes in children by preventing violence in families and communities; improving public awareness of the causes, consequences, and financial costs of violence; and enhancing screening within schools and other settings to identify child abuse, domestic violence, and community violence victims should, of course, be a clearly stated priority for policy makers and program planners (Middlebrooks & Audage, 2008). Additionally, there are various model programs that have shown promise for reducing violence within communities and others for reducing risks associated with violence within schools and families (Herrenkohl, Chung, & Catalano, 2004; Middlebrooks & Audage, 2008) (see also Chapters 7 and 8). For children already impacted by violence, a range of clinical and support services are warranted, including those that address the immediate and enduring psychological trauma of abuse and other forms of exposure (Garbarino, Hammon, Mercy, & Yung, 2004; Haugaard & Feerick, 2002; McCloskey, Figueredo, & Koss, 1995). Additionally, programs that focus on promoting caring communities by mobilizing families and building social cohesion among neighborhood residents within disadvantaged areas hold promise for lessening violence by reducing stress on families and by promoting shared expectations for healthy (prosocial) norms and standards within neighborhoods. In their review of research on community development as a response to community-level adversity, Perkins and colleagues (2004) argue for a comprehensive, empowerment-based approach to prevention that addresses the root causes of violence by maximizing participation from within the community and by building social cohesion and trust among residents (p. 333). This approach is consistent with what Sampson and colleagues (Sampson, Morenoff, & Gannon-Rowley, 2002; Sampson, Raudenbush, & Earls, 1997) have shown to be important determinants of violence within disadvantaged communities (namely the lack of cohesion, trust, and collective action among residents). In this model, residents work on shared concerns for the betterment of the community, improve their and others' safety through surveillance and monitoring of activities in the neighborhood, and promote a general sense of neighborliness and optimism. Economic and physical development efforts are also viewed as viable strategies of community crime prevention and revitalization. However, any such effort would require collaboration among a range of constituents, including local government, program developers, and private funders. While the challenges of these types of collaborations could prove notable, the gains over the long term would likely be significant.

Prevention programs focused primarily on reducing the risk of child maltreatment also are needed and several already have been tested and shown to have positive effects. For example, the home-visiting program—Nurse-Family Partnership (NFP)—of Olds and colleagues (Olds et al.,

1997), is a well-known, widely referenced, and rigorously evaluated program that targets young, low-income, and first-time mothers in an attempt to improve their prenatal health and outcomes after pregnancy. The program has been tested on diverse samples and shown to be successful in lowering rates of child maltreatment and improving outcomes for children into their adolescent years (including lower rates of running away from home, less substance use, and fewer arrests among children at age 15) (CSPV, 2008). A report by the Washington State Institute for Public Policy (Aos, Miller, & Drake, 2006) found significant cost-savings associated with the NFP model, due to reductions in crime associated with mothers and their children. Yet, there is some debate about the overall effectiveness of the NFP-type approach in preventing self-reported or officially recorded child maltreatment per se, particularly in cases where domestic violence and other acute risk factors for children are present in families involved in the intervention (Chaffin, 2004).

Prevention and intervention programs that seek to promote child safety, improve parent-child attachments, provide parenting education, and restore functioning within families have been advocated by child abuse researchers and practitioners as means to reduce the primary risks of maltreatment in young families (Cicchetti & Toth, 1998; WCPCAN, 2005). These programs can be nested within larger family-based interventions that address parenting skills and other risks within the home, such as parent substance abuse and mental illness.

Finally, programs that target social and emotional skill-building in children—both selective and more universal approaches—have been tested and appear to hold promise for improving child outcomes in the general population and in high-risk samples, although few have been tailored or tested specifically with children exposed to overlapping forms of violence (CSPV, 2008; Hawkins et al., 1999; Herrenkohl et al., 2004). It is possible, however, that a more general approach to prevention and positive youth development within schools and other primary settings could benefit children exposed to violence, particularly if other individualized services (e.g., cognitive and behavioral therapies) are also received (Cicchetti & Toth, 1998; Haugaard & Feerick, 2002). Universal, school-based programs include work with teachers to improve classroom management and lessen misbehavior, increase opportunities for prosocial peer interactions, and teach conflict resolution and problem-solving skills. Family-based prevention and intervention programs, including those serving vulnerable children already involved with the juvenile justice system, also are documented in the literature (CSPV, 2008) and may hold promise for changing behaviors in youth that are linked in part to early risks and violence exposure within and outside the family.

The need in all cases for culturally responsive interventions tailored to ethnic families and communities should be considered (Harden & Nzinga-Johnson, 2006). Examples include carefully examining the role of extended family in programs serving the African-American children and their families and attending to socialization and child-rearing values specific to the various ethnic groups within parenting programs and support services (Harden & Nzinga-Johnson, 2006).

ACKNOWLEDGMENTS   The author would like to thank Cynthia Sousa, J. Bart Klika, and Lisa Stewart for their help in compiling research for this review and for commenting on earlier drafts of this manuscript.

REFERENCES

Aos, S., Miller, M., & Drake, E. (2006). *Evidence-based public policy options to reduce future prison construction, criminal justice costs, and crime rates.* Olympia, WA: Washington State Institute for Public Policy.

Bogar, C. B., & Hulse-Killacky, D. (2006). Resiliency determinants and resiliency processes among female adult survivors of childhood sexual abuse. *Journal of Counseling and Development, 84,* 318–327.

Bolger, K. E., & Patterson, C. J. (2001). Pathways from child maltreatment to internalizing problems: Perceptions of control as mediators and moderators. *Development and Psychopathology, 13*(4), 913–940.

Burton, L., & Jarrett, R. (2000). In the mix, yet on the margins: The place of families in urban neighborhoods and child development research. *Journal of Marriage and Family, 62,* 1114–1135.

Catalano, R. F., & Hawkins, J. D. (1996). The social development model: A theory of antisocial behavior. In J. D. Hawkins (Ed.), *Delinquency and crime: Current theories* (pp. 149–197). New York: Cambridge University Press.

Ceballo, R., McLoyd, V. C., & Toyokawa, T. (2004). The influence of neighborhood quality on adolescents' educational values and school effort. *Journal of Adolescent Research, 19,* 698–715.

Chaffin, M. (2004). Is it time to rethink Healthy Start/Healthy Families? *Child Abuse and Neglect, 28,* 590–595.

Chung, H. L., & Steinberg, L. (2006). Relations between neighborhood factors, parenting behaviors, peer deviance, and delinquency among serious juvenile offenders. *Developmental Psychology, 42*(2), 319–331.

Cicchetti, D., & Rogosch, F. A. (1997). The role of self-organization in the promotion of resilience in maltreated children. *Development and Psychopathology, 9,* 797–815.

Cicchetti, D., & Toth, S. L. (1998). Perspectives on research and practice in developmental psychopathology. In W. Damon (Ed.), *Handbook of child psychology* (Vol. 4, pp. 479–583). New York: John Wiley & Sons.

Cicchetti, D., Toth, S. L., & Rogosch, F. A. (2000). The development of psychological wellness in maltreated children. In D. Cicchetti, J. Rappaport, I. Sandler, & R. P. Weissberg (Eds.), *The promotion of wellness in children and adolescents* (pp. 395–426). Washington, DC: Child Welfare League of America, Inc.

Cowen, E. L., Wyman, P. A., Work, W. C., Kim, J. Y., Fagen, D. B., & Magnus, K. B. (1997). Follow-up study of young stress-affected and stress-resilient urban children. *Development and Psychopathology, 9,* 565–577.

CSPV. (2008). *Blueprints for violence prevention* (Vol. 2008). Boulder: Center for the Study of Violence Prevention, Institute of Behavior Science, University of Colorado. Prevention of Violence.

DiRago, A. C., & Vaillant, G. E. (2007). Resilience in inner city youth: Childhood predictors of occupational status across the lifespan. *Journal of Youth and Adolescence, 36,* 61–70.

Dubow, E. F., Edwards, S., & Ippolito, M. F. (1997). Life stressors, neighborhood disadvantage, and resources: A focus on inner-city children's adjustment. *Journal of Clinical Child Psychology, 26*(2), 130–144.

Finkelhor, D. (1990). Early and long-term effects of child sexual abuse: An update. *Professional Psychology: Research and Practice, 21,* 325–330.

Furstenberg, F. F. (1993). How families manage risk and opportunity in dangerous neighborhoods. In W. J. Wilson (Ed.), *Sociology and the public agenda* (pp. 231–258). Newbury Park, CA: Sage.

Garbarino, J., Hammon, W. R., Mercy, J., & Yung, B. R. (2004). Community violence and children: Preventing exposure and reducing harm. In K. I. Maton, C. J. Schellenbach, B. J. Leadbeater & A. L. Solarz (Eds.), *Investing in children, youth, families, and communities: Strengths-based research and policy* (pp. 303–320). Washington, DC: American Psychological Association.

Gewirtz, A. H., & Edleson, J. L. (2007). Young children's exposure to intimate partner violence: Towards a developmental risk and resilience framework for research and intervention. *Journal of Family Violence, 22*(151–163).

Gorman-Smith, D., Henry, D. B., & Tolan, P. H. (2004). Exposure to community violence and violence perpetration: The protective effects of family functioning. *Journal of Clinical Child and Adolescent Psychology, 33,* 439–449.

Harden, B. J., & Nzinga-Johnson, S. (2006). Young, wounded, and black: The maltreatment of African-American children in the early years. In R. L. Hampton & T. P. Gullotta (Eds.), *Interpersonal violence in the African-American community* (pp. 17–46). New York: Springer.

Haugaard, J. J., & Feerick, M. (2002). Interventions for maltreated children to reduce their likelihood of engaging in juvenile delinquency. *Children's Services: Social Policy, Research, and Practice, 5*(4), 285–297.

Hawkins, J. D., Catalano, R. F., Kosterman, R., Abbott, R., & Hill, K. G. (1999). Preventing adolescent health-risk behaviors by strengthening protection during childhood. *Archives of Pediatrics and Adolescent Medicine, 153*(3), 226–234.

Heller, S. S., Heller, J. A., Larrieu, R., D'Imperio, & Boris, N. W. (1999). Research on resilience to child maltreatment: Empirical considerations. *Child Abuse and Neglect, 23,* 321–338.

Herrenkohl, E. C., Herrenkohl, R. C., & Egolf, B. (1994). Resilient early school-age children from maltreating homes: Outcomes in late adolescence. *American Journal of Orthopsychiatry, 64*(2), 301–309.

Herrenkohl, T. I., Chung, I.-J., & Catalano, R. F. (2004). Review of research on predictors of youth violence and school-based and community-based prevention approaches. In P. Allen-Meares & M. W. Fraser (Eds.), *Intervention with children and adolescents: An interdisciplinary perspective* (pp. 449–476). Boston: Allyn & Bacon.

Herrenkohl, T. I., Sousa, C., Tajima, E. A., Herrenkohl, R. C., & Moylan, C. A. (2008). Intersection of child abuse and children's exposure to domestic violence. *Trauma, Violence, & Abuse, 9*(2), 84–99.

Hill, N. E., & Herman-Stahl, M. A. (2002). Neighborhood safety and social involvement: Associations with parenting behaviors and depressive symptoms among African American and Euro-American mothers. *Journal of Family Psychology, 16*(2), 209–219.

Hughes, H. M., Graham-Bermann, S. A., & Gruber, G. (2001). Resilience in children exposed to domestic violence. In S. A. Graham-Bermann & J. L. Edleson (Eds.), *Domestic violence in the lives of children: The future of research, intervention, and social policy* (pp. 67–90). Washington, DC: American Psychological Association.

Jencks, C., & Mayer, S. E. (1990). The social consequences of growing up in a poor neighborhood. In L. E. L. G. H. McGeary (Ed.), *Inner-city in the United States* (pp. 86–111). Washington, DC: National Academy Press.

Kaplan, H. B. (2005). Understanding the concept of resilience. In S. Goldstein & R. B. Brooks (Eds.), *Handbook of resilience in children* (pp. 39–48). New York: Springer.

Katz, L. F., & Gottman, J. M. (1997). Buffering children from marital conflict and dissolution. *Journal of Clinical Child Psychology, 26,* 157–171.

Kaufman, J., & Zigler, E. F. (1989). The intergenerational transmission of child abuse. In D. Cicchetti & V. Carlson (Eds.), *Child maltreatment: Theory and research on the causes and consequences of child abuse and neglect* (pp. 129–150). New York: Cambridge University Press.

Kohen, D. E., Dahinten, V. S., Lenventhal, T., & McIntosh, C., N. (2008). Neighborhood disadvantage: Pathways for effects for young children. *Child Development, 79*(1), 156–169.

Leadbeater, B. J., Schellenbach, C. J., Maton, K. I., & Dodgen, D. W. (2004). Research and policy for building strengths: Processes and contexts of individual, family, and community development. In K. I. Maton, C. J. Schellenbach, B. J. Leadbeater & A. L. Solarz (Eds.), *Investing in children, youth, families, and communities: Strengths-based research and policy* (pp. 13–30). Washington, DC: American Psychological Association.

Luthar, S. (1993). Annotation: Methodological and conceptual issues in research on childhood resilience. *Journal of Child Psychology and Psychiatry, 34*(4), 441–453.

Luthar, S. (2006). Resilience in development: A synthesis of research across five decades. In D. Cicchetti & D. J. Cohen (Eds.), *Development and psychopathology: Risk, disorder, and adaptation* (pp. 740–795). New York: John Wiley.

Luthar, S., Cicchetti, D., & Becker, B. (2000). The construct of resilience: A critical evaluation and guidelines for future work. *Child Development, 71*(3), 543–562.

Masten, A. S. (2001). Ordinary magic: Resilience processes in development. *American Psychologist, 56*(3), 227–238.

Masten, A. S., Best, K. M., & Garmezy, N. (1990). Resilience and development: Contributions from the study of children who overcome adversity. *Development and Psychopathology, 2*(4), 425–444.

Masten, A. S., Hubbard, J. J., Gest, S. D., Tellegen, A., Garmezy, N., & Ramirez, M. (1999). Competence in the context of adversity: Pathways to resilience and maladaptation from childhood to late adolescence. *Development and Psychopathology, 11,* 143–169.

McCloskey, L. A., Figueredo, A. J., & Koss, M. P. (1995). The effects of systemic family violence on children's mental health. *Child Development, 66*(5), 1239–1261.

McGloin, J. M., & Widom, C. S. (2001). Resilience among abused and neglected children grown up. *Development and Psychopathology, 13*(4), 1021–1038.

Middlebrooks, J. S., & Audage, N. C. (2008). *The effects of childhood stress on health across the lifespan*. Atlanta, GA: Centers for Disease Control and Prevention, National Center for Injury Prevention and Control.

Mrazek, P. J., & Mrazek, D. A. (1987). Resilience in child maltreatment victims: A conceptual exploration. *Child Abuse & Neglect, 11*, 357–366.

O'Donnell, D. A., Schwab-Stone, M. E., & Muyeed, A. Z. (2004). Multidimensional resilience in urban children exposed to community violence. *Child Development, 73*(4), 1265–1282.

Olds, D. L., Eckenrode, J., Henderson, C. R., Kitzman, H., Powers, J., Cole, R., et al. (1997). Long-term effects of home visitation on maternal life course and child abuse and neglect. *JAMA, 278*(8), 637–643.

Ozer, E. J., & Weinstein, R. S. (2004). Urban adolescents' exposure to community violence: The role of support, school safety, and social constraints in a school-based sample of boys. *Journal of Child and Adolescent Psychology, 33*, 463–486.

Perkins, D. D., Crim, B., Silberman, P., & Brown, B. B. (2004). Community development as a response to community-level adversity: Ecological theory and research and strengths-based policy. In K. I. Maton, C. J. Schellenbach, B. J. Leadbeater & A. L. Solarz (Eds.), *Investing in children, youth, families, and communities: Strengths-based research and policy* (pp. 321–340). Washington, DC: American Psychological Association.

Pollard, J. A., Hawkins, J. D., & Arthur, M. W. (1999). Risk and protection: Are both necessary to understand diverse behavioral outcomes in adolescence? *Social Work Research, 23*(3), 145–158.

Rutter, M. (2001). Psychosocial adversity: Risk, resilience and recovery. In J. M. Richman & M. W. Fraser (Eds.), *The context of youth violence: Resilience, risk and protection* (pp. 13–42). Westport, CT: Praeger Publishers.

Sampson, R. J., Morenoff, J. D., & Gannon-Rowley, T. (2002). Assessing neighborhood effects: Social processes and new directions in research. *Annual Review of Sociology, 28*, 443–478.

Sampson, R. J., Raudenbush, S. W., & Earls, F. J. (1997). Neighborhoods and violent crime: A multilevel study of collective efficacy. *Science, 277*, 918–924.

Silk, J. S., Morris, A. S., Sessa, F. M., Steinberg, L., & Avenevoli, S. (2004). Neighborhood cohesion as a buffer against hostile maternal parenting. *Journal of Family Psychology, 18*(1), 135–146.

Sousa, C., Herrenkohl, T. I., Moylan, C. A., Tajima, E. A., Russo, M. J., & Herrenkohl, R. C. (in press). Longitudinal study on the effects of child abuse and children's exposure to domestic violence on parent-child relationships. *Journal of Interpersonal Violence*.

Tajima, E. A., Herrenkohl, T. I., & Moylan, C. A. (In press). Moderating the effects of childhood exposure to domestic violence: Examining the roles of parenting characteristics and adolescent peer support. *Journal of Adolescent Research*.

Tolan, P. H., Sherrod, L. R., Gorman-Smith, D., & Henry, D. (2004). Building protection, support, and opportunity for inner-city children and youth and their families. In K. I. Maton, C. J. Schellenbach, B. J. Leadbeater & A. L. Solarz (Eds.), *Investing in children, youth, families, and communities: Strengths-based research and policy* (pp. 193–212). Washington, DC: American Psychological Association.

Trickett, P. K., Kurtz, D. A., & Pizzigati, K. (2004). Resilient outcomes in abused and neglected children: Bases for strengths-based intervention and prevention policies. In K. I. Maton, C. J. Schellenbach, B. J. Leadbeater & A. L. Solarz (Eds.), *Investing in children, youth, families, and communities: Strengths-based research and policy* (pp. 73–95). Washington, DC: American Psychological Association.

WCPCAN. (2005). *Got prevention?* Seattle, WA: Washington Council for Prevention of Child Abuse and Neglect.

Werner, E. E. (2005). What can we learn about resilience from large-scale longitudinal studies. In S. Goldstein & R. B. Brooks (Eds.), *Handbook of resilience in children* (pp. 91–106). New York: Springer.

Werner, E. E., & Smith, R. S. (1992). *Overcoming the odds: High risk children from birth to adulthood.* Ithaca, NY: Cornell University Press.

Werner, E. E., & Smith, R. S. (2001). *Journeys from childhood to midlife. Risk, resilience, and recovery.* Ithaca, NY: Cornell University Press.

White, K. S., Bruce, S. E., Farrell, A. D., & Kllewer, W. (1998). Impact of exposure to community violence on anxiety: A longitudinal study of family social support as a protective factor for urban children. *Journal of Child and Family Studies, 7*(2), 187–203.

Wilson, W. J. (1987). *The truly disadvantaged.* Chicago: The University of Chicago Press.

Wolin, S. J., & Wolin, S. (1993). *The resilient self. How survivors of troubled families rise above adversity.* New York: Villard Books.

Wright, M. O., & Masten, A. S. (2005). Resilience processes in development. In S. Goldstein & R. B. Brooks (Eds.), *Handbook of Resilience in Children* (pp. 17–38). New York: Springer.

IV

PREVENTING YOUTH VIOLENCE IN FAMILY, SCHOOL, AND COMMUNITY CONTEXTS

Implications for Integrated Programs
and Policy Development

7

ADVANCES AND CHALLENGES IN THE PREVENTION OF YOUTH VIOLENCE

JEFFREY M. JENSON

In earlier sections of this book we explored the complexities associated with defining and understanding violent behavior. We also identified and examined correlates of violence and reviewed important personal and demographic differences related to the onset and persistence of violent conduct. Previous chapters by Herrenkohl, Aisenberg, Williams, and colleagues reveal a complex picture of how one's risk exposure, personal characteristics, and social and environmental context are related to violent behavior and victimization.

Each chapter in the first three sections raises important questions about the responsibility of social institutions to help prevent acts of interpersonal violence, child maltreatment, intimate partner violence, and community violence. In the current section, we examine ways in which schools, families, and communities have attempted to prevent aggression and violence. The history of violence prevention and recent advances in the efficacy of programs seeking to prevent aggression and violence are discussed in Chapter 7. In Chapter 8, we identify effective violence prevention programs across educational, family, and community settings. This review is intended to help readers understand, select, and implement efficacious programs in the context of school, family, and community settings.

The commission of violent acts by the nation's youth is a particularly troubling phenomenon. While most children and adolescents grow up to

111

be healthy adults, a significant portion of young people are exposed to violence during their formative developmental years. Unfortunately, some children and adolescents go on to commit aggressive and violent acts as they form interpersonal relationships and enter adulthood. As noted in previous chapters, early onset of aggressive behavior among children and adolescents is among the most significant risks for committing serious and/or persistent violent behavior as an adult. Therefore, to reduce rates of violence we must begin with efforts aimed at preventing early forms of aggression in children and adolescents. Importantly, results from controlled trials of violence prevention programs have recently shed light on ways to effectively prevent or reduce violence among young people. These approaches, and the complex issues associated with implementing and adapting prevention programs, are reviewed in the following two chapters. Policy implications associated with advances in violence prevention are noted.

> The research base for prevention policy and practice has grown
> over the last three decades to the point that exponential growth
> in professionalism and effective practice are now a wise and
> cost-effective public and private investment.
>
> Catalano, 2007, p. 377

Violence prevention programs in the United States have paralleled the country's general approach to preventing adolescent problem behaviors such as delinquency, substance abuse, and school dropout. Historically, programs aimed at preventing youth violence have been developed locally and have seldom been subjected to rigorous evaluation criteria. In recent years, however, schools and communities have placed greater emphasis on implementing tested and effective violence prevention approaches. The growing interest in selecting effective programs has been influenced by well-known incidents of school violence and by a growing recognition of the importance attached to implementing evidence-based practice strategies in schools and communities. In this chapter, we trace the history of childhood and adolescent violence prevention. The introduction and evolution of a public health approach to preventing aggression and violent conduct are reviewed. Current approaches to preventing violence in the context of schools, families, and communities are described. Consistent with definitions of violence put forward by Aisenberg and colleagues in Chapter 2, our discussion focuses on the evolution of preventing *interpersonal* forms of violence among children and youth.

THE HISTORY AND EVOLUTION OF VIOLENCE PREVENTION

Early Prevention Approaches

Violence prevention programs in the United States can be traced to the 1960s. The earliest efforts to prevent aggression and violence were coupled with broader interventions that used information dissemination and fear-arousal approaches to combat substance use, delinquency, and school dropout (Jenson, 2006). These strategies stressed the adverse consequences and dramatized the dangers of antisocial conduct in an attempt to discourage young people from participating in problem behaviors. Experts agree that conveying information about the consequences and risks associated with problem behaviors such as violence is an important component of prevention programs. However, the effects of knowledge-based or fear-arousal techniques were largely unsuccessful in changing attitudes, intentions, or individual aggressive behaviors in children and youth (Bangert-Drowns, 1988; Moskowitz, 1989; Tobler, 1986).

Affective education strategies and alternative programs and structured activities for children and youth were emphasized in schools and communities during the 1970s. Affective education was designed to increase responsible decision-making skills and enhance self-esteem. In this model, students were exposed to problem-solving and experiential activities based on the assumption that effective decision-making skills would deter involvement in aggressive and violent behavior. Unfortunately, early affective education programs did not prevent or reduce antisocial behavior itself (Botvin & Griffin, 2003).

Alternative programming was based on a belief that involvement in extracurricular activities in schools and positive activities in communities could serve as a deterrent to antisocial behavior. This assumption implied that students who participated in after-school programs such as sports, arts, academic tutoring, or community activities would be less likely to participate in aggressive and violent behavior. Programs were intended to improve participants' relationships with positive peers and adults through experiential learning and cooperation. Studies, however, revealed that this approach had only a limited effect on preventing violence and other problem behaviors (e.g., Schaps, Bartolo, Moskowitz, Palley, & Churgin, 1981).

Early violence prevention approaches suffered from a relatively weak theoretical foundation and from very limited intensity and implementation. Prevention activities in schools were often relegated to inconsequential aspects of the curricula and often taught by untrained professionals. Few prevention activities were conducted in the context of families and communities between 1960 and 1980. It is not surprising, therefore, that early efforts produced little in the way of positive outcomes.

Public Health and Violence Prevention

The 1980s marked a significant shift in the nature of violence prevention programs. In contrast to initial approaches, prevention strategies began to incorporate tenets of social learning theory to teach social, behavioral, and cognitive skills to children and youth. Manualized prevention curricula using structured skills-training techniques and lesson plans became an essential part of this new strategy. Also important, practitioners and researchers began to recognize the value of developing programs that targeted known risk and protective factors for childhood and adolescent problem behaviors (Hawkins, Jenson, Catalano, & Lishner, 1988; Hawkins, Catalano, & Miller, 1992).

Risk Factors

The principles underlying the importance of understanding risk factors for youth violence were introduced to readers in earlier sections of this book. For example, in Chapters 3 and 4, Williams, Bright, and colleagues discussed causes and correlates of violent behavior by examining a variety of types, settings, and ages. They also focused their discussion of risk in the context of race, ethnicity, and gender. Similarly, Herrenkohl and associates reviewed the complex interplay between exposure to family violence and subsequent involvement in violent conduct in Chapters 5 and 6.

Knowledge of the causes and correlates of aggression and violence is critical to designing prevention and treatment approaches that are likely to be effective in preventing or reducing violent behavior. Understanding the characteristics and conditions that elevate the likelihood of aggression is particularly important in the context of preventing childhood and adolescent violence. As noted in earlier chapters, these characteristics and conditions are now commonly referred to as risk factors by public health and prevention experts.

Risk factors are individual, family, school, peer, community, and situational level influences that increase the likelihood of becoming involved in aggressive or violent behaviors. The identification of risk factors for a variety of childhood and adolescent problems has gained widespread acceptance in the prevention field in the past decade (Biglan, Brennan, Foster, & Holden, 2004; Gottfredson & Wilson, 2003). Its origins, however, date to the late 1970s and early 1980s when researchers and policy makers began placing greater importance on understanding the individual, family, social, and community factors that commonly occurred in the lives of troubled children and youth (Rutter, 1979, 1987). The emphasis on understanding the underlying causes of childhood and youth problems led investigators to identify specific factors that were consistently associated with the occurrence of aggression, violence, and other adolescent problem behaviors. This approach, adapted from public health efforts to identify risk factors associated with problems such as smoking and heart disease, led to the use of risk-based strategies to preventing a host of childhood and adolescent problems (Hawkins et al., 1992).

The earliest risk factor models were primarily lists of the known correlates of adolescent problems (e.g., Garmezy, 1971; Hawkins et al., 1988). Early models often failed to consider the temporal relationship of risk factors to the occurrence of specific behaviors or to examine the additive and interactive effects of risk factors. Recent reviews of risk factors for adolescent problem behaviors (e.g., Fraser, Kirby, & Smokowski, 2004; Hawkins, Herrenkohl, Farrington, Brewer, Catalano, & Harachi, 1998; Herrenkohl, Hawkins, Chung, Hill, & Battin-Pearson, 2001; Herrenkohl, Chung, & Catalano, 2004; Jenson & Howard, 1999, 2001; Thornberry, 1998) have improved on earlier efforts by limiting their selection of studies to those in which the risk factor clearly preceded a problem behavior. Longitudinal studies have also been conducted to better understand the processes by which risk factors influence behavior over the course of childhood and adolescence (e.g., Hawkins, Catalano, Kosterman, Abbott, & Hill, 1999; Loeber, Farrington, Stouthamer-Loeber, & Van Kammen, 1998). Common risk factors for aggressive and violent behavior by level of influence are shown in Table 7.1.

Table 7.1. Risk Factors for Youth Violence by Level of Influence

Individual Factors

Biological Factors

  Heredity
  Being male
  High testosterone levels
  Low CNS serotonin levels

Psychological Characteristics

  Impulsivity, hyperactivity, restlessness
  Risk-taking or sensation-seeking orientation
  Early onset of aggression
  Mental health problems

Family Factors

  Parental criminality
  Child neglect and abuse
  Marital and family conflict
  Low levels of parent-child interaction and family bonding
  Excessively punitive or permissive family management practices
  Frequent residential changes
  Leaving home prior to age 16

School Factors

  High rates of truancy
  Suspension from school
  Dropout
  Low academic expectations
  Low bonding to school
  Poor school performance

Peer Factors

  Delinquent or violent peers
  Delinquent or violent siblings
  Gang membership

(Conitnued)

Table 7.1.   (continued)

Community Factors

Neighborhood poverty and population density
High residential mobility among neighborhood residents
Community disorganization
Media influences

Situational Factors

Victim-victimizer relationship
Substance abuse
Presence/availability of a weapon

Note: Adapted from Herrenkohl, Chung, and Catalano, 2004; Jenson and Howard, 1999; and U.S. Department of Health and Human Services, 2001. (Jenson & Fraser, 2006)

Protective Factors

Experts favoring less of a deficit-based model to understanding childhood and adolescent problems have advocated for a framework that is based on characteristics that protect youth from engaging in violence. Most investigators agree that protective factors are attributes or characteristics that lower the probability of an undesirable outcome (Rutter, 2001; Werner & Smith, 1992). The knowledge base associated with the concept of protection emerged in the early 1980s when investigators such as Rutter (1979) and Werner and Smith (1982) expressed the idea that certain positive attributes or characteristics appeared to operate in the presence of risk or adversity. The exact definition of a protective factor, however, quickly became a topic of debate. Most of this debate has centered on the confusion created when both risk and protective factors are conceptualized as representing the opposite ends of a single continuum (Pollard, Hawkins, & Arthur, 1999).

Currently, most interpretations of protection imply that protective traits are individual characteristics or environmental conditions that interact with specific risk factors present in a child or in her or his environment (Fraser et al., 2004). Consistent with this interpretation is the belief that protective factors serve to reduce or *buffer* the impact of risk in a child's life. Common protective factors by individual, family, school, peer, and community level of influence are shown in Table 7.2.

A Public Health Approach to Violence Prevention

Empirical evidence of the risk and protective factors associated with youth violence created an entirely new approach to violence prevention in the late 1980s and early 1990s. Importantly, practitioners and researchers recognized the practical utility of applying knowledge gained from identifying the risk and protective factors associated with problems such as

Table 7.2.   Protective Factors for Youth Violence by Level of Influence

---

Individual Factors

   Positive attitude
   Temperament
   High intelligence
   Being female
   Low childhood stress
   Social and problem-solving skills
   Belief in prosocial norms and values

Family Factors

   Attachment to parents
   Low parental conflict
   Parental monitoring

School Factors

   High levels of commitment to school
   Involvement in school activities

Peer Factors

   Friends who engage in conventional activities
   Caring relationships with siblings

Community Factors

   Opportunities for education, employment, and other pro-social activities
   Caring relationships with adults or extended family members
   Social support from nonfamily members

Note: Adapted from Jenson and Fraser, 2006; and U.S. Department of Health and Human Services, 2001.

substance use, delinquency, and violence to intervention and program design. Subsequently, the promise of a risk and protection approach to preventing a host of childhood and youth problems, including violence, was recognized by national organizations such as the Centers for Disease Control and Prevention (CDC), National Institutes of Health, and the National Institute of Justice (Hawkins, 2006; Hawkins, Catalano, & Arthur, 2002). By 1995, a public health approach to violence prevention based on understanding the risk and protective factors associated with aggression became the dominant guiding prevention framework in the country (Jenson, 2006).

A public health approach to ameliorating problems like youth violence is one that considers the presence or absence of risk and protective factors for aggression when designing and selecting interventions. As shown in Figure 7.1, this four-step framework is used to (1) define violence as an individual and social problem; (2) identify risk and protective factors associated with violent behavior; (3) develop and test violence prevention strategies; and (4) ensure widespread adoption of efficacious programs (CDC, 2008). Interventions based on a public health approach

Figure 7.1. A public health approach to violence prevention.
Adapted from Centers for Disease Control and Prevention (2008).

to violence prevention are implemented at three levels (Biglan et al., 2004; Hawkins, 2006). *Universal* prevention programs are aimed at general child and youth populations without regard to the level of risk shown among children and youth in such groups. An anti-bullying program delivered to all elementary students in a local school district is an example of a universal program. A second level of intervention is commonly known as *selected* or tertiary prevention. Selected programs target youth who evidence elevated levels of risk for aggression or violence. Selected program strategies may include parent training, skills training, or mentoring approaches. Finally, *indicated* intervention strategies target children and adolescents who have displayed aggressive or violent behavior. Youth employment, skills training, and juvenile justice responses may be considered examples of indicated intervention approaches.

Summary

Significant strides in violence prevention occurred following the ineffective nature of programs in the 1960s and 1970s. In recent years, a public health framework based on knowledge of the risk and protective factors associated with aggressive behavior has become the guiding theoretical model for violence prevention programs (CDC, 2008; Hawkins, 2006; Jenson, 2006). The adoption of a public health approach to violence prevention has also contributed to the creation of a relatively new field of practice and research known as *prevention science.*

PREVENTION SCIENCE AND VIOLENCE
PREVENTION APPROACHES

The tenants of risk and protection found in the public health approach to prevention offer a systematic way of thinking about strategies and approaches to preventing childhood and adolescent aggression. Acceptance of this approach has led to the formal establishment of prevention science and to a formal and informal network of practitioners, policy makers, and researchers who define elements of risk and protection as cornerstones of prevention practice and policy (Coie et al., 1992; Cicchetti, Rappaport, Sandler, & Weissberg, 2000; Kaftarian, Robinson, Compton, Davis, & Volkow, 2004). The common elements of prevention science imply that (1) factors associated with a problem behavior must be changed in order to prevent that behavior; (2) malleable risk and protective factors identi-fied in empirical studies should be the targets of prevention efforts; (3) prevention programs should be rigorously tested; and (4) efficacious programs should be disseminated and implemented with fidelity in school and community settings.

The core elements of prevention science acknowledge the importance of context by targeting aggressive and violent conduct in school, family, and community settings (O'Connell, Boat, & Warner, 2009). In previous chapters we discussed the importance of individual, social, and environ-mental context in understanding the onset and persistence of aggression and violence. Importantly, a number of ineffective and effective violence prevention approaches have been identified in each of these contexts in recent years. Universal, selected, and indicated prevention strategies—ineffective and effective—are reviewed below and shown in Table 7.3. Specific program examples that illustrate many of these approaches are examined in Chapter 8.

Ineffective Violence Prevention Approaches

Prior to understanding effective violence prevention programs, it may be helpful to acknowledge program approaches that have had little or no pos-itive effect on preventing aggression in children and youth. Several univer-sal prevention strategies—programs targeting all children in a given setting or location regardless of risk status—have failed to prevent violent behav-ior. Among these approaches is peer counseling, peer mediation, and peer leadership strategies (U.S. Department of Health and Human Services, 2001). As noted in an earlier section of this chapter, programs that provide information about the consequences of violence or interventions that seek to arouse fear about the potential of violence have also been ineffective in preventing aggressive and violent conduct (Moskowitz, 1989).

A number of ineffective selected prevention strategies aimed at youth or communities identified to be at high-risk for violence have also been identified. For example, gun buyback programs, firearm training, mandatory gun ownership strategies, and firearm training programs have

Table 7.3.   Ineffective and Effective Violence Prevention Approaches by Level of Intervention

---

Ineffective Prevention Strategies

Universal (General Populations)
   Peer counseling and mediation
   Peer leaders

Selected (High-Risk Populations)
   Gun buyback programs
   Firearm training
   Redirecting antisocial behavior
   Altering peer group norms

Indicated (Aggressive or Violent Populations)
   Boot camps
   Social casework
   Individual counseling
   Waivers to adult court

Effective Prevention Strategies

Universal (General Populations)
   Early childhood education
   Anti-bullying programs in schools
   Classroom management and school organization
   Social, behavioral, and cognitive skills training
   Changing community norms about violence

Selected (High-Risk Populations)
   Prenatal and infancy home visitation
   Family support
   Social, behavioral, and cognitive skills training
   Parent training
   Increasing parent-child bonding
   Reducing family conflict
   Mentoring

Indicated (Aggressive or Violent Populations)
   Social, behavioral, and cognitive skills training
   Wraparound services
   Youth employment

Adapted from Biglan et al., 2004; Limbos et al., 2007; U.S. Department of Health and Human Services, 2001; and Wilson and Lipsey, 2007.

failed to produce any significant effects in preventing or reducing violence (U.S. Department of Health and Human Services, 2001). In addition, school- and community-based efforts that strive to redirect youth behavior or change negative peer group norms have shown little or no positive impact on violent behavior (Limbos et al., 2007; Patterson & Yoerger, 1997).

Ineffective violence prevention and intervention approaches have also been identified at the indicated level. Indicated strategies target young people who have already displayed violent behavior and include juvenile boot camps, social casework, individual counseling, and using waivers to adult court for more serious young offenders (U.S. Department of Health and Human Services, 2001).

Effective Prevention Strategies

Effective universal, selected, and indicated violence prevention approaches have been identified in family, school, and community settings in the past several decades. Universal and selected family-based violence prevention approaches now begin in the earliest years of life and include prenatal and infancy programs, early childhood education, and parent training strategies. Prenatal and infancy programs target high-risk parents and children and offer a variety of tangible supports and education to support families during the critical years of infancy. Early childhood education programs aim to teach young children and their parents the requisite skills to begin school with good social, cognitive, and emotional skills. Similarly, parent training approaches target parents of high-risk youth as part of an effort to equip parents with consistent family management skills. Systematic and meta-analytic reviews of longitudinal investigations that have tested these approaches have revealed positive program effects in increasing skills and preventing the onset of aggression and violence in young children (e.g., Hahn et al., 2007; Limbos et al., 2007; Wilson & Lipsey, 2007).

Effective universal and selected school-based violence prevention approaches come in many forms. One common approach is to help teachers better organize and manage their classrooms. This strategy encourages teachers to use principles such as cooperative learning, small-group instruction, and peer learning to improve classroom climate and create conditions that are conducive to learning and positive behaviors. Social and emotional learning curricula represent a second common violence prevention approach. Social and emotional learning programs aim to teach social, cognitive, and emotional skills to students. Increases in these skills are hypothesized to produce reductions in problem behaviors such as aggression and bullying. Social and emotional learning programs typically take the form of skills training and rely heavily on the cognitive-behavioral strategies of modeling, rehearsal, and feedback. Meta-analytic reviews of longitudinal tests of classroom management and social and emotional learning approaches have shown positive effects in student learning and fewer classroom behavior problems (e.g., Wilson, Lipsey, & Derzon, 2003; Wilson & Lipsey, 2007).

Community-based prevention programs include a diverse set of strategies aimed at the individual, neighborhood, and community levels. Effective strategies include mentoring, youth employment, and community mobilization. Mentoring typically involves a one-to-one relationship between an individual youth and an adult. Mentoring programs aim to increase healthy social bonds between youth at risk of violence and seek to promote positive social norms regarding antisocial conduct. Youth employ-ment approaches have had a somewhat uneven history of effectiveness in the United States. While some prior efforts have produced little evidence with regard to effectiveness, more recent strategies have indicated that employment coupled with education can be an efficacious approach to preventing aggression and other problems. Reviews of studies assessing the effects of mentoring, youth employment, and other community strate-gies indicate that each of these approaches can prevent or reduce aggres-sion, violence, and other childhood and adolescent problem behaviors (e.g., Limbos et al., 2007).

Summary

The prevention approaches reviewed here and summarized in Table 7.3 offer practitioners, administrators, and policy makers a broad template for implementing effective violence prevention strategies in family, school, and community contexts. Significant advances in identifying ineffective and effective violence prevention approaches have been made in the past several decades. Important challenges remain, however, in increasing the overall impact of prevention efforts for children and youth at risk of vio-lent behavior.

INCREASING THE IMPACT OF VIOLENCE PREVENTION

Selecting and disseminating effective violence prevention programs, assess-ing the benefits and costs of alternative prevention approaches, and pro-moting public health violence prevention strategies in social policy directives are currently three of the field's most pressing issues.

Selection and Dissemination of Effective Programs

We earlier noted that recent increases in the number of violent incidents committed by young people have accelerated interest in violence preven-tion programs. Unfortunately, many of the nation's educational systems, human service agencies, and community organizations fail to consider, select, or implement tested or effective prevention programs (Elliott & Michalic, 2004). Subsequently, several key national policy groups and research entities have developed strategies to disseminate information about efficacious school, family, and community interventions to practi-tioners and other interested parties.

The CDC has suggested that four prevention strategies be the focal point of intervention efforts. These strategies include (1) parent- and family-based interventions aimed at improving family relations and parenting skills deemed to be important in helping children solve problems using non-violent means; (2) social learning and social development strategies that seek to teach children how to resolve problems and use appropriate social and cognitive skills in situations that place them at risk for aggres-sion or violence; (3) mentoring programs that pair positive adults with young people who are at risk for aggression and violence; and (4) physical changes in communities and neighborhoods that may reduce the likelihood of violent behavior among child and adult residents (CDC, 2008; Thornton, Craft, Dahlberg, Lynch, & Baer, 2002). The CDC has listed a number of specific programs within these four broad approaches as exemplary interventions (Thornton et al., 2002).

A second national center that aims to disseminate information about effective prevention programs is the Center for the Study and Prevention of Violence (CSPV) at the University of Colorado. The Blueprints for Violence Prevention initiative at CSPV is an ongoing effort aimed at identifying violence prevention programs that meet a high scientific standard of effectiveness (http://www.colorado.edu/cspv/blueprints/index.html). To date, more than 600 programs have been reviewed by CSPV. Interestingly, only 11 *model* programs currently meet the rigorous scientific standards established by investigators in Blueprints project; another 17 programs reach *promising* program status and await further empirical validation. Model and promising programs parallel the program approaches identified by the CDC and include school-, family-, and community-level interventions. Descriptions of model and promising programs identified by the Blueprints initiative are available at http://www.colorado.edu/cspv/blueprints/index.html. Several of these programs are reviewed in the following chapter.

Practitioners can turn to several other resources to learn about effective violence prevention programs. For example, the Coalition for Evidence-Based Policy has identified early childhood, educational, and youth development programs that are effective in preventing violence and other childhood and adolescent programs (http://www.evidencebasedprograms. org/static/). Similarly, the Center for Mental Health Services (http:// mentalhealth.samhsa.gov/) and the National Registry of Effective Programs (http://www.nrepp.samhsa.gov/) maintained by the Substance Abuse and Mental Health Services Administration offer practitioners lists of tested and effective prevention programs. These and other national initiatives are important because they represent a systematic approach to disseminating information about proven programs to schools, families, communities, and policy officials.

Benefits and Costs of Violence Prevention Programs

Another important factor in increasing the impact of violence prevention requires an understanding of the benefits and costs of prevention programs for children and youth. Historically, there has been little credible empirical evidence about the benefits and costs of prevention approaches to help practitioners or policy officials select or fund programs. This deficit has been addressed in recent years through work conducted by Aos and colleagues at the Washington State Institute for Public Policy (Aos, Lieb, Mayfield, Miller, & Pennucci, 2004).

Aos et al. (2004) reviewed the benefits and costs of a wide range of programs for preventing problems such as aggression, delinquency, school failure, and substance abuse. All programs included in their review had been previously tested using an experimental design or a well-constructed quasi-experimental design. Findings from the study reveal that some prevention programs produce cost savings and prevent or delay the onset of problem behaviors. Importantly, Aos and colleagues produce tangible evidence in the form of a *benefit-per-dollar cost figure* for early childhood, prenatal and infant home visitation, youth development, mentoring, substance abuse, teen pregnancy, and juvenile offender programs. Benefits were greatest for juvenile offender programs. In these programs the cost savings ranged from $1,900 to more than $31,000 per individual youth. Substantial benefits were also found among prenatal and infant home visitation programs; $6,200 to $17,200 in savings per individual youth were realized in this category. Significant benefits were also found for early childhood education programs and for selected youth development programs.

This important study demonstrates that effective prevention programs can also be cost-effective. The cost-saving figures generated by the authors point to the importance of investing in effective programs and to the danger of spending money on ineffective program approaches. Policy makers and other decision makers are well-advised to consider the findings and to implement the recommendations offered by Aos et al. (2004).

Social Policy and Violence Prevention

A logical next step in the application of the public health model to the field of violence prevention requires extending the framework to a broader cross-section of programs and public policies (Jenson & Fraser, 2006). To date, only limited examples of this process exist. For example, investigators in the public health field have applied principles of risk and protection to design prevention policies that target known risk factors for AIDS. Evidence suggests that the implementation of these approaches have led to reductions in the spread of AIDS in many parts of the world (Sorenson, Masson, & Perlman, 2002). A similar emphasis on social policy is needed to expand the impact of violence prevention programs (Woolf, 2008). Empirical evidence and public support for prevention suggest that the timing is right to incorporate elements of risk and protection into federal policy. In this regard, establishing a national office for the prevention of childhood and adolescent problems may be an important step.

SUMMARY

Early violence prevention programs in the United States had little impact on preventing or reducing childhood and adolescent aggression. The introduction of a public health approach to violence prevention in the

1980s improved the conceptual and methodological rigor of prevention activities and has served as a foundation for the new field of prevention science (Botvin, 2004; Greenberg, 2004; Kaftarian et al., 2004). Importantly, an emphasis on the scientific rigor of testing violence prevention approaches has followed the adoption of the public health framework (Hawkins, 2006; Jenson, 2006). Controlled studies assessing the short- and long-term outcomes of children and youth who have been exposed to a variety of school, family, and community prevention approaches have yielded positive effects in preventing or reducing aggression or violence. Many of these effective programs have also demonstrated significant cost savings when compared to more expensive treatment or incarceration alternatives (Aos et al., 2004). Finally, research and governmental entities, concerned with implementing and disseminating effective violence prevention programs, have generated lists of efficacious interventions that are available to practitioners, educators, and the general public (Campbell Collaboration Library, 2009; CSPV, 2009; Schinke, Brounstein, & Garnder, 2002). This, in turn, has increased the use of empirically based interventions among practitioners.

Evidence gained in the past two decades suggests that empirically-based and theoretically sound prevention programs can prevent the onset of aggression, violence, and other child and adolescent problems (Catalano, Arthur, Hawkins, Berglund, & Olson, 1998; Catalano, Loeber, & McKinney, 1999; Foxcroft, Ireland, Lister-Sharp, Lowe, & Breen, 2003; Gottfredson & Wilson, 2003; Jenson & Dieterich, 2007; Wilson, Lipsey, & Derzon, 2003). We review the empirical evidence pertaining to the efficacy and effectiveness of school, family, and community violence prevention approaches in the following chapter.

REFERENCES

Aos, S., Lieb, R., Mayfield, J., Miller, M., & Pennucci, A. (2004). *Benefits and costs of prevention and early intervention programs for youth.* Olympia: Washington State Institute for Public Policy.

Bangert-Drowns, R. L. (1988). The effects of school-based substance abuse education: A meta-analysis. *Journal of Drug Education, 18,* 243–264.

Biglan, A., Brennan, P. A., Foster, S. L., & Holden, H. D. (2004). *Helping adolescents at risk. Prevention of multiple problem behaviors.* New York: The Guilford Press.

Botvin, G. J. (2004). Advancing prevention science and practice: Challenges, critical issues, and future directions. *Prevention Science, 5,* 69–72.

Botvin, G. J., & Griffin, K. W. (2003). Drug abuse curricula in schools. In Z. Sloboda & W. J. Bukoski (Eds.), *Handbook of drug abuse prevention: Theory, science, and practice* (pp. 45–69). New York: Kluwer Academic.

Campbell Collaboration Library. (2009). Retrieved on May 24, 2009, from http://www.campbellcollaboration.org/

Catalano, R. F. (2007). Prevention is a sound public and private investment. *Criminology, 6,* 377–398.

Catalano, R. F., Arthur, M. W., Hawkins, J. D., Berglund, L., & Olson, J. J. (1998). Comprehensive community and school based interventions to prevent antisocial behavior. In R. Loeber & D. P. Farrington (Eds.), *Serious and violent juvenile offenders: Risk factors and successful interventions* (pp. 248–283). Thousand Oaks, CA: Sage.

Catalano, R. F., Loeber, R., & McKinney, K. (1999). School and community interventions to prevent serious and violent offending. *Juvenile Justice Bulletin*, October. Washington, DC: Office of Juvenile Justice and Delinquency Prevention.

Center for the Study and Prevention of Violence. (2009). *Blueprints for violence prevention*. Retrieved on May 26, 2009, from http://www.colorado.edu/cspv/

Center for Mental Health Services. (2009). Retrieved on May 26, 2009, from http://mentalhealth.samhsa.gov/

Centers for Disease Control and Prevention. (2008). *Understanding youth violence. Fact sheet*. Atlanta, GA: Centers for Disease Control and Prevention, National Center for Injury Prevention and Control.

Cicchetti, D., Rapparport, J., Sandler, L., & Weissberg, R. P. (Eds.). (2000). *The promotion of wellness in children and adolescents*. Washington, DC: Child Welfare League of America.

Coalition for Evidence-Based Policy (2009). Retrieved on May 15, 2009, from http://www.evidencebasedprograms.org/

Coie, J. D., Watt, N. F., West, S. G., Hawkins, J. D., Asarnow, J. R., Markman, H. J., Ramey, S. L., Shure, M. B., & Long, B. (1993). The science of prevention: A conceptual framework and some directions for a national research program. *American Psychologist, 48,* 1013–1022.

Elliott, D. S., & Mihalic, S. (2004). Issues in disseminating and replicating effective prevention programs. *Prevention Science, 5,* 47–54.

Foxcroft, D. R., Ireland, D., Lister-Sharp, D. J., Lowe, G., & Breen, R. (2003). Longer term primary prevention for alcohol misuse in young people: A systematic review. *Addiction, 98,* 397–411.

Fraser, M. W., Kirby, L. D., & Smokowski, P. R. (2004). Risk and resilience in childhood. In M. W. Fraser (Ed.), *Risk and resilience in childhood: An ecological perspective* (2nd ed., pp. 13–66). Washington, DC: NASW Press.

Garmezy, N. (1971). Vulnerability research and the issue of primary prevention. *American Journal of Orthopsychiatry, 41,* 101–116.

Gottfredson, D. C., & Wilson, D. B. (2003). Characteristics of effective school-based substance abuse prevention. *Prevention Science, 4,* 27–38.

Greenberg, M. (2004). Current and future challenges in school-based prevention: The researcher perspective. *Prevention Science, 5,* 5–13.

Hahn, R., Fuqua-Whitley, D., Wethington, H., Lowy, J., Crosby, A., Fullilove, M., et al. (2007). Effectiveness of universal school-based programs to prevent violent and aggressive behavior. *American Journal of Preventive Medicine, 33,* S114–S129.

Hawkins, J. D. (2006). Science, social work, prevention: Finding the intersection. *Social Work Research, 30,* 137–152.

Hawkins, J. D., Catalano, R. F., & Arthur, M. W. (2002). Promoting science-based prevention in communities. *Addictive Behaviors, 27,* 951–976.

Hawkins, J. D., Catalano, R. F., Kosterman, R., Abbott, R., & Hill, K. G. (1999). Preventing adolescent health-risk behaviors by strengthening protection during childhood. *Archives of Pediatrics and Adolescent Medicine, 153,* 226–234.

Hawkins, J. D., Catalano, R. F., & Miller, J. Y. (1992). Risk and protective factors for alcohol and other drug problems in adolescence and early adulthood: Implications for substance abuse prevention. *Psychological Bulletin, 112,* 64–105.

Hawkins, J. D., Herrenkohl, T., Farrington, D. P., Brewer, D. D., Catalano, R. F., & Harachi, T. W. (1998). A review of predictors of youth violence. In R. Loeber & D.P. Farrington (Eds.), *Serious and violent juvenile offenders: Risk factors and successful interventions* (pp. 106–146). Thousand Oaks, CA: Sage.

Hawkins, J. D., Jenson, J. M., Catalano, R. F., & Lishner, D. L. (1988). Delinquency and drug abuse: Implications for social services. *Social Service Review, 62,* 258–284.

Herrenkohl, T. I., Chung, I.-J., & Catalano, R. F. (2004). Review of research on predictors of youth violence and school-based and community-based prevention approaches. In P. Allen-Meares & M. W. Fraser (Eds.), *Intervention with children and adolescents: An interdisciplinary perspective* (pp. 449–476). Boston: Allyn & Bacon.

Herrenkohl, T. I., Hawkins, J. D., Chung, I.-J., Hill, K. G., & Battin-Pearson, S. (2001). School and community risk factors and interventions. In R. Loeber & D. P. Farrington (Eds.), *Child delinquents: Development, intervention, and service needs* (pp. 211–246). Thousand Oaks, CA: Sage Publications, Inc.

Jenson, J. M. (2006). Advances and challenges in preventing childhood and adolescent problem behavior. *Social Work Research, 30,* 131–134.

Jenson, J. M., & Dieterich, W. A. (2007). Effects of a skills-based prevention program on bullying and bully victimization among elementary school children. *Prevention Science, 8,* 285–296.

Jenson, J. M., & Fraser, M. W. (2006). *Social policy for children and families: A risk and resilience perspective.* Thousand Oaks, CA: Sage Publications.

Jenson, J. M., & Howard, M. O. (1999). *Youth violence. Current research and recent practice innovations.* Washington, DC: NASW Press.

Kaftarian, S, Robinson, E, Compton, W, Davis, B., & Volkow, N. (2004). Blending prevention research and practice in schools: Critical issues and suggestions. *Prevention Science, 5,* 1–3.

Limbos, M. A., Chan, L. S., Warf, C., Schneir, A., Iverson, E., Shekelle, P., & Kipke, M. D. (2007). Effectiveness of interventions to prevent youth violence. A systematic review. *American Journal of Preventive Medicine, 33,* 65–74.

Loeber, R., Farrington, D. P., Stouthamer-Loeber, M., & Van Kammen, W. B. (1998). *Antisocial behavior and mental health problems.* Mahwah, NJ: Lawrence Erlbaum.

Moskowitz, J. M. (1989). The primary prevention of alcohol problems: A critical review of the literature. *Journal of Studies on Alcohol, 50,* 54–88.

National Registry of Effective Programs. (2009). Retrieved on May 26, 2009, from http://www.nrepp.samhsa.gov/

O'Connell, M. E., Boat, T., & Warner, K. E. (Eds). (2009). Preventing mental, emotional, and behavioral disorders among young people: Progress and possibilities. Washington, DC: National Academies Press.

Patterson, G. R., & Yoerger, K. (1997). A developmental model for late-onset delinquency. In D. W. Osgood (Ed.), *Motivation and delinquency* (pp. 119–177). Lincoln, NE: University of Nebraska Press.

Pollard, J. A., Hawkins, J. D., & Arthur, M. W. (1999). Risk and protection: Are both necessary to understand diverse behavioral outcomes in adolescence? *Social Work Research, 23,* 145–158.

Rutter, M. (1979). Protective factors in children's responses to stress and disadvantage. In M. W. Kent & J. E. Rolf (Eds.), *Primary prevention of psychopathology: Vol 3, Social competence in children* (pp. 49–74). Lebanon, NH: University Press of New England.

Rutter, M. (1987). Psychosocial resilience and protective mechanisms. *American Journal of Orthopsychiatry, 57,* 316–331.

Rutter, M. (2001). Psychosocial adversity: Risk, resilience, and recovery. In J. M. Richman & M. W. Fraser (Eds.), *The context of youth violence: Resilience, risk, and protection* (pp. 13–41). Westport, CT: Praeger Publishers.

Schaps, E., Bartolo, R. D., Moskowitz, J., Palley, C. S., & Churgin, S. (1981). A review of 127 drug abuse prevention program evaluations. *Journal of Drug Issues, 11,* 17–43.

Schinke, S., Brounstein, P., & Gardner, S. (2002). *Science-based prevention programs and principles, 2002.* Rockville, MD: Substance Abuse and Mental Health Services Administration. DHHS Pub. No. (SMA) 03-3764.

Sorenson, J. L., Masson, C. L., & Perlman, D. C. (2002). HIV/hepatitis prevention in drug abuse treatment programs: Guidance from research. *NIDA Science and Practice Perspectives, 1,* 4–12. Washington, DC: National Institute on Drug Abuse.

Thornberry, T. P. (1998). Membership in youth gangs and involvement in serious and violent offending. In R. Loeber & D.P. Farrington (Eds.), *Serious & violent juvenile offenders. Risk factors and successful interventions* (pp. 147–166). New York: Sage.

Thornton, T. N., Craft, C.A., Dahlberg, L. L., Lynch, B.S., & Baer, K. (2002). *Best practices of youth violence prevention: A sourcebook for community action* (Rev.). Atlanta, GA: Centers for Disease Control and Prevention, National Center for Injury Prevention and Control.

Tobler, N. S. (1986). Meta-analysis of 143 adolescent drug prevention programs: Quantitative outcome results of program participants compared to a control comparison group. *Journal of Drug Issues, 16,* 537–567.

United States Department of Health and Human Services. (2001). *Youth violence: A report of the Surgeon General.* Rockville, MD: U.S. Department of Health and Human Services, Centers for Disease Control and Prevention, National Center for Injury Prevention and Control; Substance Abuse and Mental Health Services Administration, Center for Mental Health Services; and National Institutes of Health, National Institute of Mental Health.

Werner, E. E., & Smith, R. S. (1982). *Vulnerable but invincible: A longitudinal study of resilient children and youth.* New York: Adams, Bannister, and Cox.

Werner, E. E., & Smith, R. S. (1992). *Overcoming the odds: High risk children from birth to adulthood.* New York: Cornell University Press.

Wilson, S. J., & Lipsey, M. W. (2007). School-based interventions for aggressive and disruptive behavior: Update of a meta-analysis. *American Journal of Preventive Medicine, 33,* S130–S143.

Wilson, S. J., Lipsey, M. W., & Derzon, J. H. (2003). The effects of school-based intervention programs on aggressive behavior: A meta-analysis. *Journal of Consulting and Clinical Psychology, 71*, 136–149.

Woolf, S. H. (2008). The power of prevention and what it requires. *Journal of the American Medical Association, 299*, 2437–2439.

8

EFFECTIVE VIOLENCE PREVENTION APPROACHES IN SCHOOL, FAMILY, AND COMMUNITY SETTINGS

JEFFREY M. JENSON, ANNE POWELL, &

SHANDRA FORREST-BANK

Advances in the field of prevention described in the previous chapter offer great promise for practitioners and policy makers interested in preventing violent behavior in children and youth. Importantly, the adoption of a risk and protection model of prevention has increased the quality and availability of interventions aimed at preventing violence. In this chapter, we describe effective school-, family-, and community-level violence prevention approaches. Strategies to diffuse effective programs to school, family, and community contexts are delineated. We focus our review on interpersonal forms of aggression and violent conduct among children and youth.

SCHOOL-BASED VIOLENCE PREVENTION

Risk, Protection, and School Context

Aggression and violence committed and experienced by children and youth occur frequently in school settings. In 2007, 6% of American high school students reported carrying a weapon to school (Centers for Disease Control and Prevention [CDC], 2008). Twelve percent of students participated in a physical fight on school property. Sadly, 6% of students stayed home from school at times because they felt unsafe (CDC, 2008). In extreme and isolated cases, school violence has led to tragic incidents involving multiple student and teacher injuries and deaths (Vossekull, Fein, Reddy, Borum, & Modseleski, 2002). Clearly, education is a critical context for preventing aggressive and violent behavior.

Numerous risk and protective factors for aggression and violence are embedded in school settings. Academic failure, low levels of school commitment, antisocial peer influence, and environmental norms that encourage antisocial behavior are common risk factors associated with the onset and persistence of violence among children and youth (Farrell & Camou, 2006; Jenson & Fraser, 2006; Jenson & Howard, 1999). Conversely, conditions and traits such as high levels of attachment to teachers, parental involvement in children's education, and individual social and problem-solving skills constitute important protective factors that buffer exposure to risk and reduce the likelihood of violence (Herrenkohl, Chung, & Catalano, 2004). School based-prevention efforts offer the promise of reaching nearly all American youth and play a critical role in the nation's effort to reduce aggression, violence, and victimization among young people.

Effective School-Based Prevention Strategies

Systematic reviews, meta-analyses, and controlled trials provide considerable evidence about effective and promising school-based prevention strategies (e.g., Hahn et al., 2007; Jenson & Dieterich, 2007; Limbos et al., 2007; Wilson & Lipsey, 2007; Wilson, Lipsey, & Derzon, 2003). We use this evidence to classify and describe efficacious approaches to school-based violence prevention. To be considered in this review, interventions had to be tested under randomized study conditions and target one or more aggressive or violent behaviors. Effective interventions are divided into three program types as shown in Figure 8.1: (1) *social and emotional learning programs* that enhance social, cognitive, and behavioral skills among students; (2) *integrated programs* that combine skill training, classroom management, and parent involvement strategies; and (3) *school-wide approaches* that target social norms and cultural influences associated with violence. School-based *universal* programs for general student populations (i.e., an entire grade level within a particular school), *selective* programs targeting high-risk students, and *indicated* programs delivered to children and youth exhibiting violent or aggressive behavior are described next and summarized in Table 8.1.

Figure 8.1. School-based violence prevention programs by type, strategies, and intended outcomes.

Social and Emotional Learning Programs

Social and emotional school-based programs use skills training strategies to enhance social competence, promote emotional regulation, and develop cognitive and behavioral skills aimed at reducing violence. Importantly, many programs also concentrate on teaching students ways to avoid becoming a victim of peer aggression and violence. Common elements of skills-based interventions include a reliance on cognitive-behavioral training techniques such as modeling, rehearsal, practice, and feedback (Jenson, Dieterich, Rinner, Washington, & Burgoyne, 2006). Skills-based programs are typically delivered by teachers or trained intervention specialists using a structured or manualized curriculum.

I Can Problem Solve (ICPS) is a *universal* school-based prevention program that incorporates cognitive and problem-solving techniques to enhance prosocial behavior and reduce aggressive behavior among children in preschool through sixth grade. ICPS interventions target children's cognitive processes and problem-solving skills rather than focusing on specific antisocial behavior per se. Early controlled studies of ICPS revealed significant reductions in impulsivity, improvements in classroom behaviors, and increases in problem-solving skills among participants (Shure & Spivack, 1980, 1982). A recent two-year outcome study examined the impact of ICPS on children in kindergarten and first grade who were enrolled in a racially diverse and economically disadvantaged urban school district (Boyle & Hassert-Walker, 2008). Schools in the district were matched on several criteria including racial, ethnic, and socioeconomic composition and assigned to either an instruction or control condition. ICPS participants exhibited significantly less relational and physical aggression compared with control group participants at posttest. Results were most positive for participants who received the intervention during

Table 8.1. Effective School-Based Violence Prevention Programs

Program and Author(s)	Intervention Modality	Program Description	Risk and Protective Factors	Findings
A. Social and Emotional Learning Programs				
I Can Problem Solve Boyle & Hassert-Walker, 2008	Classroom-based skills training, generally at the *universal* level	*I Can Problem Solve* seeks to improve social competency, increase cognitive and problem-solving skills, and promote effective conflict resolution for children in elementary school.	Early onset of conduct problems, including aggression and violence	Significantly less relational and physical aggression among subjects in the intervention group compared with the control group. Results are most significant for participants who receive two years of the program.
Life Skills Training Botvin et al., 2004, 2006	Classroom-based skills training, generally at the *universal* level	*Life Skills Training* aims to prevent aggression, drug use, and other problem behaviors by enhancing self-regulation skills, social competence, and refusal skills.	Early onset of aggression and substance use	Significant reductions in verbal and physical aggression, fighting, and delinquency among intervention participants. Investigations have also shown significant reductions in alcohol, tobacco, and other drug use after program completion, at one-year, two-year, three-year, and six-year follow-up.
Promoting Alternative THinking Strategies (PATHS) Greenberg et al., 1995	Classroom-based skills training at the *universal* level for children and classroom management strategies for teachers	*PATHS* seeks to improve social competence and emotional regulation and reduce aggressive and other disruptive behaviors in preschool and elementary school-aged.	Early onset of aggression, conduct problems, and other disruptive behaviors	Significantly lower rates of aggressive and disruptive behaviors among intervention subjects compared with control subjects in regular and special education school classrooms.
Youth Matters Jenson & Dieterich, 2007	*Universal* classroom-based skills training aimed at bullying and aggression	*Youth Matters* curriculum seeks to improve social and cognitive skills necessary to prevent bullying and bully victimization among elementary school-aged children	Early onset of aggression and antisocial peer influence	Significantly lower rates of bully victimization among experimental subjects relative to controls following two-years of program participation.

(Continued)

Table 8.1. continued

Program and Author(s)	Intervention Modality	Program Description	Risk and Protective Factors	Findings
B. Integrated Programs				
Early Risers August et al., 2004	Multimodal program includes skills training, peer mentoring, and family activities at the *selective* or *indicated* level	*Early Risers* aims to improve academic competence, behavioral self-regulation, social competence, and parent involvement in children's lives.	Early onset of aggressive behavior, exposure to adverse environmental conditions, and poor family management skills	Significant improvements in academic achievement and behavioral self-regulation and reductions in disruptive classroom behavior among aggressive students. Significant gains in parent discipline skills after three years of exposure to the intervention.
FAST Track The Conduct Problems Prevention Research Group, 2004	Multimodal training at the *selective* or *indicated* level includes parent training, home visitations, social skills training for high-risk children and academic tutoring and universal classroom interventions when delivered in coordination with the PATHS curriculum	*FAST Track* seeks to improve social, cognitive, and emotional competencies, reading skills, and family, peer, and teacher responses to conduct problems among children in elementary school.	Early onset of conduct problems, including violence and aggression	Significantly improvements in classroom conduct, lower levels of peer aggression and victimization, and fewer disruptive behaviors at school for experimental participants at one-year post intervention. Significantly less problem behavior for *indicated* samples at three-year follow-up.
Good Behavior Game Kellam et al., 2008	Classroom management and skills training intervention elements, generally at the *universal* level	*Good Behavior Game* is designed to promote a positive classroom climate by reducing aggressive and disruptive behavior, establishing clear rules and consequences, and promoting teamwork among students in early elementary school.	Early onset of aggressive and disruptive behavior in the classroom	Significantly less aggressive behavior at the end of first grade among subjects in the intervention condition compared with controls. Significantly less aggressive behavior, drug use, and mental health problems among 6th grade boys in the experimental group who were assessed as aggressive in the first grade.

kindergarten and first grade compared with children who participated in only one year of the study (Boyle & Hassert-Walker, 2008).

Promoting Alternative THinking Strategies (PATHS) is a classroom-based skills training program that seeks to improve social competence and emotional regulation and reduce aggressive and other disruptive behaviors. An initial group-randomized trial revealed significant improvements in ability to regulate emotional responses to antisocial behavior exhibited by peers among intervention participants relative to controls (Greenberg, Kusché, Cook, & Quamma, 1995). Experimental subjects also had higher overall levels of social competence relative to control subjects. A subsequent investigation conducted in the context of the *FAST Track* program, a more comprehensive prevention program that uses *PATHS* as the classroom-based curriculum, revealed significant reductions in aggressive behavior, disruptive behavior in the classroom, and enhanced classroom climate among intervention subjects (Conduct Problems Prevention Research Group, 1999a). Originally designed for children in elementary school classrooms, PATHS is also an effective program for children in preschool (Domitrovich, Cortes, & Greenberg, 2007) and special education settings (Kam, Greenberg, & Kusché, 2004).

Life Skills Training (LST) was originally designed and tested as an alcohol, tobacco, and other drug abuse prevention program (Botvin & Griffin, 2004). LST assists youth in middle school to gain key social and emotional competencies that buffer risks associated with drug use and other forms of antisocial conduct. Substantial evidence exists to support the effectiveness of LST in reducing alcohol, tobacco, and other drug use (Botvin & Griffin, 2004). Importantly, a recent group-randomized trial indicated that participation in LST also led to significant reductions in verbal and physical aggression, fighting, and delinquency among experimental subjects (Botvin, Griffin, & Nichols, 2006). These results suggest that LST may be an effective prevention strategy for preventing several types of antisocial conduct, including aggression and violence.

Youth Matters is a classroom-based skills training program designed to improve social and cognitive skills necessary to prevent bullying and bully victimization among elementary school-aged children. The program includes a manualized curriculum that teaches a variety of social, cognitive, and behavioral skills deemed necessary to prevent bullying and aggression (Jenson et al., 2006). Jenson and Dieterich (2007) examined the effects of four *Youth Matters* program modules in a group-randomized trial of 28 elementary schools. Results showed significant reductions in bully victimization among intervention participants relative to controls after two years of program participation.

Integrated Programs

Some school-based violence prevention programs combine skills training approaches with additional program components designed to improve classroom management, academic achievement, and parenting skills. In addition to skills training, these programs typically use academic tutoring, cooperative learning, and parent training techniques to reduce or mitigate disruptive and aggressive behavior. For example, the *Good Behavior Game* promotes positive classroom climate by establishing clear rules and expectations for behavior, setting firm consequences for antisocial behavior, and promoting positive teamwork among students (Embry, 2002). The program encourages teachers to consistently reinforce behavioral expectations and consequences in the classroom. Using baseball analogies, the *Good Behavior Game* is played in segments or innings by teams of students during a portion of the school day. The team that has the fewest "fouls" wins the game for the day and receives an activity prize. A group-randomized trial of the program in first- and second-grade classrooms in 19 public elementary schools in Baltimore revealed significant reductions in aggressive behavior by the end of first grade for the intervention group as compared with controls (Kellam et al., 1991). At the end of sixth grade, significant reductions in aggressive behavior were also found among boys who were identified as acting aggressively in first grade. Finally, young adults who participated in the *Good Behavior Game* as first-grade students evidenced significantly less drug use and fewer mental health problems compared with young adults in the original control group sample (Kellam et al., 2008).

The *Seattle Social Development Project* (SSDP) combines skills training, classroom management training for teachers, and parent involvement (Catalano & Hawkins, 1996; Hawkins, Von Cleve, & Catalano, 1991; Hawkins, Catalano, Kosterman, Abbott & Hill, 1999; Hawkins, Kosterman, Catalano, Hill & Abbott, 2005; Hawkins, Smith, Hill, Kosterman & Catalano, 2007). SSDP is a comprehensive intervention designed to increase positive social bonds, decrease aggression, and promote school commitment and attachment among children in elementary and middle school. The classroom-based component offers students developmentally appropriate lessons on effective communication, decision-making, problem-solving, conflict resolution, and conflict avoidance skills. The teacher component addresses classroom management, interactive teaching, and cooperative learning strategies. The parent training component of the intervention strives to increase family communication, discipline, and monitoring skills. Tests of the intervention reveal significantly less aggressive behavior, higher levels of attachment and commitment to school, and less antisocial peer influence among boys who participated in the program (Hawkins et al., 1991; O'Donnell, Hawkins, Catalano, Abbot, & Day, 1995). Follow-up analyses conducted with intervention participants through early adulthood indicate that SSDP students are less likely to report violent delinquent acts, heavy drinking, and risky sexual behavior than control subjects. Experimental subjects also report more favorable work outcomes, higher levels of emotional regulation, and less criminal involvement than control subjects (Hawkins et al., 1999, 2005, 2007).

Social and emotional programs are combined frequently with academic or educational services such as tutoring or reading instruction. For example, *FAST Track* incorporates tri-weekly academic tutoring with social skills training and classroom management techniques for children in first to sixth grade (Conduct Problems Prevention Research Group, 1999a, 1999b, 2002a). In some settings, *FAST Track* is combined with the previously described *PATHS* curriculum to teach social, emotional, and cognitive skills to students. The *FAST Track* program provides academic tutoring, teacher training, parent training, and home visits to enhance skill development. Results from group-randomized trials of the program reveal improvements in classroom atmosphere and less aggression, victimization, and disruptive behavior at school among experimental subjects compared with control group students (Conduct Problems Prevention Research Group, 1999a, 1999b, 2002a, 2002b, 2002c, 2004).

The *Second Step Program* combines classroom-based training designed to enhance empathy, problem-solving and impulse control skills with teacher training strategies (Frey, Hirschstein, & Guzzo, 2000). Classroom training provides children and youth in preschool through middle school instruction on empathy and perspective taking, problem-solving and conflict resolution, and anger management with the intention of fostering the social and emotional skills necessary to reduce aggression. The classroom component trains teachers in effective program delivery and offers strategies for positively impacting the environmental context of the classroom and school. Tests of the intervention reveal significant increases in coping and anger control skills and in prosocial and cooperative behaviors among youth in the experimental group. Reductions in aggressive behavior have also been reported among experimental subjects (Cooke, Ford, Levine, Bourke, Newell, & Lapidus, 2007; Frey, Nolen, Edstrom, & Hirschstein, 2005).

Other integrated programs combine school-based strategies with techniques that target family and community risk factors for aggression and violence. For example, the *Incredible Years* combines training for teachers and parents with classroom-based skills training for children in preschool and early elementary school (Webster-Stratton, 1998, 2001; Webster-Stratton & Hammond, 1997; Webster-Stratton & Reid, 2003; Webster-Stratton, Reid, & Hammond, 2001, 2004; Webster-Stratton, Reid, & Stoolmiller, 2008). The program is designed for high-risk children who are exhibiting early aggression and other conduct problems. The program's *Dinosaur* curriculum promotes social, emotional, and academic competencies through training that attempts to enhance positive peer friendships and increase empathy, perspective-taking, anger, and conflict management skills. Group-randomized trials of the intervention reveal significant increases in family communication and problem solving skills, improved classroom management among teachers, and fewer conduct problems at home and at school among experimental subjects compared with controls (Webster-Stratton & Hammond, 1997; Webster-Stratton & Reid, 2003; Webster-Stratton et al., 2008).

The *Early Risers Program* combines skills-based training with peer mentoring, classroom management strategies, and family involvement (August, Hektner, Egan, Realmuto, & Bloomquist, 2002; August, Lee, Bloomquist, Realmuto, & Hektner, 2004; August, Realmuto, Hektner, & Bloomquist, 2001). The intervention is designed to enhance parent discipline, improve family communication, increase parent involvement, and enhance parent-child attachment. Evaluations indicate that children and families who participate in the program for at least two years show increases in social competence, academic achievement, parent involvement, and discipline practices (August et al., 2004).

Linking the Interests of Families and Teachers (LIFT) uses classroom-based skills training, behavior modification, and parent training strategies to reduce aggression and violence among elementary school children residing in low-income, high-crime neighborhoods. The classroom component incorporates experiential learning exercises designed to enhance social competence and problem-solving skills (Eddy, Reid, & Fetrow, 2000). The playground component uses a modified version of the previously described *Good Behavior Game* to foster positive peer relations and prosocial behavior on school playgrounds. Finally, a parent training component offers developmentally appropriate strategies for parents to encourage positive play behavior and promote effective problem-solving and negotiation skills (Eddy et al., 2000). Randomized trials have been conducted to assess program impacts at posttest and at one- and three-year follow-up (Eddy, Reid, Stoolmiller, & Fetrow 2003; Reid, Eddy, Fetrow, & Stoolmiller, 1999). Results reveal significantly greater social competence and less physical aggression among experimental subjects compared with control subjects. Importantly, program effects appear to be stronger for participants with high levels of aggression at the beginning of the intervention, indicating that the most aggressive children demonstrated the greatest improvement (Stoolmiller, Eddy, & Reid, 2000). At three-year follow-up, experimental subjects were significantly less likely than control subjects to be arrested or to use alcohol (Eddy et al., 2003).

Schoolwide Programs

Effective violence prevention programs targeting social norms related to violence and aggression have emerged in school settings in recent years. These programs promote positive social norms that in turn lead to a school climate that discourages aggression and violence. For example, the *Olweus Bullying Prevention Program* (Olweus, 1993) uses classroom management techniques and schoolwide components designed to impact norms about bullying behavior. Closely related to aggression, bullying is a distinct form of antisocial behavior that includes direct and indirect tactics intended to inflict harm on a weaker victim (Crick, Bigbee, & Howes, 1996; Haynie, Nansel, Eitel, Crump, Saylor, Yu, & Simons-Morton, 2001; Solberg, Olweus, & Endresen, 2007). An important component or distinguishing factor of bullying behavior is the presence of a power imbalance in which the bully exerts actual or perceived power over a victim who struggles to defend her or himself (Olweus 1993; Solberg et al., 2007). Evaluations of the *Olweus Bullying Prevention Program* reveal significant reductions in bullying and bully victimization for intervention participants as compared with controls and significant improvements in classroom and school climate following program completion (Olweus, 1993).

The *Steps to Respect Program*, similar to the Olweus program, includes classroom-based skills training for children in grades 3 to 6, classroom management, and schoolwide intervention components. The classroom-based curriculum offers 10 structured lessons designed to increase social competence, emotional regulation, positive peer interactions, conflict avoidance, and disclosure of bullying behavior. The classroom and school-wide components seek to modify classroom and school climate by promoting anti-bullying norms and by providing training to teachers, counselors, and administrators in appropriately coaching children involved in bullying and bully victimization. A group-randomized trial of the program (Frey, Hirschstein, Snell, Edstrom, MacKenzie, & Broderick, 2005) revealed that intervention participants demonstrated significant reductions in bullying and argumentative behavior compared with control subjects. Youth in the experimental group also demonstrated significant increases in positive peer interactions on the playground and in positive behaviors aimed at assisting victims.

Summary of School-Based Programs

School-based prevention programs have made significant inroads in reducing aggression and violence in the past decade. Moderating characteristics of effective school-based prevention programs including length of intervention, program content and delivery method, developmental age, and race, ethnicity, and gender are examined next.

Length of Intervention

Evidence examining the relationship between program length and aggressive behavior following intervention generally supports the intuitive belief that programs delivered over longer periods of time or that contain more sessions achieve the greatest reductions in aggressive or violent behavior (Wilson & Lipsey, 2007). For example, evidence from longitudinal studies suggests that interventions introduced and taught over the course of several years are more likely to yield positive outcomes compared with interventions of relatively brief duration. The combination of multiyear programs and environmental support from teachers appears to be particularly effective (Gottfredson & Wilson, 2003). Environmental support strategies such as school-level planning and the creation of whole-school community activities—when implemented consistently and repeatedly—have also been identified as among the most efficacious prevention strategies (Greenberg, 2004).

Program Content and Delivery

Violence prevention programs typically incorporate one or a combination of strategies including skills-training, behavioral and classroom management techniques, academic support services, and schoolwide change strategies. Among single-component programs, skills-based interventions demonstrate the largest effect sizes in reducing violence, aggression, and victimization, particularly in comparison to other intervention strategies (Wilson & Lipsey, 2007; Wilson et al., 2003). Recent reviews, however, suggest that programs with multiple intervention components are most effective in reducing the likelihood of violence among children and youth (e.g., Hahn et al., 2007).

The position and training of individuals delivering prevention programs have been identified as potential moderator variables in the delivery of prevention programs. In one review of school-based prevention, Gottfredson and Wilson (2003) found that most prevention programs were delivered by classroom teachers followed by outside trainers and peers. Interestingly, effect sizes by trainer type were somewhat inconclusive suggesting that additional research is needed to understand the relationship between locus of training and student outcomes. Other investigators have focused on the training and background of leaders. For example, Tobler (1992) found that mental health professionals and counselors produced the largest effect sizes in programs designed to prevent problem behavior. A more recent review reported that using school administrators or counselors as trainers in prevention programs is not associated with reductions in violent or aggressive behavior (Hahn et al., 2007).

Age, Race, Ethnicity, and Gender

The question of intervention timing has been discussed extensively in the prevention field. It appears that effects in preventing or reducing aggression or violence are largest for programs targeting young children in preschool and elementary school settings.

Strategies to best meet the needs of racial and ethnic groups in prevention programs have also been the topic of considerable discussion in recent years (Botvin, 2004; Kumpher, Alvarado, Smith, & Bellamy, 2002). While evidence suggests that effective prevention programs work with a broad range of students (e.g., Botvin, Griffin, Diaz, Ifill-Williams, 2001), tailoring interventions to specific populations does tend to increase efficacy for racial and ethnic subgroups (Castro, Barrera, & Martinez, 2004). Based on such evidence, the most common approach to ensuring relevance to different racial and ethnic groups is to adapt or modify an existing curriculum to meet the needs of particular groups. Given the fact that cultural adaptation is common, the task for investigators and the field becomes one of how to accomplish adaptation while maintaining program fidelity.

Evidence suggests that prevention programs demonstrate similar rates of effectiveness for male and female participants, with several exceptions. For example, evaluations of the *Good Behavior Game* reveal significantly less aggressive behavior at the end of sixth grade for participating boys (Kellam & Anthony, 1998; Kellam et al., 2008). Boys in the experimental group also reported significantly less drug use and fewer mental health problems. Similar results were not reported for girls in these investigations.

Tests of the *Seattle Social Development Project (SSDP)* also reveal significant gender effects among intervention participants. For example, after six years of program participation boys in the intervention group reported significantly less involvement with antisocial peers, less delinquency, and higher levels of social competence than boys in the control condition. Female participants in a high-risk, low-income intervention group reported significantly greater school attachment and less drug use than their control group counterparts (Hawkins et al., 2007; O'Donnell et al., 1995).

In sum, efficacious school-based violence prevention programs offer an important set of templates for the nation's educational institutions. Sufficient evidence now exists to support the implementation of a number of social and emotional learning, integrated, and schoolwide interventions. Family-based violence prevention strategies are reviewed in the following section.

FAMILY-BASED VIOLENCE PREVENTION

Risk, Protection, and Family Context

In Chapter 6, Herrenkohl and associates noted that many risk factors for youth violence are embedded in the context of the family. For example, children whose parents have committed crimes are more likely themselves to engage in violent crimes (Hawkins, Herrenkohl, Farrington, Brewer, Catalano, & Harachi, 1998). Harsh discipline practices, maltreatment, and domestic violence place children at risk for violence later in life (Smith & Landreth, 2003). In addition, parental attitudes that are tolerant of violent behavior are associated with aggressive conduct by youth (Hawkins et al., 1998).

Parenting practices and relationships between parents and children present a number of potential risk factors for violence. For example, insufficient parental monitoring and discipline are associated with youth violence (Ikeda, Simon, & Swahn, 2001), as are high conflict, poor communication, and inadequate problem-solving skills (Hogue, Liddle, Becker, & Johnson-Leckrone, 2002). Lack of parental involvement and low levels of attachment between parents and children are also risk factors for childhood and adolescent violence (Hawkins et al., 1998; Hogue, et al., 2002). Importantly, there is greater risk of aggressive and antisocial behavior in children who experience rejection, neglect, or indifference from parents. Finally, stressful family events, frequent moves, and disruption of parent-child relationships have all been linked to violent behavior in young people (Hawkins et al., 1998).

Effective Family-Based Prevention Strategies

The strong relationship between family risk factors and violence implies a need for violence prevention programs that reduce risk and increase protection in the context of the family environment. The importance of family-based programs is also supported by proponents who argue that any intervention that intends to impact the attitudes, beliefs and behaviors of youth are limited if family members are not involved (Ikeda et al., 2001). Applying the same criteria used to examine school-based programs, we review three types of effective family-based prevention strategies: (1) *prenatal and perinatal* programs; (2) *parent training* programs; and (3) *family-focused interventions* for individual youth. Figure 8.2 illustrates family-based programs by type, strategy, and intended outcomes. A summary of effective programs is found in Table 8.2.

Prenatal and Perinatal Programs

Aggression and violence generally become more resistant to change as children enter adolescence. However, in some cases aggressive behavior begins before children even enter school (Webster-Stratton & Hammond, 1997). The early onset of aggressive behavior suggests that family-based interventions should begin at the earliest possible point in a child's development, before problems occur and when destructive pathways can be altered.

Prenatal and perinatal programs are based on empirical evidence suggesting that prenatal parenting skills and the initial months of an infant's

Figure 8.2. Family-based violence prevention programs by type, strategies, and intended outcomes.

Table 8.2. Effective Family-Based Violence Prevention Programs

Program and Author(s)	Intervention Modality	Program Description	Risk and Protective Factors	Findings
A. Prenatal and Perinatal Programs				
Nurse Family Partnership Olds et al., 1998	Prenatal and perinatal home visitation and support services at the *universal* and *selected* levels	The *Nurse-Family Partnership* uses trained nurses to conduct home visits aimed at educating and counseling first time mothers to be healthy, responsible, and competent parents.	Prenatal health, parent attachment, and antisocial conduct by parents	Adolescent children of mothers who received home visitation were significantly less likely to be involved in criminal behavior and the legal system at 15-year follow-up. Mothers in the experimental group were 48% less likely than mothers in the control group to be perpetrators of abuse or neglect.
B. Parent Training Strategies				
Adolescents Transitions Program Dishion et al., 1992	Tiered intervention that includes school- and family-based interventions at the *universal, selected,* and *indicated* levels	*Adolescents Transitions Program* provides *universal* level prevention services in schools, *selected* parent training interventions based on motivational interviewing, and *indicated* strategies aimed at improving family management practices.	Early onset of antisocial behavior and substance use, commitment to school, and poor family management practices	Significant reductions in parent-child conflict, and negative engagement, substance use, and aggressive behavior among experimental subjects.
Guiding Good Choices (formerly *Preparing for the Drug Free Years*) Park et al., 2000	Structured parent training, generally at the *universal* or *indicated* level, for parents of children in middle school	*Guiding Good Choices* seeks to reduce risk factors and enhance protective factors associated with aggression and other antisocial behaviors by improving parenting skills and family communication patterns.	Early onset of antisocial behavior and substance use, commitment to school, and poor family management practices	Significant improvements in child management skills, improved parent-child relationships, and increased self-efficacy among participants.

(Continued)

Table 8.2. continued

Program and Author(s)	Intervention Modality	Program Description	Risk and Protective Factors	Findings
Parent-Child Interaction Therapy Brinkmeyer & Eyberg, 2003	Structured parent training, generally at the *indicated* level, for parents of children two to seven years old	*Parent-Child Interaction Therapy* seeks to strengthen parent-child attachments and increase parental discipline practices.	Early onset of aggression and disruptive behavior	Significant improvements in parent-child interactions, child compliance, and child behavior among experimental subjects compared with a waitlist comparison group condition.
Parent Management Treatment Training (Oregon Model) Patterson et al., 1982	Structured parent training, generally at the *selected* or *indicated* level for parents with children between three and 12 years old	Parent training interventions based on the *Oregon Model* seek to break cycles of negative child-parent coercive practices by teaching effective family management and parent communication skills.	Parental discipline, inconsistent parental monitoring, and attachment to parents	Significant reductions in childhood disruptive behavior, including aggression, among experimental subjects compared with youth in a control condition.
Preventive Treatment Program Tremblay et al., 1992, 1996	Parent training and school-based strategies, generally at the *universal* level, with parents of elementary school children	The *Preventive Treatment Program* aims to decrease aggression and promote positive behaviors through parent training, home visits, and teacher support.	Parental discipline, inconsistent parental monitoring, and attachment to parents	Experimental subjects evidence significantly less involvement in antisocial conduct at age 12 and lower rates of gang involvement, substance use, and delinquency at age 15 than controls.
Strengthening Families Program for Parents and Youth 10-14 Spoth et al., 2000	Parent and child life skills training at the *universal* or *indicated* level for children and youth between 3 and 16 years old	*Strengthening Families* aims to reduce aggression and substance use by exposing parents and youth to separate and integrated parent, child, and family training sessions.	Parental discipline, inconsistent parental monitoring, and attachment to parents	Lower rates of aggression, hostility, and substance use resulted in youth who participated in the intervention. Significant improvements in parent's ability to set appropriate limits for their children.

Program	Description	Risk Factors Targeted	Outcomes
The *Triple P – Positive Parenting Program* Sanders et al., 2000	Parent training at the *universal level* for parents of children between two and nine years old	The *Triple P – Positive Parenting Program* uses structured parent training and didactic presentations to change adverse parenting practices and family management strategies.	Parental discipline, inconsistent parental monitoring, and attachment to parents	Significant reductions in childhood problem behavior and improvements in parenting skills among experimental subjects at six-month follow-up. Significantly higher levels of self-efficacy and less stress among parents receiving the intervention compared with controls.

C. Family-Focused Interventions

Program	Description	Risk Factors Targeted	Outcomes
Brief Strategic Family Therapy Szapocznik & Williams, 2000	Individual and family therapy at the *indicated* level for children and youth with behavior problems	*Brief Strategic Family Therapy* targets maladaptive family interaction processes through practical problem-solving therapy approaches.	Early onset of antisocial behavior and substance use, commitment to school, poor family management practices, and antisocial peer influence	Significant reductions in conduct problems, delinquency, and substance abuse among BSFT participants compared with youth in control group conditions.
Functional Family Therapy Alexander & Parsons, 1982	Family therapy at the *indicated* level for youth between 11 and 18 years old	*Functional Family Therapy* helps at-risk and troubled youth and their parents to use unique family strengths in specific phases that include engagement, targeted change, and maintenance of change.	Early involvement in delinquency and other antisocial behaviors and intervention with older youth with serious problematic behavior	Significant reductions in recidivism for status and serious offenders in the experimental group compared with youth in a no treatment control condition.

(Continued)

Table 8.2. continued

Program and Author(s)	Intervention Modality	Program Description	Risk and Protective Factors	Findings
Multidimensional Family Therapy Liddle et al., 2001, 2004	Family therapy at the *indicated* level for middle and high school youth	*Multidimensional Family Therapy* is a solution-focused intervention that strives to find practical solutions to child and youth problems in home and school settings.	Early involvement in delinquency, substance use, and other antisocial behaviors, antisocial peer influence, commitment to school, and family management practices	Significant decreases in aggression, substance use, and other antisocial behavior among experimental subjects compared with controls at one-year follow-up.
Multidimensional Treatment Foster Care Chamberlain & Smith, 2003	Individual and family therapy at the *indicated* level for children and youth with severe behavior problems	*Multidimensional Treatment Foster Care* provides intense counseling to youth in foster placements and teaches foster, biological, and adoptive parents practical parenting skills.	Early involvement in delinquency and other antisocial behaviors, antisocial peer influence, commitment to school, and family management practices	Youth participating in MTFC evidence significantly less incarceration, fewer arrests, and less drug use than control subjects. Girls in the experimental group had significantly fewer days in locked settings and in caregiver-reported delinquency compared with girls in a control condition.
Multisystemic Therapy Henggeler et al., 1992, 2002	Individual and family therapy at the *indicated* level for children and youth with behavior problems	*Multisystemic Therapy* aims to reduce aggressive and antisocial conduct using a structured therapeutic process in community and home settings.	Early involvement in delinquency and substance use, antisocial peer influence, and family management practices	Significant reductions in child and adolescent emotional and behavior problems, improvements in parent-child relationships, and decreases in aggression and criminal and violent arrests up to four years following intervention.

life are related to subsequent aggression and violence (Booth, Spieker, Barnard, & Morisset, 1992; Ikeda et al., 2001; Olds, Sadler, & Kitzman, 2007). At least one American early prevention program uses trained nurses to conduct visits to the homes of pregnant or perinatal parents (Olds, Henderson et al., 1998). In Europe, however, many universal home visitation programs are available to all childbearing families regardless of their risk level (Bilukha, Hahn et al., 2005).

The *Nurse-Family Partnership Program* has produced positive effects in preventing antisocial and delinquent conduct among children and adolescents (Olds et al., 2007). This program sends nurses to the homes of single mothers during pregnancy and after childbirth to provide education and advice to parents about prenatal and infant care. One randomized investigation in New York indicated that single and low-income mothers who participated in the program had healthier babies and fewer reports of recorded child abuse and neglect than mothers in the control group during the first two years of home visitation (Olds, Henderson et al., 1998). Analyses of follow-up data revealed that mothers who participated in the intervention were 48% less likely than mothers in the control group to be identified as perpetrators of abuse or neglect at 15-year follow-up. Experimental subjects also showed significant improvements in other parenting competencies and responsibilities. Particularly relevant to this review are the long-term findings for adolescents whose mothers participated in the program as infants and young children; adolescents in the experimental condition had 59% fewer arrests and 90% fewer adjudications than control group subjects. Notably, the effects were most significant for children who were at greatest risk for problem behavior at the onset of intervention (Olds et al., 2007).

To date, no other nurse visitation programs have been rigorously tested in the United States. This is unfortunate because existing evidence suggests that home visitation programs prevent child abuse and neglect, improve parenting skills, increase social and cognitive abilities of children, and reduce criminality among adolescents (Bilukha, Hahn et al., 2005). Additional studies assessing long-term indicators of aggression and violent conduct among older adolescents and young adults whose parents received home visitation interventions are needed.

Parent Training Programs

Several family-oriented parent training interventions have been successful in preventing or reducing antisocial conduct and violent behavior among children and youth. Family-based parent training programs place emphasis on the role parents play in the development and perpetuation of childhood and adolescent antisocial conduct. One important parent training model is based on a theory of *coercive family process* articulated by Patterson and colleagues (Dishion, Patterson, & Kavanagh, 1992; Patterson, Chamberlain, & Reid, 1982). Patterson and associates view the development of oppositional behavior and aggression in children as a direct function of inadequate parenting skills. The process begins when young children initiate social and behavioral demands on parents. Confronted with increasing child demands, parents with poor monitoring and supervision skills often make inconsistent decisions that reinforce a children's inappropriate requests. This in turn leads to a *coercive process* in which children learn to get their way by becoming more and more demanding of their parent's attention. The cycle is completed through the actions of frustrated parents who repeatedly give in to their children's requests in order to keep peace in the family environment. Unfortunately, when children enter school and make similar demands on teachers or peers they are often met with resistance or rejection.

Parent training interventions recognize that interrupting early patterns of poor parenting is critical to preventing conduct problems in young children. In such programs, parents are taught to develop effective supervision practices and behavioral strategies that are hypothesized to reduce oppositional and disruptive behaviors in children (Farrington & Welsh, 1999; Thomas & Zimmer-Gembeck, 2007; Webster-Stratton et al., 2004). Several programs have demonstrated significant effects in reducing behavioral problems in children including interventions developed and tested by Patterson and colleagues at the University of Oregon (Dishion et al., 1992; Patterson et al., 1982; Patterson, Reid, Jones, & Conger, 1975). Patterson identified five core parenting skills necessary to improve serious behavior problems in children. These skills are encouragement, limit-setting, monitoring and supervision, family problem-solving, and positive parent involvement. Tests of this model consistently reveal significant reductions in childhood disruptive behavior among experimental subjects compared with controls (e.g., Dishion et al., 1992).

The *Adolescents Transitions Program* (ATP) focuses on parent practices in relationship to the school performance and behavior of young adolescents (Dishion & Kavanagh, 2000; Dishion, Kavanagh, Schneiger, Nelson, & Kaufman, 2002; Dishion et al., 1992). An ecological framework is used to deliver multimodal interventions with increasing intensity as children age developmentally. Program components include school-based family resource rooms, professional support to parents whose children are experiencing academic and behavioral problems, and a structured curriculum designed to increase parent's skills in helping their children at school (Dishion et al., 1992). Evaluations of ATP indicate that the program is effective in reducing parent-child conflict, substance abuse, and antisocial conduct including aggressive behavior (e.g., Dishion et al., 1992, 2002).

Positive outcomes have also been reported in evaluative studies of the *Preventive Treatment Program* (PTP), an intervention that targets disruptive boys from low socioeconomic families with high levels of antisocial behavior in kindergarten (Tremblay, Vitaro, Bertrand, LeBlanc, Beauchesne, Bioleau, & David, 1992). PTP provides parent-training classes and school-based skills training sessions with children. Longitudinal analyses reveal that boys who receive the intensive multi-faceted treatment exhibit less aggression, higher academic performance, fewer difficulties in adjusting to school, and fewer delinquent acts than control group subjects (Begin, 1995; Tremblay, Masse, Pagani, & Vitaro, 1996).

Parent-Child Interaction Therapy (PCIT) developed by Eyberg and associates applies a behavioral approach to parent training that relies heavily on in-vivo coaching (Eyberg et al., 2008). The program seeks to strengthen parent-child attachment and decrease dysfunctional parent-child interactions by enhancing discipline skills (Herschell, Calzada, Eyberg, & McNeil, 2002). Didactic skills training sessions are followed by sessions in which therapists watch parent-child interactions from behind a one-way mirror. This intervention component is followed by extensive parent coaching through a device attached to a parent's ear (Thomas & Zimmer-Gembeck, 2007). At least one study noted that PCIT was superior to a control group in reducing disruptive behavior in children (Brinkmeyer & Eyberg, 2003).

The *Triple P-Positive Parenting Program* developed by Sanders and colleagues at the University of Queensland, Australia promotes positive parent-child relationships by enhancing parenting skills (Sanders, Markie-Dadds, Tully, & Bor, 2000; Thomas & Zimmer-Gembeck, 2007). The intervention can be delivered at five developmental levels depending on the intensity of problem symptoms displayed by youth. Several evaluations have yielded significant reductions in childhood disruptive behavior and aggression among experimental subjects compared with children placed in comparison or control groups (Martin & Sanders, 2003; Sanders & McFarland, 2000).

Webster-Stratton (2001) created the *Incredible Years* (IY) program to help children who display early signs of conduct disorders such as aggression and oppositional behaviors. The IY series includes curricula for parents, teachers, and children that seek to promote social and emotional efficacy and treat emotional problems in children in preschool and early elementary grades. We reviewed the efficacy of the school-based IY *Dinosaur* curriculum in the previous section. Importantly, the IY parenting program views parents as collaborators and builds on the strengths and expertise of family members. Controlled investigations of the IY have demonstrated the program's ability to increase parenting skills, prevent and reduce disruptive and aggressive behavior, and improve children's mental health functioning (Gardner, Burton, & Klimes, 2006; Hutchings, Bywater, Daley, Gardner, Whitaker, Jones, Eames, & Edwards, 2007; Jones, Daley, Hutchings, Bywater, & Eames, 2007; Webster-Stratton, 1998; Webster-Stratton, Hollingsworth, & Kolpacoff, 1989). Importantly, investigators have found that combined child and parent trainings are more effective than either the child or parent component alone (Webster-Stratton & Hammond, 1997).

The Strengthening Families Program for Parents and Youth 10-14 (SFP) aims to prevent aggression, delinquency, and substance abuse during adolescence by increasing parent's management skills and by improving interpersonal and personal competencies among youth. Parents and children attend separate skill-building groups and also spend time together in supervised family activities (Spoth, Redmond, & Shin, 1998). A controlled evaluation of SFP in Iowa indicated that youth participants experienced significantly less substance use, fewer conduct problems, and improved resistance to negative peer pressure than control subjects (Spoth, Redmond, & Shin, 2000). In addition, SFP parents were better able to show affection and support and to set appropriate limits for their children than control group parents (Molgaard, Spoth, & Redmond, 2000).

Guiding Good Choices (GGC) (formally called *Preparing for the Drug Free Years*) is a structured curriculum designed to help parents improve family management skills. Based on the social development model of antisocial conduct (Catalano & Hawkins, 1996), the program asserts that parents play an important role in reducing risk and increasing protection in the lives of their children. Family workshops provide education to parents and children about risk and protection and emphasize the importance of communicating positive attitudes to children. Additional program components seek to strengthen peer resistance, anger control, and relationship skills among parents and children. A randomized trial examining the effects of GGC on families and children in 33 public schools in Iowa revealed positive effects on family bonding, drug use, and delinquency among experimental subjects (Park, Kosterman, Hawkins, Haggerty, Duncan, Duncan, & Spoth, 2000).

Family-Focused Interventions with Individual Adolescents

Family-based violence prevention strategies also include interventions for children and youth who have already displayed aggressive behavior. For example, *Functional Family Therapy* (FFT) targets youth aged 11–18 with histories of delinquency, violence, and substance abuse (Alexander & Parsons, 1982). The intervention is based on social learning and systems theories and is applied in three phases, starting with engaging and motivating, then targeting behavior change, and then generalizing new skills to broader contexts. Controlled trials of the intervention have yielded significant reductions in delinquent and criminal behavior among experimental subjects (Sexton & Alexander, 2000). Importantly, FFT has worked effectively with young people from a variety of criminal and cultural backgrounds (Gordon, Graves, & Arbuthnot, 1995).

Multidimensional Family Therapy (MDFT) uses an ecological approach to decrease problem symptoms and promote healthy development in youth experiencing antisocial conduct such as aggression. MDFT clinicians conduct therapy with individual youth and family members, coordinate school services, and help families assess neighborhood risks and resources. Youth participating in MDFT evidence significantly less antisocial, delinquent, and drug using behaviors compared with young people in comparison groups. MDFT participants have also shown significant improvements in family competence and school functioning (Liddle, Dakof, Parker, Diamond, Barrett, & Tejeda, 2001; Liddle, Rowe, Dakof, Ungaro, & Henderson, 2004).

Multidimensional Treatment Foster Care (MTFC) targets aggressive, delinquent, and emotionally disturbed children and youth at risk of residential treatment, incarceration, or hospitalization (Chamberlain & Mihalic, 1998). Youth participating in MTFC are placed with families in the community who have received intensive training in parent management skills. In addition, the biological parents of participating youth attend skills training classes in preparation for their child's return home (Eddy, Whaley, & Chamberlain, 2004). Youth participating in MTFC evidence significantly less incarceration, fewer arrests, and less drug use than control subjects (Chamberlain & Smith, 2003). Girls in MTFC programs report significantly fewer days in locked settings and in caregiver-reported delinquency compared with girls in a control condition (Leve, Chamberlain, & Reid, 2005).

Brief Strategic Family Therapy (BSFT) uses principles from family system theory (Szapocznik & Williams, 2000) to teach practical problem-solving techniques for improving maladaptive family interaction processes. Controlled studies of BSFT with Hispanic families have yielded high engagement and retention rates and significant reductions in conduct problems, delinquency, and self-reported drug use (Coatsworth, Santisteban, McBride, & Szapocznik, 2001; Santisteban, Coatsworth, Perez-Vidal, Kurtines, Schwartz, LaPierriere, & Szapocznik, 2003).

Henggeler and colleagues have been implementing and testing a comprehensive, manualized intervention called *Multi-Systemic Therapy* (MST) since the early 1990s (Henggeler, Melton, & Smith, 1992; Henggeler, Mihalic, Rone, Thomas, & Timmons-Mitchell, 1998). MST is a multimodal intervention that addresses violent, delinquent, and substance abusing behaviors. Intervention is based on nine core principles that emphasize parental skill building, youth responsibility, and school and community involvement. Controlled trials of MST with samples of violent and chronic offenders reveal significant reductions in violent offense arrests and significantly lower self-reports of aggression and violent conduct among experimental subjects compared with controls (Borduin, Mann, Cone, Henggeler, Fucci, Blaske, & Williams, 1995; Henggeler, Clingempeel, Brondino, & Pickrel, 2002). Furthermore, follow-up studies as long as 14 years after MST participation reveal significantly lower arrest rates among experimental subjects compared with control subjects (Schaeffer & Borduin, 2005).

Summary of Family-Based Programs

Significant strides have been made in family-based violence prevention approaches in recent years. However, implementation and fidelity remain critical concerns in family-based programs targeting aggression and violence among children and youth. Age, gender, race, and ethnicity concerns are also important moderating factors to consider in family-based interventions.

Implementation and Intervention Fidelity

The implementation of family-based prevention programs involves a number of significant challenges. For example, studies show that parents with high levels of risk and low levels of protection – adults who are most likely to benefit from intervention - often do not seek services (Prinz & Sanders, 2007). Further, attrition rates are high among family members who do enroll in programs (Coatsworth et al., 2001; Hogue et al., 2002; Ikeda et al., 2001). Finally, many parents of youth at risk for violent behavior experience significant logistical, employment, and financial barriers that prevent them from participating fully in services.

Program fidelity associated with the implementation of family-based interventions presents another important challenge. Efficacious programs are often difficult to replicate in high-risk communities because local resources necessary to ensure intervention fidelity are limited or simply do not exist (Elliot & Mihalic, 2004). In other cases, program and agency administrators fail to understand the importance of ensuring fidelity when they adopt efficacious programs. These challenges are particularly difficult in the context of family-based prevention strategies because multiple individual needs as well as complex family dynamics must be addressed.

Age, Race, Ethnicity, and Gender

The age of onset for aggression is an important consideration when thinking about ways to advance family-based prevention strategies. Evidence suggests that aggression begins very early in life for some children. Thus, interventions such as the *Nurse Family Partnership* program that provide prenatal care to parents may hold the greatest promise for preventing aggressive behavior that may escalate to violence over time. Significantly, the *Nurse Family Partnership* demonstrated the most positive, long-term outcomes among all family programs reviewed. These results, coupled with the need to address aggression early in a child's development, suggest that home visitation programs should be expanded in the United States.

Parent training interventions, a second program category, are implemented with children and adolescents from preschool through high school graduation. As noted above, these programs vary in intensity and are often contingent on the level of risk, protection, and problem behavior evident in children. Parent training programs seek to change parenting practices while children are quite young. Thus, they provide a promising mechanism for producing positive and long-lasting changes in children. However, longitudinal studies are needed to assess the long-term impact of parent training on aggression and violence.

Family-focused interventions targeting older youth with demonstrated histories of behavior problems must also be available to combat aggression and violence. This review suggests that interventions with older adolescents can reduce or prevent further aggression and violence. However, additional research is necessary to measure the impact of these programs into adulthood.

The issue of how to best address race and ethnic differences in family-based programs is a critical question. To date, many programs have created standardized or manualized interventions that strive to be applicable to the broadest possible populations. Unfortunately, a number of investigators have noted that such programs are often based on white, middle class values that do not adequately consider important cultural differences in family structure and behavior (Acoca, 1999; Kumpfer et al., 2002). This is particularly important in the context of family-based interventions. Thus, more research is necessary to discern the effects of race and ethnicity on training strategies and outcomes such as antisocial conduct and violence.

There is very little discussion of gender effects in the context of family-based prevention programs (Acoca, 1999). The lack of attention to gender seems to be true for both the development of interventions and the evaluation of outcomes. This is somewhat surprising in view of recent evidence revealing an increase in the number of girls who are arrested for committing violent crimes (Snyder & Sickmund, 2006). Future studies should address the topic of program adaptation for girls and assess the long-term outcomes of girls who participate in controlled prevention trials.

In sum, family-based violence prevention strategies offer great promise in reducing childhood and adolescent aggression. Unique recruitment and implementation challenges, however, pose significant programmatic and logistical concerns that are less evident in school-based approaches. Practitioners, policy makers, and researchers should strive to solve these problems in an effort to advance the efficacy of family-based interventions. Community level violence prevention approaches are reviewed next.

COMMUNITY-BASED VIOLENCE PREVENTION

Risk, Protection, and Community Context

It is impossible to understand the onset or persistence of youth aggression and violence without assessing the influence of community-level risk factors on childhood and adolescent behavior. Numerous studies reveal a significant relationship between neighborhood and community characteristics and rates of delinquency, crime, and violence. Consequently, neighborhood and community characteristics that elevate risk for aggression and violence have been the subject of renewed research and policy attention in the past decade (e.g., Liberman, 2007).

Neighborhood and community characteristics associated with elevated levels of violence include a range of demographic, economic, and structural characteristics. For example, Sampson and colleagues have consistently shown that violence is more likely to occur in neighborhoods characterized by poverty and limited economic opportunity than in more affluent communities (Morenoff, Sampson, & Raudenbush, 2001; Sampson, Morenoff, & Gannon-Rowely, 2002). Community-level characteristics such as residential instability, high substance abuse rates, and low community participation are associated with violent behavior among young people (Proctor & Dalaker, 2003; Reiss & Roth, 1993). Children and youth growing up in disadvantaged neighborhoods also experience fewer economic resources and have a limited range of public and social services compared with youth in other neighborhoods (Sampson et al., 2002). These conditions lead to fewer opportunities for involvement in prosocial activities and, in turn, may elevate a young person's likelihood of becoming involved in violence and other forms of antisocial conduct.

Individual behaviors in neighborhoods and communities also influence youth violence. Results from the *Project on Human Development in Chicago Neighborhoods* reveal that adult behaviors in neighborhoods have a significant impact on adolescent violence (Liberman, 2007). Particularly salient is a finding from this Chicago-based longitudinal study of more than 6,000 young people indicating that witnessing or experiencing gun violence in the community significantly increases a young person's risk for committing serious violent acts during adolescence (Bingenheimer, Brennan, & Earls, 2005). Studies also show the importance of mentoring by adults – and the frequent unavailability of positive adult role models – for youth growing up in disadvantaged neighborhoods (e.g., Thornton, Craft, Dahlberg, Lynch, & Baer, 2002).

A limited number of investigations have identified community-level protective traits that buffer youth from involvement in aggressive and violent behavior. Laws and norms that promote limited access to handguns and weapons and high levels of community attachment and involvement are among the factors that appear to reduce risk and protect young people from violent conduct (e.g., Hawkins et al., 1998; Jenson & Fraser, 2006).

Effective Community-Based Prevention Approaches

Community approaches to preventing aggression and violent conduct among children and youth are frequently part of a comprehensive prevention approach that includes individual, school, and family strategies. In this sense, it is difficult to isolate community-level interventions from comprehensive strategies that target a range of individual, school, and family risk and protective factors associated with violence and other types of antisocial conduct. However, several specific community-level violence prevention strategies have been tested in the past decade. These strategies have yielded mixed or promising outcomes and include mass media campaigns to discourage aggression (e.g., Hausman, Spivak, & Prothrow-Stith, 1995; Pentz, Mares, Schinke, & Rohrbach, 2004; Perry, Kelder, Murray, & Klepp, 1992), mentoring interventions that link community members to high-risk youth (e.g., Cheng, Haynie, Brenner, Wright, Chung, & Simons-Morton, 2008), community policing (Office of Juvenile Justice & Delinquency Prevention, 2008), and after-school programs in high-risk neighborhoods (Anthony, Alter, & Jenson, 2009; Gottfredson, Gerstenblith, Soule, Worner, & Lu, 2004). Controlled trials of these approaches are needed to better inform the practice and policy community of the efficacy of community-level interventions.

A relatively new direction in community-level violence prevention stems from increased attention to what is commonly called translational research. In the context of prevention practice and science, the translation of research involves making practitioners and policy makers aware of effective school, family, and community intervention approaches. Translational research has also taken the form of creating *community prevention systems* that have the capacity to help community leaders identify and prevent child and youth problems such as youth violence in less controlled research environments. Notably, Hawkins (2006) describes efforts to use the *Communities That Care* (CTC) model developed by the Social Development Research Group at the University of Washington. CTC is a system that provides tools for communities to plan, implement, and evaluate a comprehensive community prevention plan. In the CTC model, coalitions are formed to engage in systematic prevention planning that requires communities to identify prevalent risk and protective factors for adolescent problems in their localities. Following the assessment of such factors, communities are encouraged to select prevention strategies on the basis of available empirical evidence (Hawkins & Catalano, 1992). Recent findings from a longitudinal study called the Community Youth Development Study, a randomized trial that uses principles of CTC, have revealed significantly lower rates of delinquency and drug use among students in experimental communities compared with control communities (Hawkins, Brown, Oesterle, Arthur, Abbot, & Catalano, 2008). These groundbreaking findings suggest that well-organized and implemented community planning efforts can lead to positive outcomes for young people. Hopefully, future analyses from the study will focus on indicators of youth violence. Translation efforts involving the application of findings from efficacy to community prevention systems are also being undertaken in Pennsylvania and Iowa (Spoth, Greenberg, Bierman, & Redmond, 2004).

Implications for Research, Practice, and Policy

As noted by Aisenberg and colleagues in Chapter 2, interpersonal violence is the product of daily interactions occurring in people's lives at individual, school, family, and community levels of influence. Our review, and earlier discussions by Williams, Bright, Herrenkohl,and colleagues found in Sections 1 and 2, illustrate that disentangling and organizing the salient risk and protective factors for violence as targets of intervention is a complicated and time-consuming endeavor. Given such complexity, it is encouraging to note that a number of well-designed and rigorously-tested school, family, and community prevention programs have demonstrated significant reductions in violence, aggression, bullying, and victimization. Yet a number of research, practice, and policy challenges related to preventing and reducing violent conduct among youth remain.

Implementing Effective Prevention Approaches

Empirical studies and anecdotal evidence indicate that a majority of public school districts and communities implement untested or ineffective prevention strategies (Elliott & Mihalic, 2004). Prevention curricula are often developed in response to local school district or community concerns and are seldom based on theory or empirical evidence. Evidence suggests that less than 30% of American schools implement tested or evidence-based prevention programs (Ringwalt, Ennett, Nincus, Thorne, Rohrbach, & Simmons-Rudolph, 2002). To maximize the effects of prevention approaches, practitioners should be encouraged to select and implement effective strategies.

Assessing Implementation Fidelity

Researchers interested in examining the effects of interventions are well acquainted with the problems associated with implementation fidelity. Implementation studies of prevention curricula show that high program fidelity is associated with positive outcomes for children and youth (Elliott & Mihalic, 2004). Inadequate training, limited resources, competing academic demands, classroom overcrowding, and insufficient time have been identified as persistent barriers to achieving high implementation in schools and communities (Botvin, 2004). Tailoring and Adapting Prevention Curricula for Racial and Ethnic Differences.

In Chapters 3 and 4, Williams, Bright, and colleagues note the importance of understanding racial, ethnic, and gender differences in both the onset and persistence of violence. It is critical that knowledge of such differential risks associated with violence be considered in the design of school, family, and community prevention programs. An important topic in this regard relates to program adaptation, the practice of modifying established curricula content to meet subgroup or local environmental needs.

Adaptation is a complex issue with two competing viewpoints. Critics of adaptation argue strongly that prevention content should be implemented with high levels of fidelity and should not be adapted for local conditions (Elliott & Mihalic, 2004). Advocates, however, cite evidence indicating that tailoring interventions actually increases efficacy for certain racial and ethnic subgroups (Ringwalt, Vincus, Ennett, Johnson, & Rohrbach, 2004). This evidence has been used as a rationale for adaptations that strive to meet the needs of particular groups. Given that cultural adaptation is common, the task for investigators and the field is how to accomplish adaptation while maintaining program fidelity. Backer (2001) and Castro et al. (2004) have developed approaches that seek to maintain the delicate balance between program fidelity and adaptation. The adaptation of prevention curricula is controversial, however, and little research exists to indicate how adaptations in established prevention curricula affect outcomes.

Summary

This review identifies a number of effective violence prevention programs. These programs should be considered by the nation's school administrators, family practitioners, community officials, elected representatives, and researchers. To be effective across settings, programs must be selected to match school, family, and community context and local needs and implemented with a high degree of fidelity. Funding efforts at the national, state, and local levels should prioritize violence prevention during early and middle childhood as an effective alternative to traditional forms of adolescent treatment and incarceration.

WEBSITES FOR VIOLENCE PREVENTION PROGRAMS

School-Based Prevention Programs

Early Risers http://www.findyouthinfo.gov/cf_pages/programdetail.cfm?id=320
Fast Track www.fasttrackproject.org
Good Behavior Game http://www.hazelden.org/web/public/pax.page
I Can Problem Solve http://www.thinkingpreteen.com/icps.htm
Incredible Years www.incredibleyears.com
Life Skills Training (LST) http://www.lifeskillstraining.com
Linking the Interests of Families and Teachers (LIFT) http://www.oslc.org/
    projects/popups-projects/link-family-teacher.html
Olweus Bullying Prevention Program http://www.hazelden.org/web/go/olweus
Promoting Alternative THinking Strategies (PATHS) http://www.channing-bete.
    com/prevention-programs/paths/
Seattle Social Development Project (SSDP) http://depts.washington.edu/ssdp/
Second Step http://www.cfchildren.org/programs/ssp/overview/
Steps to Respect http://www.cfchildren.org/programs/str/overview/
Youth Matters http://www.discoveryeducation.com/products/health/resources.cfm

Family-Based Prevention Programs

Adolescents Transitions Program http://www.strengtheningfamilies.org/html/
    programs
Brief Strategic Family Therapy http://www.brief-strategic-family-therapy.com/bsft
Functional Family Therapy http://www.fftinc.com/

Guiding Good Choices (GGC) http://www.channing-bete.com/prevention-programs/guiding-good-choices/

Incredible Years http://www.incredibleyears.com/

Multidimensional Family Therapy http://www.med.miami.edu/ctrada

Multidimensional Treatment Foster Care http://www.mtfc.com/

Multi-Systemic Therapy http://www.mstservices.com/

Nurse Family Partnership http://www.nursefamilypartnership.org/index.cfm?fuseaction=home

Parent Management Treatment Training (Oregon Social Learning Center) http://www.oslc.org/home.html

Preventive Treatment Program http://www.findyouthinfo.gov/cf_pages/programdetail.cfm

Parent-Child Interaction Therapy http://pcit.phhp.ufl.edu/

Strengthening Families for Program for Parents and Youth Ages 10-14 http://www.extension.iastate.edu/sfp/

Triple P – Positive Parenting Program http://www5.triplep.net/

REFERENCES

Acoca, L. (1999). Investing in girls: A 21st century strategy. *Juvenile Justice, 6,* 3–13.

Alexander, J. F., & Parsons, B. V. (1982). *Functional family therapy.* Monterey, CA: Brooks Cole.

Andrews, D. W., & Dishion, T. (1995). The adolescent transitions program for high-risk teens and their parents: Toward a school-based intervention. *Education and Treatment of Children, 18,* 478–491.

Anthony, E. K., Alter, C. A., & Jenson, J. M. (2009). Development of a risk and resilience-based out-of-school time program for children and youth. *Social Work, 54,* 45–55.

August, G. J., Hektner, J. M., Egan, E. A., Realmuto, G. M., & Bloomquist, M. L. (2002). The Early Risers longitudinal prevention trial: Examination of 3-year outcomes in aggressive children with intent-to-treat and as-intended analysis. *Psychology of Addictive Behaviors, 16,* S27–S39.

August, G. J., Lee, S. S., Bloomquist, M. L., Realmuto, G. M., & Hektner, J. M. (2004). Maintenance effects of an evidence-based prevention innovation for aggressive children living in culturally diverse urban neighborhoods: The Early Risers effectiveness study. *Journal of Emotional and Behavioral Disorders, 12,* 194–205.

August, G. J., Realmuto, G. M., Hektner, J. M., & Bloomquist, M. L. (2001). An integrated components preventive intervention for aggressive elementary school children: The Early Risers program. *Journal of Consulting and Clinical Psychology, 69,* 614–626.

Backer, T. E. (2001). *Finding the balance: Program fidelity and adaptation in substance abuse prevention: A state-of-the-art review.* Rockville, MD: Substance Abuse and Mental Health Services Administration, Center for Substance Abuse Prevention.

Begin, P. (1995). Delinquency prevention: The Montreal longitudinal-experimental study. Parliamentary Research Branch. Political and Social Affairs Division. http://dsp-psd.tpsgc.gc.ca/Collection-R/LoPBdP/MR/mr132-e.htm

Bilukha, O., Hahn, R. A., Crosby, A., Fullilove, M. T., Liberman, A., Moscicki, E., Snyder, S., Turna, F., Corso, P., Schofield, A., Briss, P., & Task Force on Community Preventive Services. (2005). The effectiveness of early childhood home visitation in preventing violence: A systematic review. *American Journal of Preventive Medicine, 28*, Supplement 1, 11–39.

Bingenheimer, J. B., Brennan, R. T., & Earls, F. J. (2005). Firearm violence exposure and serious violent behavior. *Science, 308*, 1323–1326.

Booth, C. L., Spieker, S. J., Barnard, K. E., & Morisset, C. E. (1992). In J. McCord & R. E. Tremblay (Eds.), *Preventing antisocial behavior: Interventions from birth through adolescence.* New York: Guilford Press.

Borduin, C. M., Mann, B. J., Cone, L. T., Henggeler, S. W., Fucci, B. R., Blaske, D. M., & Williams, R. A. (1995). Multisystemic treatment of serious juvenile offenders: Long-term prevention of criminality and violence. *Journal of Consulting and Clinical Psychology, 63*, 569–578.

Botvin, G. J. (2004). Advancing prevention science and practice: Challenges, critical issues, and future directions. *Prevention Science, 5*, 69–72.

Botvin, G. J., & Griffin, K. W. (2004). Life Skills training: Empirical findings and future directions. *The Journal of Primary Prevention, 25B*, 211–232.

Botvin, G. J., Griffin, K. W., Diaz, T., & Ifill-Williams, M. (2001). Drug abuse prevention among minority adolescents: Posttest and one-year follow-up of a school-based preventive intervention. *Prevention Science, 2*, 1–13.

Botvin, G. J., Griffin, K. W., & Nichols, T. D. (2006). Preventing youth violence and delinquency through a universal school-based prevention approach. *Prevention Science, 7*, 403–408.

Boyle, D., & Hassert-Walker, C. (2008). Reducing overt and relational aggression among young children: The results from a two-year outcome evaluation. *Journal of School Violence, 7*, 27–42.

Brinkmeyer, M. Y., & Eyberg, S. M. (2003). Parent-child interaction therapy for oppositional children. In A. E. Kazdin & J. R. Weisz (Eds.), *Evidenced-based psychotherapies for children and adolescents* (pp. 204–223). New York: Guilford.

Castro, F. G., Barrera, M., & Martinez, C. R. (2004). The cultural adaptation of prevention interventions: Resolving tensions between fidelity and fit. *Prevention Science, 5*, 41–45.

Catalano, R. F., & Hawkins, J. D. (1996). The social development model: A theory of antisocial behavior. In J. D. Hawkins (Ed.), *Delinquency and crime: Current theories* (pp. 149–197). Cambridge: Cambridge University Press.

Centers for Disease Control and Prevention. (2008). Youth risk behavior surveillance: United States, 2007. *Morbidity and Mortality Weekly Report, 57*, 1–131.

Chamberlain, P., & Mihalic, S. F. (1998). Multidimensional treatment foster care. In D. S. Elliott (Ed.), *Book eight: Blueprints for violence prevention.* Boulder: Institute of Behavioral Science, University of Colorado at Boulder.

Chamberlain, P., & Smith, D. K. (2003). Antisocial behavior in children and adolescents: The Oregon Multidimensional Treatment Foster Care model. In A. E. Kazdin & J. R. Weisz (Eds.), *Evidence-based psychotherapies for children and adolescents* (pp. 282–300). New York: Guilford.

Cheng, T. L., Haynie, D., Brenner, R., Wright, J. L., Chung, S. E., & Simons-Morton, B. (2008). Effectiveness of a mentor-implemented, violence prevention intervention for assault-injured youths presenting to the emergency department: Results from a randomized trial. *Pediatrics, 122*, 938–946.

Coatsworth, J. D., Santisteban, D. A., McBride, C. K., & Szapocznik, J. (2001). Brief strategic family therapy versus community control: Engagement, retention, and an exploration of the moderating role of the adolescent symptom severity. *Family Process, 40,* 313–332.

Conduct Problems Prevention Research Group. (1999a). Initial impact of the Fast Track prevention trial for conduct problems: I. The high-risk sample. *Journal of Consulting and Clinical Psychology, 67,* 631–647.

Conduct Problems Prevention Research Group. (1999b). Initial impact of the Fast Track prevention trial for conduct problems: II. Classroom effects. *Journal of Consulting and Clinical Psychology, 67,* 648–657.

Conduct Problems Prevention Research Group. (2002a). The implementation of the Fast Track program: An example of a large-scale prevention science efficacy trial. *Journal of Abnormal Child Psychology, 30,* 1–17.

Conduct Problems Prevention Research Group. (2002b). Evaluation of the first 3 years of the Fast Track prevention trial with children at high risk for adolescent conduct problems. *Journal of Abnormal Child Psychology, 30,* 19–35.

Conduct Problems Prevention Research Group. (2002c). Predictor variables associated with positive Fast Track outcomes at the end of third grade. *Journal of Abnormal Child Psychology, 30,* 37–52.

Conduct Problems Prevention Research Group. (2004). The effects of the Fast Track program on serious problem outcomes at the end of elementary school. *Journal of Clinical Child and Adolescent Psychiatry, 33,* 650–661.

Cooke, M. B., Ford, J., Levine, J., Bourke, C., Newell, L., & Lapidus, G. (2007). The effects of city-wide implementation of Second Step on elementary school students' prosocial and aggressive behaviors. *The Journal of Primary Prevention, 28,* 93–115.

Crick, N. R., Bigbee, M. A., & Howes, C. (1996). Gender differences in children's normative beliefs about aggression: How do I hurt thee? Let me count the ways. *Child Development, 67,* 1003–1014.

Dishion, T. J., & Kavanaugh, K. (2000). A multilevel approach to family-centered prevention in schools: Process and outcome. *Addictive Behaviors, 25,* 899–911.

Dishion, T. J., Kavanagh, K., Schneiger, A., Nelson, S., & Kaufman, N. K. (2002). Preventing early adolescent substance use: A family-centered strategy for the public middle school. *Prevention Science, 3,* 191–201.

Dishion, T. J., Patterson, G. R., & Kavanagh, K. (1992). An experimental test of the coercion model: Linking theory, measurement, and intervention. In J. McCord & R. Trembley (Eds.), *The interaction of theory and practice: Experimental studies of interventions* (pp. 253–282). New York: Guilford.

Domitrovich, C., Cortes, R., & Greenberg, M. (2007). Improving young children's social and emotional competence: A randomized trial of the preschool 'PATHS' curriculum. *Journal of Primary Prevention, 28,* 67–91.

Eddy, J. M., Reid, J. B., & Fetrow, R. A (2000). An elementary school-based prevention program targeting antecedents of youth delinquency and violence: Linking the Interests of Families and Teachers (LIFT). *Journal of Emotional and Behavioral Disorders, 8,* 165–176.

Eddy, J. M., Reid, J. B., Stoolmiller, M., & Fetrow, R. A. (2003). Outcomes during middle school for an elementary school-based preventive intervention for conduct problems: Follow-up results from a randomized trial. *Behavior Therapy, 34,* 535–552.

Eddy, J. M., Whaley, R. B., & Chamberlain, P. (2004). The prevention of violent behavior by chronic and serious male juvenile offenders: A 2-year follow-up of a randomized clinical trial. *Journal of Emotional & Behavioral Disorders, 12,* 2–8.

Elliott, D. S., & Mihalic, S. (2004). Issues in disseminating and replicating effective prevention programs. *Prevention Science, 5,* 47–53.

Embry, D. D. (2002). The Good Behavior Game: A best practice candidate as a universal behavioral vaccine. *Clinical Child and Family Psychology Review, 5,* 273–297.

Eyberg, S. M., Nelson, M. M., & Bogs, S. R. (2008). Evidence-based psychosocial treatments for children and adolescents with disruptive behavior. *Journal of Clinical Child and Adolescent Psychology, 37,* 215–237.

Farrell, A. D., & Camou, S. (2006). School-based interventions for youth violence prevention. In J. R. Lutzker (Ed.), *Preventing violence: Research and evidence-based intervention strategies* (pp. 125–145). Washington, DC: American Psychological Association.

Farrington, D. P., & Welsh, B. C. (1999). Delinquency prevention using family-based interventions. *Children & Society, 13,* 287–303.

Frey, K., Hirschstein, M., & Guzzo, B. (2000). Second Step: Preventing aggression by promoting social competence. *Journal of Emotional and Behavioral Disorders, 8,* 102–112.

Frey, K. S., Hirschstein, M. K., Snell, J. L., Edstrom, L. V., MacKenzie, E. P., & Broderick, C. J. (2005). Reducing playground bullying and supporting beliefs: An experimental trial of the Steps to Respect program. *Developmental Psychology, 41,* 479–491.

Frey, K. S., Nolen, S. B., Edstrom, L. V., & Hirschstein, M. K. (2005). Effects of a school-based social-emotional competence program: Linking children's goals, attributions, and behavior. *Journal of Applied Developmental Psychology, 26,* 171–200.

Gardner, F., Burton, J., & Klimes, I. (2006). Randomized controlled trial of a parenting intervention in the voluntary sector for reducing child conduct problems: Outcomes and mechanisms of change. *Journal of Child Psychology and Psychiatry, 47,* 1123–1132.

Gordon, D. A., Graves, K., & Arbuthnot, J. (1995). The effect of functional family therapy for delinquents on adult criminal behavior. *Criminal Justice and Behavior, 22,* 60–73.

Gottfredson, D. C., Gerstenblith, S. A., Soule, D. A., Worner, S. C., & Lu, S. (2004). Do afterschool programs reduce delinquency? *Prevention Science, 5,* 253–266.

Gottfredson, D. C., & Wilson, D. B. (2003). Characteristics of effective school-based substance abuse prevention. *Prevention Science, 4,* 27–38.

Greenberg, M. T. (2004). Current and future challenges in school-based prevention: The researcher perspective. *Prevention Science, 5,* 5–13.

Greenberg, M. T., Kusché, C. A., Cook, E. T., & Quamma, J. P. (1995). Promoting emotional competence in school-aged children: The effects of the PATHS curriculum. *Development and Psychopathology, 7,* 117–136.

Hahn, R., Fuqua-Whitley, D., Wethington, H., Lowy, J., Crosby, A., Fullilove, M., et al. (2007). Effectiveness of universal school-based programs to prevent violent and aggressive behavior. *American Journal Preventive Medicine, 33,* S114–S129.

Hausman, A. J., Spivak, H., & Prothrow-Stith, D (1995). Evaluation of a community-based youth violence prevention project. *Journal of Adolescent Health, 17,* 353–359.

Hawkins, J. D. (2006). Science, social work, prevention: Finding the intersections. *Social Work Research,* 137–152.

Hawkins, J. D., Brown, E. C., Oesterle, S., Arthur, M. W., Abbot, R. D., & Catalano, R. F. (2008). Early effects of Communities that Care on targeted risks and initiation of delinquent behavior and substance use. *Journal of Adolescent Health, 43,* 15–22.

Hawkins, J. D., & Catalano, R. F. (1992). *Communities that Care: Actions for drug abuse prevention.* San Francisco: Jossey-Boss.

Hawkins, J. D., Catalano, R. F., Kosterman, R., Abbott, R., & Hill, K. G. (1999). Preventing adolescent health-risk behaviors by strengthening protection during childhood. *Archives of Pediatric Adolescent Medicine, 153,* 226–234.

Hawkins, J. D., Herrenkohl, T., Farrington, D. P., Brewer, D., Catalano, R. F., & Harachi, T. W. (1998). A review of predictors of youth violence. In R. Loeber & D. P. Farrington (Eds.), *Serious and violent juvenile offenders: Risk factors and successful interventions* (pp. 106–146). Thousand Oaks, CA: Sage.

Hawkins, J. D., Kosterman, R., Catalano, R. F., Hill, K. G., & Abbott, R. D. (2005). Promoting positive adult functioning through social development intervention in childhood: Long-term effects from the Seattle Social Development Project. *Archives of Pediatrics and Adolescent Medicine, 159,* 25–31.

Hawkins, J. D., Smith, B. H., Hill, K. G., Kosterman, R., Catalano, R. F., & Abbott, R. D. (2007). Promoting social development and preventing health and behavior problems during the elementary grades: Results from the Seattle Social Development Project. *Victims & Offenders, 2,* 161–181.

Hawkins, J. D., Von Cleve, E., & Catalano, R. F. (1991). Reducing early child-hood aggression: Results of a primary prevention program. *Journal American Academy Child Adolescent Psychiatry, 30,* 208–217.

Haynie, D. L., Nansel, T., Eitel, P., Crump, A. D., Saylor, K., Yu, K., & Simons-Morton, B. (2001). Bullies, victims, and bully/victims: Distinct groups of at-risk youth. *Journal of Early Adolescence, 21,* 29–49.

Henggeler, S. W., Clingempeel, W. G., Brondino, M. J., & Pickrel, S. G. (2002). Four-year follow-up of multisystemic therapy with substance-abusing and substance-dependent juvenile offenders. *Journal of the American Academy of Child and Adolescent Psychiatry, 41,* 868–874.

Henggeler, S. W., Melton, G. B., & Smith, L. A. (1992). Family preservation using multisystemic therapy: An effective alternative to incarcerating serious juvenile offenders. *Journal of Consulting and Clinical Psychology, 60,* 953–961.

Henggeler, S. W., Mihalic, S. F., Rone, L., Thomas, C., & Timmons-Mitchell, J. (1998). *Multisystemic therapy: Blueprints for violence prevention, book six.* Blueprints for Violence Prevention Series (D. S. Elliott, Series Editor). Boulder: Center for the Study and Prevention of Violence, Institute of Behavioral Science, University of Colorado.

Herrenkohl, T. I., Chung, I. J., & Catalano, R. F. (2004). Review of research on predictors of youth violence and school-based and community-based prevention approaches. In P. Allen-Meares & M. W. Fraser (Eds.), *Intervention with children and adolescents: An interdisciplinary perspective* (pp. 449–476). Boston: Pearson Education Inc.

Herschell, A. D., Calzada, E. J., Eyberg, S. M., & McNeil, C. B. (2002). Parent-child interaction therapy: New directions in research. *Cognitive and Behavioral Practice, 9,* 9–16.

Hogue, A., Liddle, H. A., Becker, D., & Johnson-Leckrone, J. (2002). Family-based prevention counseling for high-risk young adolescents: Immediate outcomes. *Journal of Community Psychology, 30,* 1–22.

Hutchings, J., Bywater, T., Daley, D. Gardner, F., Whitaker, C., Jones, K., Eames, C., & Edwards, R. T. (2007). Parenting intervention in Sure Start services for children at risk of developing conduct disorder: Pragmatic randomised controlled trial. *British Medical Journal, 33,* 678–682.

Ikeda, R. M., Simon, T. R., & Swahn, M. (2001). The prevention of youth violence: The rationale for and characteristics of four evaluation projects. *American Journal of Preventative Medicine, 20,* 15–21.

Jenson, J. M., & Dieterich, W. A. (2007). Effects of a skills-based prevention program on bullying and bully victimization among elementary school children. *Prevention Science, 8,* 285–296.

Jenson, J. M., Dieterich, W. A., Rinner, J. R., Washington, F., & Burgoyne, K. (2006). Implementation and design issues in group-randomized prevention trials: Lessons from the *Youth Matters* public schools study. *Children and Schools, 28,* 207–218.

Jenson, J. M., & Fraser, M. W. (2006). *Social policy for children and families: A risk and resilience perspective.* Thousand Oaks, CA: Sage Publications.

Jenson, J. M., & Howard, M. O. (1999). *Youth violence. Current research and recent practice innovations.* Washington, DC: NASW Press.

Jones, K., Daley, D., Hutchings, J., Bywater, T., & Eames, C. (2007). Efficacy of the Incredible Years basic parent training program as an early intervention for children with conduct problems and ADHD. *Child Care Health Development, 33,* 749–756.

Kam, C., Greenberg, M. T., & Kusché, C. A. (2004). Sustained effects of the PATHS curriculum on the social and psychological adjustment of children in special education. *Journal of Emotional and Behavioral Disorders, 12,* 66–78.

Kellam, S. G., & Anthony, J. C. (1998). Targeting early antecedents to prevent tobacco smoking: Findings from an epidemiologically based randomized field trial. *American Journal of Public Health, 88,* 1490–1495.

Kellam, S. G., Brown, C. H., Poduska, J. M., Ialongo, N. S., Wang, W., Toyinbo, P., et al. (2008). Effects of a universal classroom behavior management program in first and second grades on young adult behavioral, psychiatric, and social outcomes. *Drug and Alcohol Dependence, S95,* S5–S28.

Kellam, S. G., Werthamer-Larsson, L., Dolan, L. J., Brown, C. H., Mayer, L. S., Rebok, G. W., et al. (1991). Developmental epidemiologically based preventive trials: Baseline modeling of early target behaviors and depressive symptoms. *American Journal of Community Psychology, 19,* 563–584.

Kumpfer, K. L., Alvarado, R., Smith, P., & Bellamy, N. (2002). Cultural sensitivity and adaptation in family-based prevention interventions. *Prevention Science, 3,* 241–246.

Leve, L. D., Chamberlain, P., & Reid, J. B. (2005). Intervention outcomes for girls referred from juvenile justice: Effects on delinquency. *Journal of Consulting and Clinical Psychology, 73,* 1181–1185.

Liberman, A. (2007). Adolescents, neighborhoods, and violence: Recent findings from the Project on Human Development in Chicago Neighborhoods. *Research in Brief.* Washington, DC: U.S. Department of Justice.

Liddle, H. A., Dakof, G. A., Parker, K., Diamond, G. S., Barrett, K., & Tejeda, M. (2001). Multidimensional family therapy for adolescent substance abuse: Results of a randomized clinical trial. *American Journal of Drug and Alcohol Abuse, 27,* 651–687.

Liddle, H. A., Rowe, C. L., Dakof, G. A., Ungaro, R. A., & Henderson, C. (2004). Early intervention for adolescent substance abuse: Pretreatment to post-treatment outcomes of a randomized controlled trial comparing multidimensional family therapy and peer group treatment. *Journal of Psychoactive Drugs, 36,* 2–37.

Limbos, M. A., Chan, L. S., Warf, C., Schneir, A., Iverson, E., Shekelle, P., & Kipke, M. D. (2007). Effectiveness of interventions to prevent youth violence. A systematic review. *American Journal of Preventive Medicine, 33,* 65–74.

Molgaard, V., Spoth, R., & Redmond, C. (2000). Competency training—The Strengthening Families Program: For parents and youth 10–14. *Juvenile Justice Bulletin.* Washington, DC: U.S. Department of Justice, Office of Justice Programs, Office of Juvenile Justice and Delinquency Prevention.

Morenoff, J. D., Sampson, R. J., & Raudenbush, S. W. (2001). Neighborhood inequality, collective efficacy, and spatial dynamics of urban violence. *Criminology, 39,* 517–559.

O'Donnell, J., Hawkins, J. D., Catalano, R. F., Abbot, R. D., & Day, E. (1995). Preventing school failure, drug use, and delinquency among low-income children: Long-term intervention in elementary schools. *American Journal of Orthopsychiatry, 65,* 87–100.

Office of Juvenile Justice and Delinquency Prevention. (2008). *Best practices to address community gang problems.* U.S. Department of Justice, Washington, DC

Olds, D. L., Sadler, L., & Kitzman, H. (2007). Programs for parents and infants and toddlers: Recent evidence from randomized trials. *Journal of Child Psychology and Psychiatry, 48,* 355–391.

Olds, D., Henderson, C. R., Cole, R., Eckenrode, J., Kitzman, H., Luckey, D., Pettitt, L., Sidora, K., Morris, P., & Powers, J. (1998). Long-term effects of nurse home visitation on children's criminal and antisocial behavior: 15-Year follow-up of a randomized controlled trial. *JAMA, 280,* 1238–1244.

Olweus, D. (1993). *Bullying at school.* Cambridge, MA: Blackwell.

Park, J., Kosterman, R., Hawkins, J. D., Haggerty, K. P., Duncan, T. E., Duncan, S. C., & Spoth, R. (2000). Effects of the *Preparing for the Drug Free Years* curriculum on growth in alcohol use and risk for alcohol use in early adolescence. *Prevention Science, 1,* 125–138.

Patterson, G. R., Chamberlain, P., & Reid, J. B. (1982). A comparative evaluation of a parent-training program. *Behavior Therapy, 13,* 638–650.

Patterson, G. R., Reid, J. B., Jones, R. R., & Conger, R. E. (1975). *A social learning approach to family intervention: Families with aggressive children* (Vol. I). Eugene, OR: Castalia.

Pentz, M. A., Mares, D., Schinke, S., & Rohrbach, L. (2004). Political science, public policy, and drug use prevention. *Substance Use & Misuse, 39,* 1821–1865.

Perry, C. L., Kelder, S. H., Murray, D. M., & Klepp, K. I. (1992). Community-wide smoking prevention: Long-term outcomes of the Minnesota Heart

Health Program and the Class of 1989 Study. *American Journal of Public Health, 82,* 1210–1216.

Prinz, R. J., & Sanders, M. R. (2007). Adopting a population approach to parenting and family support interventions. *Clinical Psychology Review, 27,* 739–749.

Proctor, B. D., & Dalaker, J. (2003). *Poverty in the United States: 2002.* U.S. Census Bureau, Current Population Reports, P60-222. Washington, DC: U.S. Government Printing Office.

Reid, J. B., Eddy, J. M., Fetrow, R. A., & Stoolmiller, M. (1999). Description and immediate impacts of a preventative intervention for conduct problems. *American Journal of Community Psychology, 27,* 483–517.

Reiss, A. J., & Roth, J. A. (1993). *Understanding and preventing violence* (Vol. 1). Washington, DC: National Academies Press.

Ringwalt, C. L., Ennett, S., Vincus, A., Thorne, J., Rohrbach, L. A., & Simmons-Rudolph, A. (2002). The prevalence of effective substance use prevention curricula in U.S. middle schools. *Prevention Science, 3,* 257–265.

Ringwalt, C. L., Vincus, A., Ennett, S., Johnson, R., & Rohrbach, L. A. (2004). Reasons for teachers' adaptation of substance use prevention curricula in schools with non-white student populations. *Prevention Science, 5,* 61–67.

Sampson, R. J., Morenoff, J. D., & Gannon-Rowely, T. (2002). Assessing neighborhood effects: Social processes and new directions in research. *Annual Review of Sociology, 28,* 443–478.

Sanders, M. R., Markie-Dadds, C., Tully, L. A., & Bor, W. (2000). The Triple P-Positive Parenting Program: A comparison of enhanced, standard, and self-directed behavioral family intervention for parents of children with early onset conduct problems. *Journal of Consulting and Clinical Psychology, 68,* 624–640.

Sanders, M. R., & McFarland, M. (2000). Treatment of depressed mothers with disruptive children: A controlled evaluation of a cognitive-behavioral family intervention. *Behavior Therapy, 31,* 89–112.

Santisteban, D. A., Coatsworth, J. D., Perez-Vidal, A., Kurtines, W. M., Schwartz, S. J., LaPierriere, A., & Szapocznik, J. (2003). Efficacy of brief strategic family therapy in modifying Hispanic adolescent behavior problems and substance use. *Journal of Family Psychology, 17,* 121–133.

Schaeffer, C. M., & Borduin, C. M. (2005). Long-term follow-up to a randomized clinical trial of multisystemic therapy with serious and violent juvenile offenders. *Journal of Consulting and Clinical Psychology, 73,* 445–453.

Schuhmann, E. M., Foote, R. C, Eyberg, S., Boggs, S. R., Algina, J. (1998). Efficacy of parent-child interaction therapy: Interim report of a randomized trial with short-term maintenance. *Journal of Clinical Child & Adolescent Psychology, 27*(1), 34–45.

Sexton, T. L., & Alexander, J. F (December, 2000). Functional family therapy. Office of Juvenile Justice and Delinquency Prevention. *Juvenile Justice Bulletin,* 3–7.

Sexton, T. L., & Alexander, J. F. (2003). Functional family therapy: A mature clinical model of working with at-risk adolescents and their families. In T. L. Sexton, G. R. Weeks, & M. S. Robbins (Eds.), *Handbook of family therapy* (pp. 323–348). New York: Taylor & Francis.

Shure, M. B., & Spivack, G. (1980). Interpersonal problem solving as a mediator of behavioral adjustment in pre-school and kindergarten children. *Journal of Applied Developmental Psychology, 1,* 29–44.

Shure, M. B., & Spivack, G. (1982). Interpersonal problem-solving in young children: A cognitive approach to prevention. *American Journal of Community Psychology, 10*, 341–356.

Smith, N., & Landreth, G. (2003). Intensive filial therapy with child witnesses of domestic violence: A comparison with individual and sibling group play therapy. *International Journal of Play Therapy, 12*, 67–88.

Snyder, H. N., & Sickmund, M. (2006). *Juvenile offenders and victims: 2006 National report.* Washington, DC: U.S. Department of Justice, Office of Justice Programs, Office of Juvenile Justice and Delinquency Prevention.

Solberg, M. E., Olweus, D., & Endresen, I. M. (2007). Bullies and victims at school: Are they the same pupils? *British Journal of Educational Psychology, 77*, 441–464.

Sorenson, J. L., Masson, C. L., & Perlman, D. C. (2002). HIV/hepatitis prevention in drug abuse treatment programs: Guidance from research. *NIDA Science and Practice Perspectives, 1*, 4–12. Washington, DC: National Institute on Drug Abuse.

Spoth, R., Greenberg, M., Bierman, K., & Redmond, C. (2004). PROSPER community–university partnership model for public education systems: Capacity-building for evidence-based, competence-building prevention. *Prevention Science, 5*, 31–39.

Spoth, R., Redmond, C., & Shin, C. (1998). Direct and indirect latent-variable parenting outcomes of two universal family-focused preventive interventions: Extending a public health-oriented research base. *Journal of Consulting and Clinical Psychology, 66*, 385–399.

Spoth, R. L., Redmond, C., & Shin, C. (2000). Reducing adolescents' aggressive and hostile behaviors: Randomized trial effects of a brief family intervention 4 years past baseline. *Archives of Pediatrics and Adolescent Medicine, 154*(12), 1248–1257.

Stoolmiller, M., Eddy, J. M., & Reid, J. B. (2000). Detecting and describing preventive intervention effects in a universal school-based randomized trial targeting delinquent and violent behavior. *Journal of Consulting and Clinical Psychology, 68*, 296–306.

Szapocnik, J., & Williams, R. A. (2000). Brief strategic family therapy: Twenty-five years of interplay among theory, research, and practice in adolescent behavior problems and drug abuse. *Clinical Child and Family Psychology Review, 3*, 117–134.

Tobler, N. S. (1992). Drug prevention programs can work: Research findings. *Journal of Addictive Diseases, 11*, 1–28.

Thomas, R., & Zimmer-Gembeck, M. J. (2007). Behavior outcomes of parent-child interaction therapy and Triple P–Positive Parenting Program: A review and meta-analysis. *Journal of Abnormal Psychology, 35*, 475–495.

Thornton, T. N., Craft, C. Q., Dahlberg, L. L., Lynch, B. S., & Baer, K. (2002). *Best practices of youth violence prevention: A sourcebook for community action.* Atlanta, CA: Centers for Disease Control and Prevention.

Tremblay, R. E., Masse, L., Pagani, L., & Vitaro, F. (1996). From childhood physical aggression to adolescent maladjustment: The Montreal Prevention Experiment. In R. D. Peters & R. J. McMahon (Eds.), *Preventing childhood disorders, substance abuse, and delinquency* (pp. 268–298). Thousand Oaks, CA: Sage Publications.

Tremblay, R. E., Vitaro, F., Bertrand, L., LeBlanc, M., Beauchesne, H., Bioleau, H., & David, L. (1992). Parent and child training to prevent early onset of delinquency: The Montreal Longitudinal Experimental Study. In J. McCord & R. E. Tremblay (Eds.), *Preventing antisocial behavior: Interventions from birth through adolescence* (pp. 117–138). New York: The Guilford Press.

Vossekull, B., Fein, R. A., Reddy, M., Borum, R., & Modseleski, W. (2002). *The final report and findings of the Safe School Initiative: Implications for the prevention of school attacks in the United States.* Washington, DC: U.S. Secret Service and U.S. Department of Education.

Webster-Stratton, C. (1998). Preventing conduct problems in Head Start children: Strengthening parent competencies. *Journal of Consulting and Clinical Psychology, 66,* 715–730.

Webster-Stratton, C. (2001). The Incredible Years: Parents, teachers, and children training series, *Residential Treatment for Children & Youth, 18,* 31–45.

Webster-Stratton, C., & Hammond, M. (1997). Treating children with early-onset conduct problems: A comparison of child and parent training interventions. *Journal of Clinical and Consulting Psychology, 65,* 93–109.

Webster-Stratton, C., Hollingsworth, T., & Kolpacoff, M (1989). The long-term effectiveness and clinical significance of three cost-effective training programs for families with conduct problem children. *Journal of Counseling and Clinical Psychology, 57,* 550–553.

Webster-Stratton, C., & Reid, J. (2003). Treating conduct problems and strengthening social and emotional competence in young children: The Dina Dinosaur treatment program. *Journal of Emotional and Behavioral Disorders, 11,* 130–143.

Webster-Stratton, C., Reid, J., & Hammond, M. (2001). Social skills and problem-solving training for children with early-onset conduct problems: Who benefits? *Journal of Child Psychology and Psychiatry and Allied Disciplines, 42,* 943–952.

Webster-Stratton, C., Reid, J., & Hammond, M. (2004). Treating children with early-onset conduct problems: Intervention outcomes for parent, child, and teacher training. *Journal of Clinical Child and Adolescent Psychology, 33,* 105–124.

Webster-Stratton, C., Reid, M. J., & Hammond, M. (2001). Preventing conduct problems, promoting social competence: A parent and teacher training partnership in Head Start. *Journal of Clinical Child Psychology, 30,* 283–302.

Webster-Stratton, C., Reid, M. J., & Stoolmiller, M. (2008). Preventing conduct problems and improving school readiness: Evaluation of the Incredible Years teacher and child training programs in high-risk schools. *Journal of Child Psychology and Psychiatry, 49,* 471–488.

Wells, K. C., & Egan, J. (1988). Social learning and systems family therapy for childhood oppositional disorder: Comparative treatment outcome. *Comprehensive Psychiatry, 29,* 138–146.

Wilson, S. J., & Lipsey, M. W. (2007). School-based interventions for aggressive and disruptive behavior: Update of a meta-analysis. *American Journal of Preventive Medicine, 33,* S130–S143.

Wilson, S. J., Lipsey, M. W., & Derzon, J. H. (2003). The effects of school-based intervention programs on aggressive behavior: A meta-analysis. *Journal of Consulting and Clinical Psychology, 71,* 136–149.

V

FUTURE CONSIDERATIONS FOR THE STUDY AND PREVENTION OF VIOLENCE

9

CULTURE, INTERSECTIONALITY, AND INTERRELATEDNESS OF FORMS OF VIOLENCE

Considerations in the Study of Violence and Violence Prevention

EUGENE AISENBERG, GITA MEHROTRA,
AMELIA GAVIN, & JENNIFER BOWMAN

This final section of the book returns to several of the fundamental issues raised in Chapter 2 about the conceptualization of violence, focusing particularly, in Chapter 9, on issues of culture, inequality, and power as they relate to the study of violence. Chapter 9 also continues discussion of gender and ethnicity, along with other "social identities," seeking to draw these issues closer together toward a better understanding of the different facets and meanings of violence. The goal is to refocus attention on topics that are often at the periphery of scholarly discussions about violence and that rarely enter discussion about prevention—forging a new paradigm for the field that leads with a very direct and forthright discussion of the role of oppression, dislocation, and discrimination experienced by groups within the larger population.

Chapter 10 offers several concluding remarks, pulling forward several important themes of the previous chapters and emphasizing next steps in research and practice. The authors again touch on the need for integrated models of violence etiology and applications in the field that can bring about lasting changes.

Previous chapters have highlighted aspects of context in the study of violence with respect to risk factors, protective factors, and outcomes of violence exposure in children. Authors also summarize important findings on prevention and intervention programs. Research across all areas has increased what we know about violence and how it can be addressed through planned interventions. However, fundamental questions remain about the nature of violence and its root causes, how violence is perceived, and how it is conceptualized and understood in research and practice. Also, as discussed throughout the book, gender and ethnicity are important variables that help shape the context of violence. Yet, the roles of gender, ethnicity, and other social identities in the etiology and prevention of violence remain only partly understood. Issues of culture, oppression, and discrimination also require further elucidation and analysis to arrive at a more complete understanding of violence in context.

In this chapter, we seek to highlight the role of culture in framing an individual's beliefs and understanding of violence. We also discuss issues of structural inequality, social power, and dominance of one group over others and the ways in which these factors perpetuate violence at a societal level. We posit the need for multidimensional conceptualizations of violence that take into account the salience of culture and the intersection of identity categories, such as gender, age, race, class, religion, sexual orientation, immigration history, and poverty. Rather than frame gender and ethnicity as demographic variables and view them as each intersecting with violence in a discrete manner, as is the prevailing approach of most studies, we understand gender and ethnicity as intersecting with one another, with other social identities, and with culture. Finally, we discuss the interrelatedness of various forms of violence and the link between violence and power. It is our aim to begin to center these crucial considerations that often have been neglected or minimized in the study of violence. By contextualizing violence in this manner, we seek a fundamental shift in paradigm for the field of violence. Additionally, we seek to provide a foundation for further research and practice that will help stimulate innovative violence prevention initiatives and advance practice.

In the literature, the cultural dimensions of violence—its idiom, discourse, and meaning—often receive less attention than the more obvious physical aspects of violence (see Chapter 2). As Brackley and Williams (2007) noted, "Definitions and the experience of violence seem to vary across cultures and with age and socioeconomic status ..." (p. 15). What does the act of violence signify or express? What is the cry of the perpetrator?

These questions tend to be neglected and viewed with less concern and importance (Blok, 2000). However, violence is inextricably bound to larger cultural processes that shape the interpretation and attribution of violence experiences (Peterson del Mar, 2002). The causes and significance of violence, its meaning, and interpretation cannot be fully understood without taking into account cultural factors and context.

Existing literature often reduces culture to findings on race/ethnicity or national origin. However, we understand culture more broadly to include the interplay of multiple axes of difference, such as gender, sexual orientation, family formation, geography, spirituality, immigration history, class, and race. *Culture,* defined as "the learned, shared, and transmitted values, beliefs, norms, and lifeways of a particular culture that guides thinking, decisions, and actions in patterned ways and often intergenerationally" (Leininger & McFarland, 2006, p. 13), frames a person's beliefs and values, a person's ways of seeing, thinking and behaving. Culture can affect (1) what a person considers to be violence, how an individual and community perceive and construe violence; (2) beliefs about the cause of violence; (3) the desire of an individual/family to keep the experience of violence confidential; (4) belief that violence can be prevented through personal and collective effort; (5) tendencies toward accepting violence as inevitable; (6) types of social support provided by family and community; (7) individualistic versus collectivistic cultural approaches; and (8) perception of the best method of treatment (Brackley & Williams, 2007).

Culture impacts how fear and perceived safety are related to actual threats of harm (Aisenberg, Ayón, & Orozco-Figueroa, 2008; Tolan, 2007). According to Blok (2000), "It makes sense to consider violence as a cultural category, as a historically developed cultural form or construction. How people conceive of violence and the meaning it has for them depend on time and place, vary with historical circumstances and also depend on the perspective of those involved—offenders and victims, spectators and bystanders, witnesses and authorities" (p. 26). In such a consideration, it is imperative for researchers, practitioners, and policy advocates to respectfully and competently listen to the experiences of diverse and marginalized populations. Such intentful engagement with diverse communities must also seek to understand the legacies of oppression, dislocation, and discrimination experienced by these populations, as well as their survival strategies. Often, dominant cultures fail to respect and affirm the contextual realities of the histories, languages, values, traditions, and indigenous wisdom and resources of marginalized groups. Such failure and the lack of historical and cultural understanding by many researchers and practitioners engender further isolation and marginalization as well as fear and mistrust across communities. Also, the dominant culture's failure to include and respect diverse cultures, and at times their discounting of the strengths and needs of marginalized populations or failing to believe the stories and coping strategies of marginalized people, contribute to the perpetration and transmission of violence across communities and generations.

To more deeply understand the causes and significance of violence as well as to promote effective intervention and violence prevention efforts cultural factors, economic, religious, political, psychological, and historical factors as well as social relations of power need to be taken into account. "These variations carry forward important implications for how violence is understood, how its patterns are identified, how risk factors are related, and which interventions and policies seem most appropriate" (Tolan, 2007, p. 5). Given the complexity of defining violence and the salience of social relations of power in impacting both the causes and the lived experiences of violence, further analysis is needed that helps to elucidate the ways that culture, history, and systems of oppression work together to perpetuate interrelated forms of violence among individuals and communities.

INTERSECTIONALITY

In general, researchers have paid limited attention to the ways that race, gender, sexual orientation, immigration history, poverty, and class intersect and produce and maintain unequal distribution of institutional power and privilege in the United States (Simien, 2007). In violence-related research and practice, intersections of gender, race, class, sexual orientation, and other experiences of marginalization are rarely fully assessed, addressed, and analyzed. In assessing and measuring their contributions to violence exposure researchers often make a major assumption—that the dichotomies of black/white, male/female, or disadvantaged/advantaged exist in an isolated manner. In a strict sense, they do not (Simien, 2007). According to proponents of intersectionality, race is "gendered" and gender is "racialized." Collins (2000), for instance, describes interlocking systems of oppression as structures of social inequality, such as racism and sexism, that mutually create and reinforce each other.

Rather than support a compartmentalized approach in which social categories such as race, class, gender, sexual orientation, and disability are separate and discrete, advocates of intersectionality acknowledge existing heterogeneity and interdependence within and across these categories. Also, they emphasize the simultaneity of oppression (Collins, 2000; Crenshaw, 1991, 1993; Wing, 1997). In doing so, they forcefully challenge researchers to study violence, reactions to crime, and processes of violence and criminal justice in a manner that is not divorced from the larger context of the realities of multiple forms of social injustice permeating society (Tifft, Maruna, & Elliott, 2006). One of the most severe consequences of minimizing or ignoring structural dimensions of violence and their impact is the implementation of short-sighted and ineffectual responses to violent incidents. No matter how energetically social policy makers address violence, if the society's structural dynamics are overlooked and left intact they will continue to engender violence, and violence prevention policies and programs will fail (Elliott, 1985). The examination of the dynamics of institutional arrangements and systems of stratification must be a central focus in the study of violence.

In seeking to understand violence and responses to violence, it is critical to examine the salience of multiple forms of oppression on a structural as well as individual level. Too often, for example, public policy makers have emphasized cultural values of ethnic and racial minority populations as a significant determinant of group differences in rates of violence rather than posit that violence among African Americans and Latinos, for example, is rooted in socioeconomic and class inequalities (Hawkins, 1993). Consequently, policies are implemented that seek to change the values and culture of high-risk ethnic populations rather than address the need for structural change and directly target socioeconomic inequality and oppression (Hawkins, 1993).

This narrow approach in assessment and treatment fails to acknowledge that these identities and experiences of marginalization can impact a person's life, experience of violence, and response to the provision of services and thus warrant rigorous study and examination. Focusing on individual characteristics in assessment and intervention, rather than examining and addressing the intersection of multiple aspects and determinants of violence, has further stigmatized and marginalized individuals and communities of color by failing to affirm indigenous strengths within families and communities of color and failing to adequately assess context and resources. Therefore, in youth violence prevention programs, for example, it is crucial to provide youth with the tools to deconstruct miseducation and misrepresentations of their race or ethnic group throughout history and to reconstruct knowledge of the contributions and knowledge of their race or ethnic group to construct a better life for the community (Potts, 2003).

To facilitate the examination of the intersection of multiple aspects and determinants of violence, it is crucial to expand existing definitions of violence and take into consideration that violence involves the exercise of force at the service of power. Such regard represents a critical shift. Violence involves the human exercise of power through the use of force in the interest of maintaining, destroying, or building a given order of rights and appropriations, and placing limits on, or denying, the integrity and rights of others (individually or collectively) (Agudelo, 1992, p. 368). As Agudelo (1992, p. 366) notes:

> To postulate that violence is a problem of power has serious
> implications. In the first place, it contradicts the idea that violence
> is blind brute force. It also contradicts the acceptance of violence
> as something innate, as an unavoidable destiny of humankind.
> It begins to point the finger more at the historical nature of the
> phenomenon, which includes but goes beyond the individual.

Purposeful reflection, scholarship, and decision making regarding violence should take into account both recognition of the effect of this use of destructive force and recognition of the rights, legality, and power that are in conflict (Agudelo, 1992). While the use of violence to respond to or address inequality is less addressed in social science and psychological literature nevertheless, "there are conditions of oppression, injustice, and grievous economic inequality in which violence is not a disease but rather a necessary reaction on the part of the body social—somewhat like the biological organism's response to infection. It is like fever, a mechanism for combating infection, which is the real disease" (Agudelo, pp. 367–368). In such circumstances, including colonization, violence may be a necessary and just response.

Active resistance to violence and its power to harm, shame, dominate, and oppress is an important but often overlooked aspect of violence. In instances of intimate partner violence, for example, women employ a range of resources and creative strategies to resist and escape violence from their partners (Campbell, Rose, Kub, & Nedd, 1998; Cook, Wollard, & McCollum, 2004; Hollander, 2005). Such forceful action contradicts prevailing cultural beliefs about women's inherent vulnerability that have made their successful resistance to violence invisible and helped perpetuate intimate partner violence by increasing men's confidence to overpower women and by decreasing women's sense of self-efficacy to resist it (Hollander, 2005). Also, such struggle transcends the individual level of response as collective acts of resistance have propelled important legislative and policy changes over the past several decades. This dynamic of resistance and the use of survival strategies in the face of inequality and oppression need to be incorporated and made explicit in understanding violence and its effects.

INTERRELATEDNESS OF FORMS OF VIOLENCE

Violence occurs in multiple settings such as the home, school, workplace, and community and across different populations, including youth and families. Also, it occurs in many types of relationships (e.g., between partners, family members, strangers, neighbors). The heterogeneity of violence has led to studies examining discrete subtypes of violent behavior and separate causal determinants and risk and protective factors. As noted by Herrenkohl (Chapter 5), recent research has begun to examine commonalities and interrelatedness across some forms of violence, in particular child maltreatment and domestic violence (Appel & Holden, 1998; Daro, Edleson, & Pinderhughes, 2004; Herrenkohl, Sousa, Tajima, Herrenkohl, & Moylan, 2008; Wolfe, Crooks, Lee, McIntyre-Smith, & Jaffe, 2003), as well as violence in the community and home (Maas, Herrenkohl, & Sousa, 2008; Margolin & Gordis, 2000). Overall, however, few studies have examined the interrelationships and context between exposure to different forms of violence (Mabanglo, 2002; Finkelhor, Ormrod, & Turner, 2007). Past studies have typically focused on one form of victimization and may exaggerate the contribution of single types of victimization to mental health problems and thus fail to identify victims who experience exposure to multiple and often co-occurring experiences of violence in their life-times (Aisenberg & Herrenkohl, 2008; Finkelhor et al., 2007). Also, past studies often fail to delineate the contribution of these interrelationships to mental health and behavioral problems (Finkelhor et al., 2007). A growing body of research has demonstrated that the types of violence experienced by children and adolescents are not singular, disparate experiences (Hanson et al., 2006).

This overlap presents clear challenges in studying the effects of violence because the effect of one form of violence exposure may be difficult to discern from another. For example, community violence is often over-looked in studies of domestic violence and physical child abuse (Gorman-Smith & Tolan, 1998). This lack of assessment raises the possibility that effects attributable to community violence exposure may be misattributed to other forms of violence (Aisenberg & Mennen, 2000). Similarly, studies of community violence that do not account for intrafamilial violence may overestimate the effects of violence in the community. To disentangle the co-occurring forms of violence and the effects of these stressors, often experienced on a repetitive basis, remains a serious challenge. As noted by Herrenkohl (Chapter 5), failure to account for overlapping forms of violence across settings has contributed to an incomplete understanding of the environments at risk for violence. Further examination within distinct types of violence and across these types is crucial to assess the overlap among them and to advance our understanding.

Another limitation is the lack of specification of the nature of the cultural and contextual factors that shape the varied experiences, perceptions, and interpretation of violence and outcomes across racial/ethnic populations (Bartelt, 1994; Brodsky, 1997; Guterman et al., 2000). As noted by Jenson and colleagues (Chapter 8), many evidence-based intervention programs are based on dominant culture (white, middle class) values that fail to adequately consider cultural differences. Future studies "should be guided by models sensitive to the effects of culture on developmental processes and to culture's unique contributions to how successful adaptation is achieved in the face of adversity" (Flores, Cicchetti, & Rogosch, 2005, p. 348). Such research is crucial to understand the relationship of racial, cultural, and community infrastructure and "protective" factors that reduce risk and increase resilience of specific groups with respect to mental health, and incorporate knowledge about such protective factors into the development and implementation of appropriate mental health treatments and services (National Implementation Research Network, 2003). Also, research that examines and compares the experiences and outcomes of immigrant children and children of immigrant and refugee parents is particularly needed given the pattern of trauma and violence often experienced by families who have fled war and violence in their native country. Rarely is such exposure assessed among immigrant children and families despite the fact that such violence often impels immigrant adults to uproot their families. Such exposure has significant impact upon a person and communities, including the ability to trust and feel safe, an internalized sense of marginalization and oppression, possible traumatic effects, including posttraumatic stress disorder (PTSD) and dissociation, and a lack of positive role models.

Given the importance of culture and context as considerations in the study and treatment of violence, programs and practice can be strengthened if communities themselves are involved with the conceptualization and process of research and program development. The traditional, hierarchical, top down approach in the development and dissemination of violence model programs and evidence based practices clearly reveals the lack of ties specifically between research and communities of color as well as between research and service providers. These gaps hinder engagement in authentic partnership that is mutually beneficial and promotes meaningful and sustainable change in the community and in systems of care. Such an approach perpetuates mistrust within ethnic communities that is rooted in historical experiences of marginalization and oppression by the dominant culture. Also, it is based on communities' experiences of researchers entering their community and conducting research without much respect or regard for the community or without helping to promote meaningful change through their scientific endeavor (Aisenberg, 2008).

CONCLUSION

According to WHO (2002), "Violence is a complex problem rooted in the interaction of many factors – biological, social, cultural, economic and political". Rather than view violence in static, linear, and compartmentalized ways, scholars, public officials, and practitioners are encouraged to take into account the dynamic and intersecting characteristics of culture and social power in the definition, assessment, measurement, and policy interventions of violence.

As noted above and earlier in Chapter 2, it is important that the field move towards an integrative set of definitions and approach to violence that centers on the interrelatedness of violent behaviors and intersectionality with respect to multiple identities, structural inequalities, culture, and power. Transdisciplinary research is needed along with skilled clinicians and policy makers to help address the multifaceted and multilevel factors of violence and to improve the health and well-being of people throughout the world. Also, sustained and comprehensive training in the areas of cultural competency and anti-oppression is warranted, particularly for practitioners and researchers working with diverse communities.

To be effective in goals of preventing violence and providing just and effective treatment to victims, our understanding of violence requires contextualizing the individual's social identity(ies) and social context, as well as the perceptions and social meanings constructed by the individual (Stanko, 2006). Also, such a model must take into account and address three important elements: 1) the interdependent relationships existing at multiple levels within the ecological and familial contexts of the individual's coping and functioning; 2) the pathways for intervention and prevention that deal with these contexts and work within them; and 3) the gender and other social inequalities experienced by diverse and marginalized individuals and communities.

REFERENCES

Agudelo, S. F. (1992). Violence and health: Preliminary elements for thought and action. *International Journal of Health Sciences, 22,* 365–376.

Aisenberg, E. (2008). Evidence base practice in mental health care to ethnic minority communities: Has its practice fallen short of its evidence? *Social Work, 53,* 297–306.

Aisenberg, E., Ayón, C., & Orozco-Figueroa, A. (2008). The role of young adolescents' perception in understanding severity of impact of exposure to community violence. *Journal of Interpersonal Violence, 23,* 1555–1578.

Aisenberg, E., & Herrenkohl, T. I. (2008). Community violence in context: Risk and resilience in children and families. Special Issue. *Journal of Interpersonal Violence, 23,* 296–315.

Aisenberg, E., & Mennen, F. E. (October 2000). Children exposed to community violence: Issues for assessment and treatment. *Child and Adolescent Social Work Journal, 17,* 341–360.

Appel, A. E., & Holden, G. W. (1998). The co-occurrence of spouse and physical child abuse: A review and appraisal. *Journal of Family Psychology, 12,* 578–599.

Bartelt, D. (1994). On resilience: Questions of validity. In M. Wang & E. Gordon (Eds.), *Educational resilience in inner city America* (pp. 97–108). Hillsdale, NJ: Erlbaum.

Blok, A. (2000). The enigma of senseless violence. In J. Abbink & G. Aijmer (Eds.), *Meanings of violence: A cross cultural perspective* (pp. 23–38). New York: Berg Publishers.

Brackley, M. H., & Williams, G. B. (2007). Problem/definitions of violence by women with health disparities. *Journal of Multicultural Nursing & Health, 13,* 11–12.

Brodsky, A. (1997). Why the concept of resilience is resilient. *The Community Psychologist, 30,* 29–32.

Campbell, J., Rose, L., Kub, J., & Nedd, D. (1998). Voices of strength and resistance: A contextual and longitudinal analysis of women's responses to battering. *Journal of Interpersonal Violence, 13,* 743–762.

Collins, P. H. (2000). *Black feminist thought,* 2nd edition. New York: Routledge.

Cook, S. L., Woolard, J. L., & McCollum, H. C. (2004). The strengths, competence, and resilience of women facing domestic violence: How can research and policy support them? In K. Maton, C. Schellenbach, B. Leadbeater, & A. Solarz (Eds.), *Investing in children, youth, families, and communities: Strengths-based research and policy* (pp. 97–115). Washington, DC: American Psychological Association.

Crenshaw, K. (1991). Mapping the margins: intersectionality, identity politics, and violence against women of color. *Stanford Law Review, 43,* 1241–1299.

180   FUTURE CONSIDERATIONS FOR THE STUDY AND PREVENTION

Crenshaw, K. (1993). Race, gender, and violence against women. In M. Minow (Ed.), *Family matters: Readings on family lives and the law* (pp. 230–232). New York: New Press.

Daro, D., Edleson, J. L., & Pinderhughes, H. (2004). Finding common ground in the study of child maltreatment, youth violence, and adult domestic violence. *Journal of Interpersonal Violence, 19,* 282–298.

Elliot, D. (1985). The assumption that theories can be combined with increased explanatory power: Theoretical integrations. In R. F. Meier (Ed.), *Theoretical methods in criminology* (pp. 123–149). Beverly Hills: Sage.

Finkelhor, D., Ormrod, R. K., & Turner, H. A. (2007). Poly-victimization: A neglected component in child victimization. *Child Abuse and Neglect, 31,* 7–26.

Flores, E., Cicchetti, D., & Rogosch, F. A. (2005). Predictors of resilience in maltreated and nonmaltreated Latino children. *Developmental Psychology, 41*(2), 338–351.

Gorman-Smith, D., & Tolan, P. (1998). The role of exposure to community violence and developmental problems among inner-city youth. *Development and Psychopathology, 10,* 101–116.

Guterman, N. B., Cameron, M., & Staller, K. (2000). Definitional and measurement issues in the study of community violence among children and youths. *Journal of Community Psychology, 28,* 571–587.

Hanson, R. F., Self-Brown, S., Fricker-Ethai, A. E., Kilpatrick, D. G., Saunders, B. E., & Resnick, H. S. (2006). The relations between family environment and violence exposure among youth: Findings from the National Survey of Adolescents. *Child Maltreatment, 11,* 3–15.

Hawkins, D. F. (1993). Inequality, culture, and interpersonal violence. *Health Affairs, 12,* 80–95.

Herrenkohl, T. I., Sousa, C., Tajima, E. A., Herrenkohl, R. C., & Moylan, C.A. (2008). Intersection of child abuse and children's exposure to domestic violence. *Trauma, Violence, and Abuse, 9,* 84–89.

Holland, J. A. (2005). Challenging despair: Teaching about women's resistance to violence. *Violence Against Women, 11,* 776–791.

Leininger, M. M., & McFarland, M. R. (2006). *Culture care diversity and universality: A worldwide nursing theory.* Sudbury, MA: Jones and Bartlett.

Maas, C., Herrenkohl, T. I., & Sousa, C. (2008). Review of research on child maltreatment and violence in youth. *Trauma, Violence, and Abuse. 9,* 56–67.

Mabanglo, M. (2002). Trauma and the effects of violence exposure and abuse on children: A review of the literature. *Smith College Studies in Social Work, 72,* 231–251.

Margolin, G., & Gordis, E. B. (2000). The effects of family and community violence on children. *Annual Review of Psychology, 51,* 445–479.

National Implementation Research Network, the Louis de la Parte Florida Mental Health Institute. (2003). Consensus statement on evidence based programs and cultural competence. Tampa, FL. Retrieved July 10, 2006, from http://www.epp.networkofcare.org/uploads/Consensus 6230512.pdf

Peterson del Mar, D. (2002). *Beaten down: A history of interpersonal violence in the West.* Seattle: University of Washington Press.

Potts, R. G. (2003). Emancipatory education versus school-based prevention in African American communities. *American Journal of Community Psychology, 31,* 173–183.

Simien, E. M. (2007). Doing intersectionality research: From conceptual issues to practical examples. *Politics & Gender, 3,* 264–271.

Stanko, E. A. (2006). Theorizing about violence. *Violence Against Women, 12,* 543–555.

Tiff, L., Maruna, S., & Elliott, E. (2006). The state of criminology in the 21st century: A penpal roundtable. *Contemporary Justice Review, 9,* 387–400.

Tolan, P. H. (2007). Understanding violence. In D. J. Flannery, A. T. Vazsonyi, & I. D. Waldman (Eds.), *The Cambridge handbook of violent behavior and aggression* (pp. 5–18). New York: Cambridge University Press.

U.S. Department of Health and Human Services. (2001). *Mental health: Culture, race, and ethnicity: A supplement to mental health: A report of the Surgeon General.* Rockville, MD: Author.

Wing, A. K. (Ed.). (1997). *Critical race feminism.* New York: New York University Press.

Wolfe, D. A., Crooks, C. V., Lee, V., McIntyre-Smith, A., & Jaffe, P. G. (2003). The effects of children's exposure to domestic violence: A meta-analysis and critique. *Clinical Child and Family Psychological Review, 6,* 171–187.

World Health Organization. (2002). *World report on violence and health: Summary.* Geneva: World Health Organization.

10

LESSONS AND CHALLENGES IN THE STUDY AND PREVENTION OF VIOLENCE

Todd I. Herrenkohl, Eugene Aisenberg, James
Herbert Williams, & Jeffrey M. Jenson

This book examines the context of family, youth, and community violence, including the various social and systemic macro-level causes and correlates of violence in and across settings. The book also summarizes current research on the adverse effects of violence for children, protective factors, and strengths within families, schools, and communities that can be leveraged to enhance the well-being of vulnerable children. Our primary goal in writing the book was to bring forward current ideas and evidence of the overlap in different forms of violence, to synthesize knowledge, and to motivate—by way of critical review and analysis—advances in research on topics contained in the volume. Across all chapters, we seek to keep race, ethnicity, culture, and gender at the forefront of the discussion and to analyze theories and research findings from the perspective of how these factors shape the context of violence. Authors refer to the strengths and limitations of violence and prevention research, highlight gaps in research findings, and underscore challenges that remain, in research, program development, and policy.

All chapters in this book refer to notable advances and areas of innovation in violence research and programs. Perhaps most remarkable is how far we have come in our understanding risk and protective factors for violence among youth. Much has been learned about risk factors that span the family, school, and community domains. Research has also helped identify protective factors or buffers of early risk exposure in children-variables that interact with risk factors to lessen the probability of some undesired outcome, such as the onset of conduct problems in children or the recurrence of violence in families.

While advances have come about through systematic study of violence and its effects, authors of this book are careful to point out that we have reached a point of needing to do more by way of tackling complex issues related to violence and prevention, such as racial and ethnic disparities in violent offending. Authors also point to the need for broader, more inclusive definitions of violence and models organized around ideas of dominance and discrimination. There also exist less daunting tasks, such as beginning to merge what is known about individual correlates of violence with knowledge of social, structural, and environmental influences.

Advances in the prevention of violence are notable, yet challenges also remain. For example, there is a pressing need to understand how to use what is known to work in prevention to bring about lasting changes in real-world settings and to go about that process with an eye toward cultural adaptation. In this concluding chapter, we highlight several key findings from the preceding chapters and discuss a few particularly important topics for the next generation of research studies on violence and prevention.

RISK AND PROTECTIVE FACTORS FOR VIOLENCE IN YOUTH

As noted throughout the book, young people—those in their adolescent and early adult years—are at higher risk than are individuals of other age groups for perpetrating violence, and for becoming victims of violence. We know that violence among youth is linked to a host of individual (constitutional, biological), social, and environmental factors and that in many cases children who encounter chronic violence are more likely to use violence themselves. As discussed in Chapters 4 and 5, longitudinal studies show that children who are exposed to violence in their families are at significantly higher risk for conduct problems and adulthood perpetration of violent crime and intimate partner abuse. While there is good news that many children appear resilient to some of the long-term effects of violence exposure, research reviewed by Herrenkohl in Chapter 6 suggests the need for careful and more focused analyses of resilience as a life-course pattern. Further, the study of ethnic and gender differences related to outcomes of family violence exposure and resilience—topics of a very few investigations to date—holds promise for advancing the field and strengthening the foundations of prevention and intervention programs. In our view, linking resilience research and practice applications is an important goal that requires more direct and intentional communication between those who study the issues and those who work with youth in real-world settings, including schools and neighborhood organizations. Related particularly to our focus on violence in context are interventions focused on strengthening social support networks and mentoring of vulnerable youth.

Children and families of color encounter violence disproportionately, as noted in several earlier chapters. African Americans and other ethnic minority groups are more likely than are other children to become victims of violence. Williams and colleagues (Chapter 3) report that African American youth are also more likely to perpetrate violence, to do so earlier, and to become involved in the juvenile and criminal justice systems. Indeed, research shows large disparities in rates of youth violence perpetration, arrests, and detention of juveniles for violent crimes. African American youth are arrested in much larger numbers than are Whites and are detained more often and for longer periods. Unfortunately, research is limited on how and why these disparities persist, although discrimination by law enforcement and inconsistency in court processing of juvenile offenders are proposed causes. The need for review and reform at all levels—from policing to placement of delinquent youth—must be carefully considered in light of the findings discussed.

In Chapter 4, Bright and colleagues examine what is has become a major point of discussion among violence researchers, law enforcement, and service providers: the increasing rates of violent crime arrests among girls. Boys still outnumber girls in overall prevalences of crime and arrests, although the gender gap in officially recorded violence appears to be narrowing. Why? As noted in Chapter 4, relatively little is actually known about girls and violence, which is troubling given the recent trends. Further research is needed on how patterns of violent behavior actually differ for girls, whether common risk and protective factors predict violent offending in both genders, and whether programs designed to prevent and treat violence in boys are as effective for girls. Bright et al.'s reference to gendered perspectives on violence highlights some of the current hypotheses about why boys and girls differ in their expressions of violence, but few of these hypotheses have been rigorously tested. As when considering race differences in violence, with gender, consideration must be given to ways to accommodate the needs of girls who come in contact with law enforcement, to ways of reducing systems biases, and, ultimately, to insure all youth, girls and boys, are treated equitably at all stages of intervention and systems involvement.

Race, ethnicity, and gender define individuals at higher and lower risk of being exposed to violence, for perpetrating violence, and for coming in contact with the juvenile justice system. They are also, according to Aisenberg and colleagues in Chapter 9, "identity categories" that intersect with culture and histories of dominance and oppression. Importantly, the authors urge the field to more fully consider how these factors influence youth and community violence. They also recommend further consideration of the ways in which culture and identities play into current definitions, methods of study, and proposed remedies to violence on a broad scale.

In closing this section, it is important to return to the question introduced at the start of Chapter 2: "What is violence?" A notable limitation of most studies, as Aisenberg and colleagues remind us, is that we minimize, or exclude altogether, questions of culture, discrimination, and social power—forces that can perpetuate violence at a macro, societal level. Integrated theories of violence that place these issues at the center, not at the margins, of scholarly discussion could help advance the field in important ways, but primarily by changing the way violence at the level of the individual is understood. Chapter 9 serves as a reminder that there are many points at which to begin conversations about next steps in violence research and prevention; the goal, of course, is that those conversations take place.

PREVENTION OF VIOLENCE

Despite various limitations in the study of the etiology and prevention of violence, it is well established that violence within families, schools, and communities can be prevented and that certain approaches are better aligned with the themes of this book than are others. Jenson and colleagues note in Chapters 7 and 8 that many prevention programs aim to prevent or reduce violence by targeting known risk and protective factors across settings. Skills-based programs for high-risk and vulnerable youth are used routinely in schools, targeting children at or before the point when most youth initiate violence. Prevention studies with children of elementary and middle school ages are perhaps more common than are studies of older youth. However, programs tested with adolescents also appear promising, according to outcome evaluations and cost-benefit studies. For example, programs like Multisystemic Therapy and Multidimensional Treatment Foster Care show sizable cost-savings compared with other services for chronically antisocial youth (Aos, Miller, & Drake, 2006). In fact, Aos and colleagues at the Washington State Institute for Public Policy (WSIPP) estimate the positive return from Multidimensional Treatment Foster Care—an alternative to standard group care or residential placement—at around $24,000 per individual child. Nurse Family Partnership, a widely disseminated, home visitation for low-income, at-risk pregnant women, registers cost-savings of over $17,000 per child and is known to lessen potential for child abuse, reduce crime, and strengthen families across generations. These findings in prevention are encouraging. However, questions remain as to how to bring about lasting changes using tested programs. As Jenson and colleagues note in Chapters 7 and 8, research has yet to show how to adapt and/or modify successful programs to allow implementation in different settings and how to make them culturally relevant.

CONCLUSION AND SUMMARY

We began this effort with a goal of bringing into view the many and varied aspects of context related to violence and to highlight approaches to intervention across settings. Although there are undoubtedly areas we have left unaddressed or only partially covered, we hope that issues raised in this book stimulate others to consider more fully the interrelated causes, correlates, and outcomes of violence exposure in children, as well as systems responses and innovative models of prevention. We sought to raise fundamental questions about the very constructs we study and the ways in which our methods shape the questions we can ask. There have been many notable advances in the field and equally many challenges that remain. Advances across all areas of research—from basic studies of violence risk and protective factors, to evaluation studies of comprehensive intervention programs—have helped answer the "whys" and "hows" of violence etiology and prevention. But advances and ongoing work in the field have also exposed many shortcomings, biases, and flaws in the way we go about the task of studying and acting on violence. The field continues to evolve and, with this, our theories, perspectives, and tools of research must keep pace. In returning to our opening assessment of the current state of the field: What we now know about the causes and consequences of violence—and about the tools to prevent it—place us in a good position to end this global crisis. But, as we finish, it is important to also note that, to end this global crisis, further innovation of methods is necessary. Progress will happen with debate, discussion, and refinement of ideas and approaches. For now, violence has been remains one of the more complicated and enduring problems we face.

REFERENCE

Aos, S., Miller, M., & Drake, E. (2006). *Evidence-based public policy options to reduce future prison construction, criminal justice costs, and crime rates.* Olympia, WA: Washington State Institute for Public Policy.

INDEX

Race/ethnicity, 6–10, 28, 32–38, 40, 73,
    76–78, 81–82, 84–86, 95–97, 99,
    103–104, 140, 152, 171–173,
    175, 178, 182–184
  African Americans, 6–7, 9, 40, 76–78,
    84–86, 96–97, 99, 103–104,
    175, 184
  Asian/Pacific Islanders, 76–77
  Asians, 77
  Hispanics/Latinos, 77, 96, 175
  Native Americans/Alaska Natives, 76–77
  Whites (non-Hispanic), 77
Raudenbush, S.W., 7, 20, 34, 37, 78, 95,
    102, 154
Reid, J.B., 137–138, 147–148, 157
Reiss, A.J., 15–16, 154
Resilience, 9–10, 37–38, 73, 86, 92–104,
    173, 176–177, 183
  And development, 73, 93, 101
  And implications for prevention &
    intervention, 10, 86, 92, 95
  As a dynamic process, 101
  Conceptualization/operationalization of,
    10, 73, 86, 92–93, 100–101
  Indicators of, 93, 98, 100
    Absence of criminal record, 93
    Absence of learning & behavior
      problems, 93
    Absence of psychiatric disorders, 93
    Academic achievement, 93, 98
    Affectionate/engaging temperament, 98
    Average or above average intelligence,
      98, 100
    Caring personality, 93
    Competence, 93–94
    Determination to lead a different life
      than parent, 98, 100
    Effective coping strategies, 98
    Employment success, 93
    Existence of close interpersonal
      relationships, 93, 98
    High sociability, 98
    Involvement in social activities, 93
    Low delinquency & school
      misconduct, 93
    Low depression, anxiety, &/or distress,
      93, 98
    Low emotionality, 98
    Low somatization
    Low substance use, 93
    Maternal competence, 98
    No perpetration of violence, 93
    Positive outlook on future, 93, 98, 100
    Self-confidence, 93, 98
    Self-reliance, 93

  Social stability & success, 93, 98
  Stable living environment, 93, 98
  Strong internal locus of control, 98, 100
  Measurement of, 10, 73, 100–101
  Survival strategies, 173, 176
Risk and protective factors for violence,
    6–10, 16, 19–22, 27–28,
    32–39, 50–60, 62, 73–86,
    92–104, 112, 114–117,
    121–122, 130–158, 171–177,
    179, 182–186
  Academic achievement, 37, 93, 98,
    130–158
  Affectionate/engaging temperament, 98
  Average or above average intelligence,
    98, 100
  Biological, 115
  Bonding, 34–35
  Caring personality, 93
  Community groups/religious
    organizations, 99
  Competence, 93–94
  Definitions of, 35, 37, 57
  Effective coping strategies, 98
  Environmental risks, 55, 73
  Exposure to violence, 7, 9, 54–55,
    73–86, 92–104
  Family-related, 56, 58, 115, 117, 138,
    141–142, 148, 154–155
  Gender, 6–7, 9–10, 27–28, 50–57,
    59–60, 62, 73, 80–82, 85–86, 97,
    141, 152–153, 171–174, 176,
    179, 182-184
  High sociability, 98
  Impulsive behavior, 58
  Intervention programs, 76, 94–95
  Involvement in social activities, 93
  Limitations of protective factors, 97
  Low distress, 98
  Low emotionality, 98
  Maternal competence, 98
  Neighborhood advantage/disadvantage,
    7, 19–20, 22, 34–36, 58, 77–78,
    83–84, 94–96, 99–100, 102,
    116–117, 121, 154–155
  Collective efficacy, 19–20, 34, 58,
    78, 84, 96, 99–100, 102,
    121, 155
  Peer influence, 58, 115, 117, 121, 131,
    138–139, 141, 147
  Problem-solving skills, 37–38, 103, 117,
    131, 136–138, 141, 145, 148
  Race/ethnicity, 6–10, 28, 32–38, 73,
    76–78, 81–82, 84–86, 95–97, 99,
    103–104, 140, 182–184